Skin Deep

Edited by
Marita Golden and
Susan Richards Shreve

Nan A. Talese
Doubleday
New York London Toronto Sydney Auckland

Skin Deep

Black Women
& White Women
Write About Race

PUBLISHED BY NAN A. TALESE
an imprint of Doubleday
a division of Bantam Doubleday Dell Publishing Group, Inc.
1540 Broadway, New York, New York 10036

DOUBLEDAY *is a trademark of Doubleday, a division of*
Bantam Doubleday Dell Publishing Group, Inc.

Book design by Terry Karydes

Page 310 represents a continuation of this copyright page

Library of Congress Cataloging-in-Publication Data
Skin deep : Black women and White women write about race /
  edited by Marita Golden and Susan Richards Shreve.
  p. cm.
  1. Afro-American women. 2. Racism—United States.
3. United States—Race relations.
4. Women—United States—Social conditions.
I. Golden, Marita. II. Shreve, Susan Richards.
E185.86.S6 1995
305.8' 0973—dc20
94-44606
CIP

ISBN 0-385-47409-1
Copyright © 1995 by Marita Golden and Susan Richards Shreve

July 1995

First Edition

10 9 8 7 6 5 4 3 2 1

Contents

Introduction
Marita Golden   1

Introduction
Susan Richards Shreve   7

High Yellow White Trash
Lisa Page   13

whitegirls
Marita Golden   24

The Racism of Well-Meaning White People
Naomi Wolf   37

Overhand and Underhand
Retha Powers   47

Negative
Joyce Carol Oates   60

Recitatif
Toni Morrison   87

What Tina Has to Do with It
Beverly Lowry   111

Legacies and Ghosts
Patricia Browning Griffith   118

Adjustments
Mary Morris   128

Prudential Life Insurance
Susan Richards Shreve   138

Across the Glittering Sea
Jewelle Gomez   148

Loving Across the Boundary
Ann Filemyr   162

The Revenge of Hannah Kemhuff
Alice Walker   189

Tulsa, 1921
Susan Straight   208

A Worn Path
Eudora Welty   227

Contents Under Pressure:
WHITE WOMAN/BLACK HISTORY
Catherine Clinton   238

Reaching Across the Feminist Racial Divide
Dorothy Gilliam   256

Feminism in Black and White
bell hooks   265

Hello, Stranger
Gayle Pemberton   278

"Are We So Different?"
A DIALOGUE BETWEEN AN AFRICAN-AMERICAN AND
   A WHITE SOCIAL WORKER
Cathleen Gray, Ph.D.
Shirley Bryant, D.S.W.   287

Contributors   305

Introduction

by Marita Golden

hen my friend and colleague Susan Shreve suggested we edit an anthology of writing about race by black and white women, I had several reactions. My first thought quite honestly was "Uh-oh"—you know, that primal, urgent, squishy inside feeling that synthesizes the fear you got as a child approaching a dark room in a dark house, as you clutched the hand of your girlfriend and she clutched yours and you both argued over who would knock or push the door open and then who would turn on the light. "You do it." "No, you." "You're taller." "But you're braver!"

I also felt, *about time!* and that we were as qualified and prepared to pull together such a collection as anybody else. I was fiercely, totally excited by the prospect of working with a group of women prepared to step up to the plate on the one subject in America nobody really wants to discuss. Correction: whites don't want to discuss, and blacks can't *stop* discussing.

Ironically, white America will catapult books about race to the top of the best-seller list, even as racism remains a national open wound. Obsession ain't solution, however, because reading even at its most intense and verisimilitudinous is vicarious, and once you close the book you're off the hook. Then add to the equation that this was going to be a meditation scripted and improvised by women. Women who had been raised to be polite, never to rock the boat, and even though we *had* while our parents and our men weren't looking and sometimes even when they were, subsequently mastered shaking up the dinghy and gloried in it, I wondered if race would scare the rebel, the hell raiser, the wild woman out of us. I mean who really gets down, digs deep over that four-letter word? RACE. And even bolstered by women's actual, yet often mythologized, talent for intimacy and revelation, race remains taboo even among the hippest, the most liberated, progressive, and righteous among us. The more I thought about it the more I realized that editing this anthology was going to be unsettling, frustrating, surprising, and perhaps a bit messy. I couldn't wait to get started.

The contour of the project in the beginning pretty much followed the contours of racial reality and politics in America. Several white women writers we approached were terrified (that's the only word) to broach the subject. Some said yes and then said no and meant it. The black women couldn't wait to pick up the pen or settle down in front of their computers. No fear there. Write about race? Write about my life! But pretty soon it became clear that in different ways we were *all* a little scared to write about the great continuing American reality and dilemma. Our fear, of course, was inevitable, necessary, important. We were Americans, so how could we be anything but afraid to write, which means think and talk, about race? And if we weren't afraid we sure weren't as certain or as sure as we thought we were. In the end the black women weren't automatic experts on race and the white women weren't all racial wimps.

But make no mistake about it, this was virgin territory for us all. And it is virgin for good reasons. There is so much at stake. Women are keepers of a community's faith, guardians of its deepest beliefs and lies, harbingers of its most vivid fears in a way that men can never be, in a way that men have traditionally designated women to be. And so white women of necessity have been complicit in racism, both institutional and private. Black women have been agitators and warriors against the system white women swore to uphold as passionately as white men. We have been defined as symbolic and actual opposites. The white woman weak/the black woman strong, the white woman undersexed/the black woman oversexed, the white woman the symbol of sexual desire/the black woman neutered. And this mumbo jumbo of imprisoning, corrupting imagery still rages in our heads and in our hearts, and makes it all the more difficult to throw a life or love line to one another.

Race is the tar baby in our midst; touch it and you get stuck, hold it and you get dirty, so they say. But anyone who reads the pieces that follow will discover only premeditated ruminations designed to cleanse, complete, and free. The aching honesty, the willingness to critique and unveil that mark the fiction and nonfiction herein is testimony to the bounty we could all share if we tried as hard to see each other as we try not to, or to "fess up" rather than be nice. Show me yours, I'll show you mine seems to have been the prevailing, mystically shared aesthetic these writer-conspirators adopted.

But no doubt about it, despite Technicolor and multiculturalism, our lives are still largely segregated—off limits to one another by habit, custom, and choice. Yet every word in this book attests as much to our desire for communication and conversation as to the unmitigated legacy of mythology and history that trips us up.

No way can I pretend that our past histories are not etched in the present—silent, yes, but speaking the indelible language of evidence at a crime scene. The failure of mainstream bourgeois feminism, for example, to embrace the black-brown-yellow female experience (and all the issues of class and ethnicity it represents) echoes the cowardice of early white suffragettes afraid to acknowledge bravely and vehemently that race is a woman's issue too.

I would be a timid editor indeed if I failed to interrogate the text I have aided in shaping. And so I must admit that I am disappointed that in these pages no white writer addresses race and present-day feminism. And the essays tellingly reveal how frequently the lives of conscious white women who could both see and see beyond race (that's the real trick for us all) have been enhanced and enlarged by their connections/friendships/liaisons with black women and even their fantasies *about* black women. But read the narratives of the "sisters" closely and what throbs within the arteries of the text is a bitterness, a feeling that they have received too often a much smaller bounty in return, from discourse (attempted and achieved) as well as relations public, private, and political with white women.

Still, these pieces are an unruly brew. A white woman discovers in the process of writing about race that she has an African-American female ancestor. And says *Right on!* A biracial daughter grapples with her white mother's ambivalence and anguish about the daughter's blackness.

One of the realities which make this collection possible is that Susan and I represent the first generation of black and white women who have coexisted, worked, planned to subvert the system, and lived together as virtual equals. And in some cases the traditional power relationships have been altered altogether. While black women have for generations mentored white women informally about life and everything else (including birthin' babies), like several of the black women contributors I teach on a white college campus, which makes me for the majority of my students perhaps the first or one of only a handful of black female authority figures they have dealt with in their brief lives. I give the grades, become the role model, am asked for advice; in many cases become the mentor for white students and most often white women in a way that their mamas could never have imagined a black woman being.

Over a decade ago, while living in Boston, I began as teacher and then became friend to a wonderfully talented and adventurous young white woman. When I told her about this anthology she wrote me a letter and concluded—discussing, with the openness I so love, a friendship with a black woman she knows in Boston—"I have, I think, made her see that I do not 'represent' my race, and she has made me see that in America, in many people's eyes, she represents her race every waking minute, whether she wants to or not. So we've had to talk about *it* a lot; we haven't been able to take anything for granted. Not our common gender, not our common background as children of absentee fathers and single mothers who worked too hard for too little money. And I think that's been good; there's such a tendency in our society for 'well-meaning' people to brush differences aside, from fear, ignorance, whatever. So much pressure to homogenize. I think the very existence of interracial friendships is subversive, flying in the face of all that history, all those laws and institutions that exist to keep us apart. That these friendships exist at all is a triumph of individuality, making them very special, miraculous in no small way."

Tell me, who's the teacher now?

Introduction
by Susan Richards Shreve

At the end of the Second World War, my family bought a farm in Vienna, Virginia, which is now suburban but was at that time rural and Southern. It was a small farm with a large barn, a scattering of livestock, a substantial vegetable garden, and three tenant houses behind the main house. The farm was inexpensive because of its distance from Washington, D.C., where my father worked in the Office of Censorship. And I'm sure my father, who grew up poor in the Middle West, had romantic ideas about this southeastern farm —about raising his children there (I was five and my brother a baby), about himself as farmer and the farmer's adored wife and most especially about the tenant houses.

With the purchase of the property came not only those three small wooden houses but also the people in them—an extended family: three brothers and their wives and children. African-Americans. Blacks. Colored. These were my father's chosen friends—like family, they came with the territory. He set about living on that farm in segregated, redneck Virginia, as invented kin; he played poker with the men at night, hung out in the kitchen drinking beer, worked side by side with them in the farm work that was done in their off hours from other jobs. They lived in the houses free, shared the land, toted from our fridge and worked with my mother in the house, ironing, churning butter, cleaning, cooking and, outside, milking the cows, killing the chickens, feeding the pigs. Their children were my company. Years later when my own four children were small, I lived briefly with my brother and his early-seventies hippies in a commune, and that is what the farm felt like to me then. A shared community. I did not even notice that we sat in the dining room alone, three pale white faces and a baby in a bassinet. I thought we all shared the long kitchen table. Maybe we did or maybe it's a romance to believe that, like my father's romance with the tenant houses. My parents have been dead for a long time and although I was an asker of questions, ours was a tiny family and I missed finding some essential answers.

I do not know what combination of intellectual conviction and essential humanity went into my father's efforts at building this unlikely community of blacks and whites. He was a rebel by temperament and liked the conflict such a nature creates. I'm sure he was struck to see the difference that existed between the blacks and whites in the South and the relationship he knew with blacks in rural Ohio. But essentially I believe it was a matter of the heart and not the mind with him always, a sense of the genuine. Our parents were decent people who dignified the human lives they touched. That seemed normal when we were growing up. In retrospect, given the history of the last thirty years, it seems extraordinary.

We moved to the farm in November before Thanksgiving and left for good on the fifth of July the following year. I don't know what happened in the months leading up to the Fourth of July. I assume that there were a lot of night poker games and convivial conversations over beer in the kitchen and whisperings with my mother and the women and older girls. Whatever happened, my family's way of going about a daily life was different from that of the families who had lived at the farm in the past, and as it turned out must have been unsettling and disturbing.

On the morning of the Fourth of July, my father and the men butchered a pig. It was a huge pig and they killed him with my father's shotgun, which I understand now is not a common way to kill a pig. The fact about the pig killing was that when it was over and the pig was dead, hung upside down in the cellar so as not to spoil in the summer heat, all of the ammunition in the shotgun was gone. We had a picnic in the afternoon and sparklers and firecrackers and then I went to bed. The next thing I remember, it was dark and noisy and I ran downstairs to find the kitchen full of the women and girls from the other houses and my mother in a white dress covered with the blood of Janey, the oldest of the girls, who had been shot. And there was plenty of shooting, at least the sound of it, just beyond the kitchen door. My father, a slight man not easily frightened, stood behind the door with his pig-killing gun empty of its ammunition. He called to turn off the lights, my mother told me to get under the kitchen table. And outside the door, the men from the houses shouted for my father to let the women go. He would not. The women cried not to be forced out; my father said he would not let them go until the men gave up their guns, and the men said they would break down the door and kill him. My mother called the police, who told her they would not get involved in a domestic situation, certainly not with the colored. They said to let the women go.

And finally my father did.

That night I sat in darkness between my parents, who must

have been suffering from their failure for making promises which could not be kept in Virginia in the forties. We sat in a window seat overlooking the back of the farm and watched the fireworks, the cheerful singing and dancing and shouting of our friends from the houses out back. The following day, my parents put the farm up for sale and we moved to the city.

That was my first experience with race and it seems to me a sad story full of all the possibilities and impossibilities inevitable between the races in a democracy which failed in a central way. And like all beginnings in our lives, the story has accumulated a force beyond itself, beyond I'm sure the factual truth of the circumstances.

The other night at a Fourth of July party, everyone read a small bit of the Declaration of Independence. We think of it as short. But it is in fact quite long and the length is a result of grievances against the King of England, some small, some large. But I was struck by the fact that these grievances do not hold a candle to the grievances fundamental to the paradox of our democracy, in a country which promised a safe house to the oppressed, was committed to the rights of the individual to life, liberty, and the pursuit of happiness and yet allowed slavery to exist on its soil. Race is our subject in this country. We will tell its story again and again, through the generations— and mark, this book could not have been written, nor thousands of others published today and tomorrow when I was a little girl—but we will tell the story, black and white—until, years from now, it has a happy ending.

Skin Deep had its beginnings in the office of Martha Levin of Anchor Books. I had been talking to her and to my editor Nan A. Talese about a book on race. I wanted to do an anthology about race which would have a general readership as well as a readership in colleges and universities, especially watching my children and their friends move from the innocence of genuine friendships amongst the races to the divisiveness of "political correctness" in colleges and universities. Marita Golden has been a perfect choice for a co-editor. I have known her as a colleague and a friend. We both grew up in Washington, D.C., ten years apart, and we each represent in our various ways these two cities, one black, one white, which are Washington.

This history of the relationship between black and white women—and I am speaking here in broad generalities—is one which has always been in its structure a history of the black woman in the role of mentor. Think of the plantations. Young girls grew up with slave "mammies" on whom they depended in profound and personal ways. As mothers and wives, their most important responsibilities for raising children and running a house were delegated to the slave women; their most private lives were often shared with them before or even instead of their husbands. And every woman knows, the person in charge of the house and the children is in a central way in charge of the domestic texture of the next generation. In fact, white women under slavery relegated a great deal of their personal power, their secret lives to the women who were slaves in their houses—and when those women in future generations became economically independent in spite of their poverty, providers for their own families, they gained a kind of internal freedom, a sense of themselves and their own boundaries that turned the tables and created for us, white and black women, two very different histories.

It is those histories that this anthology addresses in its various essays and works of fiction. In asking writers to be a part of this project, we gave a lot of thought to the particular people we invited, writers who had considered race in their fiction or nonfiction, writers whose backgrounds or present lives made them especially sensitive to issues of race. There were certainly a number of the writers we contacted who said they had nothing to say about the subject. We also wanted to have primarily original, unpublished material and therefore have reprinted only three stories: the often anthologized "A Worn Path" by Eudora Welty, who long before other women looked at race with a clear eye was writing about Phoenix Jackson with a compassion and empathy to break our hearts; Toni Morrison's "Recitatif," whose story of friendship invites the exploration of What is race? Projection or reality?; and Alice Walker's "The Revenge of Hannah Kemhuff." We wanted to include historians and cultural historians and so we have the African-American historians Catherine Clinton and bell hooks. We have included and concluded the book with two pieces by psychotherapists who approach the question of race in dealing with patients therapeutically. We hoped to have a range not simply of points of view—we knew we'd have that —but also of form. So we are pleased to include a chilling play of racial reversals by Joyce Carol Oates, Marita Golden's prose poem about white girls in her hair, a chapter from a novel in progress by Susan Straight, and a range of generations and professional visibility with a couple of new voices in fiction and nonfiction.

The arrangement of the anthology is fluid, generally responding to the essays themselves. We begin with a piece by Lisa Page, a biracial daughter's relationship with her white mother, and Marita Golden's white girls in her hair, and then friendship, history, mythology and fantasy, love lines, fiction, essays of definition, and conclude with paired pieces by Dr. Cathleen Gray and Dr. Shirley Bryant.

The title for this collection is not quite a fact, but, rather, a hope, that what divides us in a history of oppression and misunderstanding and exploitation can be bridged; that women of whatever color, who have carried the responsibility for the continuation of the race, will address our differences; that the issue of race in our children's generation will be, in fact, skin deep.

High Yellow White Trash
Lisa Page

I am a child of a white mother and a black father. That makes me what some people call a zebra, mulatto, or, more recently, biracial. There are a lot of names for people like me. Bright-skinned, mixed, café au lait, high yellow white trash. That last one I made up myself. It sums up for me what it is to be black yet aware of a white heritage. You get a double consciousness that never goes away. You are forever light-skinned, no matter how black you feel on the inside. You've got that bloodline that you can't deny.

For I do share the characteristics of both my parents. I have my mother's eyes, my father's hands. I am tall like the Germans of my mother's family. I am small-boned like the people in my father's African-American family. And all my life, I have looked for the strands of my heritage in the outside world. In the black and white faces of people I see on the street, I see my history, see the hatred and love that have forged who I am.

My father always talked about white people and black people. He had special names for them. "Ofays" were the white people he couldn't understand. They were the ones who could read music for days without spontaneity, without soul; they didn't know how to improvise. Ofays had no rhythm and no sense of humor half the time, he said. They were technicians; they could follow the numbers, do anything that was spelled out for them. They were so serious they couldn't relax; they didn't know how to have fun. But in business, they had it together, no question about it.

"Spooks" were the black folks who got on my father's nerves. They couldn't wait on the corner for a car to pass by. They had to walk right out in front of it and dare it not to stop. Spooks couldn't negotiate the business world; they had what my father called that "ghetto mentality" which doomed them to life forever excluded from the powers that be.

My mother was not so forthcoming on the subject of race. Black people were "Negroes." White people were "Caucasians." Otherwise, people were people and it didn't matter what color their skin happened to be. Yet she knew she had given up something by marrying my father.

The day that I was born, in 1956, she was wheeled into the colored maternity section of what is now the University of Chicago Hospital. Because she was white, the hospital staff hadn't put her there initially, when she went into labor. After my arrival, they relegated her accordingly. My mother lost a piece of her identity that day: her status as a white woman, something she'd taken for granted throughout her life. Now she had given birth to a biracial baby. She was guilty by association; she was stained, privileged no more.

To her credit, she never let on how much this disturbed her while I was a child. It was only later, during my adolescence, that she revealed how much this had hurt her. But I'm getting ahead of myself.

My parents had two more children, another girl and then, four years later, a boy. We lived in Hyde Park, an affluent, multiracial community on Chicago's south side, near the University of Chicago. The word "biracial" wasn't in anybody's vocabulary back then. My parents' marriage was referred to as interracial. As a child, I didn't understand this. It was part of the language the grown-ups used.

My father was my favorite person on earth. I waited for the sound of his laughter, the crease of his smile. To support us, he owned and managed his own drugstore and played the saxophone professionally on the side. He knew many jazz musicians: Charlie Parker, John Coltrane, Cannonball Adderley. He was always whistling be-bop tunes or practicing his saxophone. He played jazz records on the stereo, brought his flute to us at bedtime for a lullaby. Together, he and my mother prospered; they were the chocolate/vanilla yuppies of the early 1960s. He was the successful pharmacist, she was the former social worker and we were their beautiful children.

As a child, I never saw my parents' world as divided. But when they divorced in 1963, my world was shattered, cracked as if a giant quake had rendered it asunder. It was split right down the middle so that my one world became two: the white world of my mother and the black world of my father. They were never one world again.

My father moved in with his sister in the duplex apartment my grandparents owned. The divorce allotted him his business and the car, while my mother won the house, custody of us and alimony and child support payments to be made by my father in full. He saw the three of us twice a week. He was not allowed in the house when he came; he had to wait outside on the front stairs.

At about the same time the mayor of Chicago, Richard J. Daley, began what he called an "urban renewal" program; he tore down all the houses and apartment buildings around my father's drugstore, leaving a wasteland of poverty and urban blight. Gone were many of my father's regular customers who used to sit on the stools facing the soda fountain. They were replaced by drug addicts and drunks, street-gang members and the poor. My father was expelled from the middle class. He was back where he started all over again.

My mother, in the meantime, lived with us in the house. She didn't play jazz records on the stereo anymore; my father took his collection with him when he moved out. Instead she played classical music: Rachmaninoff, Beethoven, Mozart, Vivaldi. Her property values increased but her standard of living went down; she had to watch her budget to keep it in line with her alimony payments. She sent me to ballet classes, and my sister took horseback riding lessons, much like our white neighbors. I felt split in half, traversing these two worlds —one affluent and one poverty-stricken, one black, one white. It was a double life where the language changed as did the scenery.

"We were whites with defects," my sister tells me on the phone. She is describing the way my mother's family saw us. We were accepted, for the most part, but with complications. People were always trying to correct our "defects." My ballet instructor talked about my "swayback" and my "bad feet," never cognizant of the fact that that was the way black girls were built. She told me to straighten up, to point my feet harder. I held my chin up, slipping into my white-girl disguise. I wiped all expression off my face so that it was a clean slate, even as the toe shoes bit into my feet as I balanced myself. I learned to lower my voice too. This was part of the disguise. Without this costume, I was suspect and I knew it. As myself, I was always too loud around white people, too brash. My actions were sharper; I began to think I had to slow down. I didn't want to scare anybody.

And my mother's family clearly thought we were defective

too. When we visited her hometown in Michigan, relatives actually lied about us to the neighbors, claiming our father was East Indian to explain our skin color. During one family reunion the pictures weren't taken until my sister, brother, and I were out of the room. I was always conscious of my hair around them, of how unruly and dark it was, compared to their straight blond hair.

But in the black world, we weren't whites with defects. We weren't defective at all; in fact, the opposite seemed to be true. No one was scared of us in my father's drugstore. We were never too loud. People complimented our green eyes and our light skin. They asked our father, jokingly, "How'd you have some pretty children like that?" My father always said, "They're mine, aren't they? Of course they're pretty!"

There was a change in my father's language once he was away from my mother. His words took on a different slant. "Run that over next door for me right quick," he'd say. And, "Ain't that some mess? Now Grover know he ain't supposed to play that stuff in here." Away from her, he seemed to relax into another speech pattern. I tried to talk that way too, rolling the words off my tongue. I tried it out on the kids in the playground erected on one of the vacant lots. "Ain't that some mess?" I asked as they looked me up and down. "Ain't that some stuff?" This was another disguise. I learned to look tough when my father wasn't around, learned how to crack my gum when I chewed it, and how to rock my head back and forth to make my point. The world "alright" became "aahiite." "What do you mean?" became "Whatchu mean?" And when a boy liked you he said, "Can I go?" The response for which I didn't get. So that I usually lapsed back into my white-girl disguise in spite of myself, and said nothing.

This new language horrified my mother. "I told you never to use the word 'ain't.' It's improper English!" she cried. Proper English became a "white thing"; it went along with being soft-spoken and moving slowly. There were many white things coming clear to me now just as there were many black things. I was putting the world together, organizing it into its two separate files. The fathers of my white girlfriends were pipe-smoking academics with the wood-burning fireplaces and the book-lined living rooms, and opera playing in the background. They never whistled be-bop or said things like, "Ain't that some mess?" In fact, they never said very much of anything at all. The homes they lived in were large Victorian structures that usually included exotic dogs that had to be walked, a task that often fell to my girlfriends. Everything was so serious. Television was an abomination, an insult to one's intelligence. Books were everything. But not those potboilers, those murder mysteries, those Gothic romances! Steinbeck, Hawthorne, Shakespeare, Edgar Allan Poe, Charles Dickens, and Mark Twain. Bellow, Solzhenitsyn, Kafka. They were the ones worth reading.

And so I started seriously reading books, beginning in the seventh grade. Books became a passion of mine but they worried me too. They were more of those white things. Black people didn't seem to read books, and they didn't seem to write them either. The only black authors I knew of were Richard Wright and Langston Hughes. Of course black people did read the Bible; my father's family could quote scripture up and down, but they didn't know a lick of poetry and didn't care to.

Religion was a black thing. Even in the poorest neighborhoods where the only businesses were liquor stores and wig shops, there were still the storefront churches with their white-washed front doors. Hymns and gospel music. Preachers speechifying. Boys and girls in Sunday school, church picnics and retreats, youth groups . . . these were black things. My mother's religion, agnosticism, was a figment of the white imagination. Black folks just knew there was a God: ". . . for whatsoever a man soweth, that shall he also reap" and "Yea, though I walk through the valley of the shadow of death, I will fear no evil: for thou art with me . . ." These were codes to live by, beacons to follow in the dark. They provided a spotlight on the world, played up the difference between right and wrong, gave you a reason to weather the storm. Moral vision was a black thing. White folks never talked about it. Black folks did.

What white folks did talk about was their therapists, and this seemed their substitute for religion. It got you in touch with yourself. Some of the kids I knew had therapists and so did their parents. There were psychologists and marriage counselors, primal-scream therapists, psychic healing and Rolfing and eventually the spin-offs, est, and transcendental meditation.

I was sent to a child psychologist when my parents divorced. He wanted me to talk about my feelings but I told him lies instead. I didn't know what my feelings were. I just wanted my father back in the house where he belonged. It was too much for me, having to make sense of the world divided. I couldn't handle it. It wasn't fair.

Before I was out of grammar school, a new word was in the national vocabulary: integration. My mother looked up to certain black leaders, like Al Raby and Jesse Jackson. They were doing things to make Chicago a more integrated place. They were fighting a losing battle—Chicago is not now and has never been interested in racial integration. But the ideas were there, and in Hyde Park there was a genuine audience for it. The community prided itself on its racially mixed schools. But there was trouble too, especially around 1968 when King died and the west side of Chicago went up in flames. Even though Hyde Park did not burn, some families began leaving the neighborhood. And the racial makeup of my school began to change. Black faces filled up more and more of the classrooms as white people yanked their children out and sent them to private school. Whole families moved to the northern suburbs. There was a name for what they were doing: white flight. Even at the age of thirteen I understood what that meant. White fright was more like it. They were getting the heck out of Dodge.

And apparently I was what they were scared of. I was getting too close. I wasn't waiting on the front steps of the house the way my father did—I was inside the front door. I was talking too loud for them, moving too fast.

For I was turning blacker by the minute. Or so it seemed I was in my mother's eyes. I was just like my father, or so she said. I didn't appreciate all the sacrifices she'd made on my behalf. I talked back too much. I was angry all the time. I was always playing music too loud. Ballet was out the window. The boogaloo became my favorite dance.

Yet in my head, I was still white too . . . I couldn't double-Dutch to save my life—I always tripped over the jump ropes. I couldn't do the bop except by accident—I couldn't relax. I was like the ofays my father talked about who could follow the numbers but never improvise. I wasn't loud enough either. With black people, I was too soft-spoken.

But acting white was totally uncool. There were words for this: "Oreo" meant you were black on the outside but white on the inside. "Uncle Tom" meant you kissed up to white folks. In those days, black was beautiful and you had to prove yourself worthy of the definition. There was no half way to go about it.

My mother was unnerved by this. While my sister and I played James Brown's "Say It Loud, I'm Black and I'm Proud" on the stereo over and over, she said little if anything at all. But when I started referring to myself as black, she had a different reaction.

"Why do you have to refer to yourself that way?" she

asked. "Calling yourself black makes me feel like I'm invisible. Like I don't exist. Like I don't count."

She was upset when I started a subscription to *Essence*.

"Why can't you subscribe to *Mademoiselle* or *Glamour*? Why does it have to be to that magazine?" This stunned me. I didn't realize she would perceive this as a threat. But who were the women in *Essence* magazine? They surely didn't reflect my mother.

I started a new high school my junior year, one located in the downtown area. It required riding the bus every day. Every morning I caught the Jeffrey Express and it was filled with black women going to work. I admired these women, the way they wore their hair and their makeup and I told my mother this.

"Why are those women beautiful?" she asked me. Well (and this I could not tell her), they were beautiful because they were teaching me something. When I rode on the bus with them, they supplied lessons about skin color, hair texture and variety, personal style. Black-woman style. It was something my mother could not provide.

She saw this as rebellion, as ungratefulness. As her daughter, I was supposed to emulate and embrace her, not deny her. I didn't want to deny my mother. But I was different from her and I was trying to make sense of what those differences meant.

My white-girl disguise was still hanging in the closet. It was part of me; I couldn't escape it. But I found myself reaching out to my father in my late teens and early twenties. In my mind, he became the bright side of the family tree. Even then, I realize, I was organizing the world. Defensiveness was a white thing. So was manipulation, exploitation. Humor was a black thing, so were sarcasm and irony. Black was warm, white was cool, black was reefer, white was cocktails and cocaine. Black was action—finger popping, thigh slapping, selling woof tickets to make you smile. White was standing still long enough to get your point across, intellectual criticism, racial guilt. Black was differentiating between book sense and street sense, talking in the vernacular and speaking proper English too. White wasn't bilingual; it was one language, one world.

Now I live in the grownup world. I'm a mother myself. When I look back at the way I categorized the world, I think about all the nuances I missed. There were tensions in Hyde Park that were not just racial. Economic tensions, cultural differences. I couldn't see all that then. No, I saw my internal world only, and tried to project it onto the exterior. It was easier to deal with that way. That way it wasn't only my problem but everybody else's too. The breakup of my parents became the breakup of society. They were two warring factions I desperately wanted to make up.

But the black world and the white world are two very different places. That hasn't changed. I still travel between them, and most of the time I'm in an all-black situation or an all-white situation. That's reality. Making sense of that reality and my place in it has been a lifetime process.

I realize how much my mother struggled with her own identity. She thought she gave it up, in her marriage, or compromised it somehow. She couldn't help her inability to empathize with my situation. I think of this now when I look at my son. He will have different opinions from mine, different ideas. While we may not differ along racial lines, there will be other things. I only hope I can give him room to be those things. That he will know I will always accept him and love him.

I like to think I've worked certain things out for myself, but I'm still part of the larger society and we as a group have a long way to go. We still have names for each other, names for ourselves. Personally, I love the word "biracial." But it's problematic too. It has connotations that concern me—the suggestion of something slightly better than black, like the "coloreds" of South Africa. That half-white thing again. I'm not sure how different it is from the old terminology; it's a prettier word than "mulatto" but it's the same thing. The truth is, most black people in this country are biracial, with mixed white and native American blood. So I don't know about the ramifications in terms of the future.

I wish I could tell you I don't have a white-girl disguise anymore. I wish I could say I'm never schizophrenic around racial issues. But I still get confused sometimes, still feel I'm not black enough or white enough around certain people in my life. I have learned to cut myself some slack, though. Learned to accept that paradox is part of life, that being able to see two opposites existing side by side is a source of energy and strength. It's much easier to see things literally in black and white. But our lives are made up of gray areas that are not so easy to define.

I still hear my father's voice in my head and my mother's too. Spooks and ofays, Caucasians and Negroes, black people, white people. I still have a double consciousness and I expect I always will. It's part of negotiating the world divided, of maintaining a balance and being myself.

whitegirls
Marita Golden

whitegirls are a potion
slick, syrupy sweet and
dangerous
swimming
beneath
black skin
how did she get
inside me
was she hidden
in my daddy
cringing within
my mama
was she
with me
a twin
floating in the sac

was there room for us both
who kicked the hardest
so mama knew she was there
i was born
cesarian style
and already
she had infiltrated
a ghost nobody could see
but you knew she was there
cause you heard
the pictures falling from the wall
the tables pushed on their side,
the outwardly placid, still house
forever on edge
and trembling
there was the chill
of a spirit
unknown
even by itself
pre-packaged
re-packaged
bought and
sold
yes whitegirls
have been
slaves
too

my mama dreamed
of three-story
victorian-style houses
with her name on the deed
and lamb coats/fox fur throws
chevrolets and plymouths

she owned
and
before the dining-room mirror
in one of those houses
(her name was on the deed)
i stood
sentenced
before
gilt-edged mirrors
whose frames echoed the majesty
my mama yearned for
even wove into the
tattered edges that would in the end
overtake the solid seams
i stood
cursed
mama's scarves draped
round my head
scarves
draped and streaming
nylon and silk
whiteblueredgreenyelloworange colors
streaming/screaming to
reach my eight- nine- ten-year-old
shoulders
with eyes on fire
blinded eyes
pledge allegiance eyes
i saw
hair
in the mirror
cascading
blooming
falling

billowing
blowing
long hair
(not blond)
i'm too dark even in fantasy to be a blonde,
(and i knew even then BLOND
is a state of mind, a trick, a sleight of hand
a conceit plenty of whitegirls never know)
until they are old enough
to use clairol
cause it really doesn't even matter
if blondes have more fun
more men
more sex
more love
it's when you think about it that
you put the dye back on the shelf
but this hair
my hair reflected
in mama's mirror
is brown sometimes black
it is long, no
loooooooooooong
because
the world loves
long whitegirl hair
and eyes
and noses
but it is the hair
that really matters
it is the hair
black boys love whitegirl hair
on black girls
i fondle it

caress it
shake my head to toss it
(the way whitegirls really do)
with that
slight but definite movement
of shoulders neck head
and HAIR that
is the secret
the hydrogen bomb, the ace in the hole
long HAIR that
black girls
real black girls don't have.
but close my eyes
and then open them
lock my mind
and then kill it
and i have it too
mirror on the wall
who's got the longest hair of all?
dream on baby
dream on . . . .
and when I answer the telephone
pick it up to say hello
mama's friends stammer
"oh bea where'd you get that daughter
she talks so proper she sounds
just like a little whitegirl."
just like
a little whitegirl
just
like
a
whitegirl
does that explain the

awe/envy/satisfaction/surprise/glee/happiness
volcanic in their voices
what does it mean
to sound
like a little whitegirl
and look like me
they probe, pry, examine
when they visit
why no tinge of mama's north carolina
lyrical drawl
am i a talking duck
a singing bear
no
i am a little
black girl
who sounds
just like
a little whitegirl
why can't i sound
like *me?*
"this is just the way
i talk" i explain
near tears and i
don't know why
whitegirl
is the cruel norm
greedy standard
golden rule
perfect measure

read too much
think too much
want too much
live too much

earn too much
have too much
be too much
("who the hell does she think
she is, a whitegirl?")

in college
gym class i discover
whitegirls naked
look like black
girls naked
(flabby thighs,
knock knees, too small tits
too big breasts, childhood scars,
chicken-pox marks, cellulite)
look like us except the
butt no butt really
nudity
stark and unapologetic
is the great
equalizer

1969 and
BLACK
BLACKNESS
BLACKPRIDE
BLACKBLACKBLACKBLACKBLACK
stomps out colored/negro
BLACK as
in the color of the edges of fire
black panther berets
and nappy hair
BLACK
is crucible no longer

but treasure
gift
so we say so we shout so we scream so we say
one brother
confides, his afro pick stuck in hair
sprouting like a rainforest
he is wearing black sunglasses
to hide his soul
"Yeah I know the MAN is a pig
but I've talked to some of the whitegirls
here on campus
and sister
I don't
know what it is
whitegirls are different . . ."
he shakes his head
saying this
like one who once thought
the world was flat
gravity didn't exist
he knows the truth now
"whitegirls are different . . ."
voice distant
ecstatic
hollow
obsessed (but he doesn't know it)
he had sex with a whitegirl
last night
different than who?
different than what?
why do i feel this word
like a slap in the face
a punch in the groin
a slammed door

("your own paranoia sister,
you got to grow beyond that
if we gonna be free")
no it's all that damn hair

but
whitegirls
are different

whitegirls stowed
passengers
on the underground
railroad
cheered the imposition
of
jim crow laws
were burned as
witches
at the stake
packed picnic baskets
for the family to take
to alabama
georgia mississippi nigger
lynchings
have been trophy and
punching bag
of anonymous white
and black men
and ones everybody knew
i dislodged the
whitegirl who had
been squatter/trespasser
inside my head
drove her out

by washing my hair
(and my brain)
the hair
i don't press
or perm
just dry
then apply
afro sheen
which
melts her down,
her screams
are awful
her nails cling to my scalp
draw blood
(as always)
her feet scramble across my forehead
she wants to stay
she has been loved all these years
and now . . .
("wait a minute she pleads
I've got no place else
to go")

years later
with three sister friends
witnessing
thelma and louise
watching whitegirls
in the dark
we leave the theater
aghast
wondering if celluloid whitegirls
have anything to do
with

the lives of *real* whitegirls
the ones who never
got in my head
cause they live in appalachia
or in iowa and have acne
and $4.25 an hour jobs and welfare
and snot-nose kids and trailer homes
and mamas they hate and daddies they don't know
and they think feminists
just need a good man
whitegirl feminists think they
are beyond redemption
whitegirls
a noose around my neck
yours too
take off your suit honey
throw on some jeans
levi's not calvins
sit at my kitchen table
from kmart
taste *my* oppression
overdone and burnt
at the edges
which can't afford
no nanny from switzerland
or domestic
from some country
we run the communists
out of
i choke on it
sometimes
throw up too
but
what do

train tracks and ovens
and pills and ocean waves
mean when like
tomorrow may not be much
but
at least it's *something*
and if you get up early
and keep on stepping
maybe you can carve
your name on it
so *what* you're
a woman
most of the world's
got a womb
(and who *are* emma, anna,
virginia, sylvia, and anne)

we sit in the kitchen of one sister friend
dissecting
discussing
whitegirls
we
who have traveled
beyond childhood mirrors
and being battered
and so light everybody thinks you're white
and widowhood
and divorce
and generic female confusion
over coffee cake we are brimming
full of our own stories
and when
conversation circles back around
to *thelma and louise*

we vote
to always drive away from
never toward
s
   t
      e
        e
           p
cavernous elevated
f
   a
      l
        l
          s
we pass a resolution:
damn
the cliff!!!!!

The Racism of Well-Meaning White People

Naomi Wolf

y friend Elizabeth encourages her white students to write a racial autobiography. When I remember how I learned about the concept of race, I can see in my development a beginning and intensifying awareness of a racial gulf as clearly as if it were a fissure in the lifeline of my hand.

Before one learns the culture's negative associations with blackness, one is conscious as a child of a fascination with the idea of racial differences. In first grade, as for most of my primary and secondary school education, I was at a public school in which white children were a distinct minority. I wanted "Julia," the black single mother on TV, to be my mother, and I don't think it occurred to me that she couldn't. I wanted to marry Michael Jackson when I grew up. I wanted to pat Sean Wilson's Afro because it looked alluringly springy—growing mysteriously upward and outward even as my own hair grew downward.

This is what I thought about blackness: nothing at all, for it was a concept that had no objective reality. When I first heard the words "black" and "white" used in a racial context, I was confused: no one, of course, is black or white. I thought of the blackness of licorice or blackboard slate, and the whiteness of Caspar the Ghost, and I thought that this was a form of nomenclature that adults had created without examining it. I looked around me at my class of Chinese, Philippine, Japanese, "Afro-American," and scattered Nordic children, and what I beheld was ivory, biscuit, buff, brick, sandalwood, clay, tobacco, peanut, hazelnut, walnut, chestnut, and Moroccan leather, though I could hardly have named those names. When someone explained at last that the browner children were "black," I resisted, because to me, black was a hue that had no color and no warmth. What am I?, I asked, and was informed that I was "white." I stared at my hand, darker and sallower than the unpleasant peach-beige "flesh" shade in the crayon box, and I tried to merge these new concepts with the breathing evidence before my eyes. It was clear, though, from something in the voice that explained these things—or perhaps from the images around me that were starting to filter in, already beginning to structure into groups and values the chaotic, laughing, quarreling, undifferentiated tangle of childness in the school yard—that I was in by my skin; by a hair; that I was a lucky little girl indeed.

In third grade, my best friend was black; I still had little sense of what that meant. To me, Sondra's most defining quality was a kind of impudence, and an eager, squirrelly, tomboyish no-nonsense energy unlike that of the more placid girls on my block. We lay on the twin beds in her room—oh glamorous excess, twin beds, clown lamp, play lipstick—and waved our feet in the air; we planned in detail how we would be roommates in college. College meant that we would let boys come over to our room to visit.

Sondra's house was a heaven of forbidden independence, for she was what we would now call a latchkey child; we were on our own. Her mother was the only mother I knew who worked; this was right before the Second Wave hit the white houses on our block, and the mothers there were still pacing restlessly somewhere in the house while we played. Sondra's father was a handsome man in a uniform in a black-and-white full-length framed photo. Sondra's mother came home only at night and she heralded her return with a stern footfall, sterner than that of the other parents I knew. She had her reasons: once we spilled Cutex nail polish remover all over her varnished vanity and it blistered the finish. We were glad to feel it evaporate magically on our skin and breathe the lemony-druggy fumes. Another time we let the boys into the house, and, in a riot of sensuality, tasted the dessert wine kept in a glass carafe on the sideboard, fondled the glass grapes on the living-room coffee table, and pierced all the chocolates into sticky half-moons with our fingers.

In a low, private voice her mother threatened Sondra with mayhem for the badness we'd gotten up to; myself she never scolded, though the white mothers scolded me when I broke or spilled things. Sondra's mother never deigned to; she would let me out of the house with an averted face and turn away swiftly, almost shrugging, as if to say: Well, what, after all, can one expect. I learned that I was not to be treated as a member of the family.

I knew, of course, that Sondra was different from me, but the difference was in her effrontery and her bossy alertness. Her hair was long and puffy; it crimped naturally like the tassels of the woolen rugs that I surreptitiously unfurled on our living-room floor. Mine was long and lank. Her eyes tilted upward slightly at the corners and the eyelashes curled more acutely than mine did; her skin was yellow-brown and mine yellow-pink; the palms of her hands were softer and the moons of her nails showed clearer. But those differences were different the way I understood everyone was different. I could not know they would send us apart as irrevocably as train tracks diverging east and west.

Later, when I was ten or eleven, these differences were given a force that propelled us in opposite directions of the school yard. Sondra somehow was claimed by her black "group"; they played different skipping games, listened to different music, and doodled different catchphrases on their notebook covers. Suddenly she had a new body language, and wore the bomber jackets and rolled-cuff painter's pants that black girls wore then in San Francisco in the early seventies, and carried a comb with sharp teeth as an accessory of allegiance. Suddenly when I passed her outside the school-yard gates she was leaning against the brick wall, tougher and cooler than I was, tougher and cooler than I remembered she herself was; and when I passed she had her new girlfriends around her and she did not, maybe she could not, let her curly-lashed, low-lidded eyes, as familiar to me almost as my own, betray the least hint at what had been and still, still was between us. She as much as dared me not to come any closer. I was history and I knew better than to go up to her and try to claim back what she knew I knew about her: claim her back, cramp her style, complicate her new identity. I too, doubtless, in her eyes, had been claimed by my whiteness, though of course that was invisible to me. And I was history not because I had changed or because she had changed, but because somehow imperceptibly we had outgrown our goofy humanity and grown into the color of our skins.

"Why don't you ever go see Sondra anymore?" asked my mother, and it was like a cramp in my chest, though I did not have the words that could explain it.

Later still, the social valuations of blackness came home to me in even starker guise. This lesson came in the form of the boys from the Lower Haight, who would come up every spring to Parnassus Heights to steal the plums.

When the plums came out, our street was a vision: blossoms hung in clots like confectionery, showers of them cascaded down with the wind, and a few weeks later, hard, tart, carnelian-colored plums, with silver dust in the clefts, would appear among the boughs. Virtually inedible, to children they were irresistible.

The flocks of "boys from the Lower Haight"—already, we'd learned to use euphemisms—were indeed different from the boys I knew. They were louder, they shinnied up the trees and broke off the branches; the splintered boughs littered the street. Early on, the white dads leaned out of windows to confront them, and the boys looked up and put their hands on their hips and broke into peals of laughter, and let out extravagant strings of mockery that took the listening white children's breath away. The mighty dads looked utterly reduced as that laughter echoed down the helpless street. The dads quickly withdrew and never bothered to scold the boys again. (Years later, as an adult, I would see the scene of the black crows in *Dumbo* laughing just that laugh, and I would think, what white people must fear worse than what they believe to be black people's sexuality is that conflagration of black people's laughter.)

With the plum raids came petty break-ins and burglaries, and again and again a parent would see a child from outside the neighborhood dashing away from a broken window. Our house was vandalized: someone stole our toy savings banks with all the pennies and nickels in them, and someone defecated on the floor. Year after year after year this cycle recurred, and no one ever called the police. It was a liberal upper-middle-class street where you would lose your credibility as a decent person if you were to call the precinct on these children.

The children became pre-adolescents, who became youths.

Year by year the crimes grew more serious, and why not? The neighborhood, refusing to complain, was holding itself out like a plate. Finally an irascible old woman cracked, and broke the code of silence. At the arraignment, the mother of one of the boys thanked her. She hadn't known her son was running with a crowd like this.

What I saw and then absorbed in this ritual was the parallel of what I learned when Sondra's mother refused to scold me: the black kids were not to be treated as members of the family either. For when white kids brought marijuana to smoke in the hollow tree in the forest, and when my brother and his friends tried their mettle by sneaking into a local school building at night, and when a white kid showed his friends a lighter shaped like a gun at the school dance, the parents called the police. I learned that the parents had a different standard for white kids' and black kids' behavior; the flip side of this double standard was that we all understood that the black kids would get into worse trouble than the white kids if they did get caught, because for some reason their transgressions were seen as more threatening and more serious.

Most of all, I saw how the neighbors treated the blackness of the children like an alien destructive force that sweeps through, not into, a community; that it is not to be included in its laws, not enveloped in its expectations, and not held responsible for the lost tin savings banks and the broken boughs. From Sondra's mother and from the white parents, I perceived that racial difference meant the bad faith of the grown-ups' not treating the children of other races as if they were their own children, or even remotely like their own children.

Why did the white parents not bother to scold the black children? Everyone knew both that the children had nowhere else to play and that they are doomed anyway, so they might as well take possession of their pennies, their harsh too-grown-up laughter, and their fistfuls of plums.

I learned these lessons, which means that though I consciously hate racism, it is in me. But the racism of what I call WMWPs—well-meaning white people—is distinctive. It is not garden-variety, crude, explicit, guttural racism: we all know what that looks like, and white people of my demographic and ideological niche like to recognize it with a shudder because it is so far away from who we are. Its alienness makes us feel safer from the fear that racism is something that claims us too. But we WMWPs have our own codes.

As an adult, I find that my racism and that of the white people I know isn't made up, generally speaking, of what one *does;* if intention were all, I'd like to believe I would be home free. Rather, one's racism has to do with how one sees: one experiences one's own racism more often as a sort of shameful scrim, a dirty curtain made of the elaborate tissues of fears and inequities that surround and envelope the fact of race merely because one lives in a racist culture.

My racism consists of the thin, pliant, tenacious barrier that does not obtrude between me and a fellow Jew, but that does obtrude between me and people of color I encounter. (This barrier does not impose itself between me and people of color in countries in which it is I who am considered the stranger, and its absence is an unspeakable relief.)

In white people's experience, class bears an inverse discomfort ratio to race. In other words, to the extent that people of color a WMWP meets speak in an accent she shares, wear the kinds of clothes she wears, and participate in much the same social frame of reference, the tissue of the scrim is thinner and more transparent—*oh, I can see you,* and, of course, *you can see me. I am not just that pale blur, that comic rube, that ditto of oppression, a generic white person.*

This is what a white person hears about race when she travels in educated, overwhelmingly white, *very well-meaning* circles. First of all, she almost never hears overtly racist language, which is grounds for social ostracism (such language is rightly considered reprehensible; but, too, it is considered vulgar—literally low-class). What she does hear is white people talking at length about black people who are talking about racism. Or else she hears white people talking about the racism of institutions—such as the police department, or the FBI, or political parties whose views are unpopular in those enlightened circles.

In these conversations, the white people tend to assume a highly conventionalized facial expression—lots of shaking of heads, furrowing of brows, even a tsk-tsk or two. It is a little body-language set piece, stylized as the attitudes on a Greek urn, and meant to convey, "Isn't it awful? We're all in this together." More loudly it conveys, "I am a good, concerned, altruistic citizen." The tone is that of conscientious neighbors shaking their heads over the rubble left from an earthquake or a landslide—that is, a mindless, impersonal force of nature that is nothing to do with who they are. Finally, periodically and usually only when there is a black person present, she will hear a kind of equally stylized "personal" (but actually quite impersonal) breast-beating: "I was so *hurt* and *troubled* when I began to understand that our black sisters feel marginalized in this organization." What is odd about these moments is how rigid and unspontaneous they are, how repetitive. *There is a safe groove somewhere in this dangerous field,* the impulse seems to suggest; *Lord, let me find it; let me stay there; let me not stray from the path.* What one doesn't hear—what I've never read, for instance, despite the formal "we are all racists" mantra on the white left—is an anti-racist white person talking honestly about what their own racism looks like, sounds like, feels like.

Now, there have been plenty of moments when I've seen that black or brown people's invocation of racial tension is as stylized as white people's defensiveness about it. But a white person is writing this essay, and white people tend to leave the job of discussing white racism to black people, when in fact white people are the experts on it. So I'll stick to examining the racism of white people—indeed, of this white person. Not that I believe that white racism is the only kind or even always, simplistically and uniquely, worse than other kinds, but it is my kind.

This is what WMWP racism sounds like: WMWPs in conversation hear that someone of their background has been assaulted by a group of young men. The immediate next question is in code: "Was there a description of the attackers?"

Relatedly, this is the sort of anecdote that makes the WMWP rounds: "A clerk in a law firm was walking on a D.C. street and saw a group of young black men. He decided that the only reason to cross the street away from them was a racist one, and, not wanting to be racist, he did not cross the street. They called him white boy and beat him to a bloody pulp." The look in WMWPs' eyes at this: caught in the crossfire of our daily tensions, paralyzed between longing and fear.

WMWPs hear of slaughter in Bosnia and we say, "How evil"—that is, should we intervene? We hear of slaughter in Rwanda and we say, "How tragic; what chaos"—that is, "What, after all, can be done?"

WMWPs will sometimes describe an African-American's having received a coveted job, promotion, or fellowship, and the merest flicker of a glance will pass among them, and everyone knows the whole history of affirmative action legislation and debate is in that glance. And when someone finally speaks, he will say, "Of course, Harvard [The Fourth Circuit, The New York Times Op-Ed page] *should* have an African-American [man, woman]." And the unspoken sentence is: And then we can get back to a real meritocracy—that is to say, *my* career.

When a WMWP has an African-American doctor, lawyer, or stockbroker, he or she will be sure to mention it (in a context of extreme praise) to other WMWPs. If he or she employs an African-American domestic worker, it won't come up.

Everyone knows this, but it bears repeating: WMWPs unconsciously imitate the rhythms of Black speech when they are in conversation with Black people. Ironically, it makes them feel less self-conscious. And one reason WMWPs obsess about Black anti-White racism or anti-Semitism is that it makes them feel relieved.

There it is, banal and vague and choking: the racism of well-meaning white people. It means spending so much time trying to clear the scrim away—and hoping to convey that one is indeed trying to clear it away—that the Other in question is still dimmed and obscured.

If one is dishonest and white, one pretends it does not exist. But a white person who claims to have no impediment of vision in this country is not, I think, telling the whole truth. And when it comes to race relations, not telling the whole truth about the fog one inhabits slows down the work of groping forward.

I imagine that what bores black people about the racism of well-meaning white people is watching them struggle with this shroud and entangle themselves in it and blow at it and touch it and ignore it and disown it, all the while remaining rapt in the drama, the spectacle of our own anxiety, at the expense of the encounter itself.

Only connect, wrote Forster. "Only": what a glib, elusive hope—one written in a country, and at a time, when race was something that happened on the other side of the globe, not to other people's children at play or on your doorstep, or to your own child at play in the house of the familiar, perpetual stranger.

Overhand and Underhand

Retha Powers

I t is one of the incidents I would most like to go back in time and change. I was nine years old and I was riding bikes with my friend Allie on the bike path along the East River. Our afternoon had been spent racing down the hill that led from the entrance to my co-op building down to the water. Each time our small legs peddled to the mouth of the hill we counted to three, daring each other not to use our brakes to make the turn left or right away from the river's edge as we swooped down.

This time Allie moved right and I followed, gripping the handlebars of my green banana-seat bike until the momentum built by the wind of our descent expired and we came to a halt. We began laughing, exhilarated as much by the risk we took as relieved that once again we did not hit a bump or turn just a little too late and end up flying over the railing that separated land from water. Allie began to hyperventilate, not from shock but rather from the sight of a boy she liked. He was a classic

bad-boy fantasy. He was in our grade but had been left back
two times so he was really twelve or perhaps thirteen. He was
walking in our direction so she quickly turned her back and
pretended she did not see him. "Don't look," she whispered,
smiling. When he reached our general vicinity he asked her if
her name was Carol; she corrected him and stared intensely.
He looked at me, saying nothing, and then: "Hey-yo, black
girl. Let me see how fast you can ride your bike from here to
there." He pointed to a metal chain that kept cars from entering the bike path.

Who was he calling "black girl"? I stayed put, trying to
sort out my feelings and the proper response while staring into
his cold blue eyes. That was not my name. He had not called
me nigger, nigger girl, negress or coon. I was a black girl, but
that was not my name. In seconds I tried to sort out why his
calling me that made me angry and if it was more that he had
called out an order and expected me to respond.

I looked at Allie. She had been my first friend since I
moved to Roosevelt Island with my parents. We became fast
friends, as my mother would say, inseparable since the first day
we befriended each other, chatting on the phone and meeting
to play in the park or ride bikes as much as we were allowed.

"Do it. Go. Go." Allie fanned me away like she was shoo-
ing a small child and I rode as fast as I could. I had intended to
keep riding, to slip through the narrow space between the end
of the chain and the grass, ride back up the hill and go home.
But halfway there I thought about what it meant: that if I didn't
return I probably wouldn't have anyone to ride bikes with
anymore. I had just moved to the Island with my family as she
had, and I would be alone again. With this childhood priority
in mind but feeling sad and a bit hollow, I slowed down and
reluctantly made my way back, watching Allie nervously place
her blond hair behind her ears while the wind blew it around
wildly.

When I reached the two of them, there was little evidence that they had even watched, and Allie was still smiling.

Occasionally I play this scene over in my head. Not as frequently as I did throughout my childhood, but memory is funny and now and again something will bring this to the forefront of my mind. It might be something related, like the sight of a small girl riding a bicycle; other times it's something more abstract. Or it may simply be that when I am lying semi-awake in bed and tired, that allows me to access this part of myself. Why didn't I keep riding? Allie turned out to be a terrible friend and passed over lunches with me for the company of a new girl who was also white. She barely spoke to me after that, and if I tried to join the two for lunch they would speak as if I were not there. This type of breakup happens in childhood friendships regardless of race, when selfishness and cruelty are fascinating and fun. But what followed next was a letter addressed to my mother in Allie's handwriting. Enclosed was a letter written to me calling me "black slut" and accusing me of committing sexual acts I barely knew existed.

In my fantasies I say, "My name is not 'black girl'" and ride away, never speaking to Allie again. In reality, Allie did the above things and later became a skinhead. Soon after the biking incident, I resolved not to take my friendships with white girls seriously. My reasons for maintaining friendships with them were as practical as having a partner for bike riding. My parents moved to this new community, Roosevelt Island, because they wanted the best schooling possible for my brother and me. The Island was an experiment in creating a suburban experience in an urban city. It was fifteen minutes away from Manhattan by tramway, and today even closer by subway. When we moved there as one of the first residents, there were a handful of blacks in comparison to the number of white residents, but it was still described as integrated. In the school, there were very few Black or Latino or Asian students. So

wherever possible, I linked up with one of the five black children and made an attempt at strength in numbers.

But the reality of the racial imbalance made friendships
with white children an unavoidable necessity. Although I spent
much of my time alone, the thought of being alone all the time
was too painful, so I created an emotional distance between
myself and my white friends to the point where for a long time
I did not believe that friendship could exist in truth. Even
knowing better, I would eventually let my guard down and
allow myself to be hurt or surprised by an action or comment
linked to race. For example, there was the time that Kim, a girl
who was supposed to be a friend, stepped away and went home
after a white boy called me nigger. I didn't expect her to jump
in when I beat him up, but she said nothing to me when she
walked away.

When we were children, before I moved to Roosevelt Island, my friends and I in our predominantly black neighborhood in Queens developed a code to ask what someone's race
was. The need for a code was made clear to us by the way
adults turned their eyes on us, annoyed or embarrassed, when
we asked outright. "Is he overhand or underhand?" We asked
the question flipping our palms over, face up and face down
accordingly. Overhand meant the brown color of our skin, and
underhand the color of the pink fleshiness of our palms. Underhand also referred to the dubious nature of the white people of
legend we read about in our history books or saw in the streets.
It was a testament to the underhanded way that people who
looked like us were treated, which we were aware of at the start
of memory.

I grew up well after the civil rights movement, a benefi-
ciary of integration, a child who had never known legal segregation. Desegregation and the civil rights movement meant
that this was not supposed to happen. It was almost twenty
years after the March on Washington that some of the worst

experiences I had took place. But in truth, the racism of adults and this country continued to work itself through its children.

Many fistfights after being called nigger later, I stopped attending Island schools. By the time I entered high school, I had finally met up with black girls in large enough number to have a circle of friends. This was important to me, as I did not feel I had to protect myself against betrayal and was therefore able to be myself. Obviously all of these friendships were not perfect, but I never felt that I had to hold myself back or wait for them to do or say something hurtful.

On the other hand, in my liberal high school I became a desirable exotic to the white girls who befriended me. At this school, which emphasized the humanities, many of my class-mates were aspiring actresses, artists, musicians, or writers with middle-class parents who taught them at the very least that it was not polite to hate people on the basis of race. Unlike the girls of elementary school who said I was ugly because I was black, Una told me I was beautiful. She often asked if she could touch my hair and marveled at its curls, wishing her hair were like mine. Whenever we went out to a movie or dinner Una paid, especially if we were joining her group of friends, mostly nouveau hippies who were heavy into Jimi Hendrix and reggae but who knew no black people. The status of novelty soon wore off. I began testing limits by crying poor every time she asked me out. She never questioned this, even though my parents made far more money than did her mother, with whom she shared a cramped studio apartment. At first I liked playing the role of black friend, and the certain level of celebrity that came with it. Whenever a discussion about race or politics or class or anything vaguely linked to black people ensued, every-one turned to me in deference to my firsthand knowledge on all counts. Because I was now the celebrated one, I accepted the gifts with which Una frequently surprised me with entitlement mixed with contempt for her pandering. Soon I realized that she wanted me around because I increased her coolness quotient. Before we met there was no one she could point to as proof that she was not a racist. In high school my status in white friendships was transformed from easily discarded sidekick into exotic flower, a goddess on an altar of African-Americanness from which I struck the blows. It was a strange objectification, especially in contrast to my experiences with white friends who would not speak to me or become immediately distant when certain other white girls came around.

The exception to this rule came when I met Tara. Tara never treated me as dispensable or a novelty. We met at a meeting for our high school newspaper. Both of us sat in the back of the room with a cultivated haughtiness that was a combination of true feelings of superiority over our peers and a fear that we were not but had better act like it. Over long talks in the hallways and rooms of our school and our homes it was revealed that both of us had developed these façades out of feelings of alienation. For me it was the experience of being black in predominantly white environments and the ways that made me feel ever on the defensive. Tara was the child of ex-hippies who wandered Santa Fe, New Mexico, and other places she had called home for long and short periods of time. By the time she returned to New York and a decidedly more staid experience, she had become affixed in the place of outsider. Alone, we were lonely and bored; together, we were powerful and angry, a unified voice against anything we agreed upon or needed to protest in the name of each other. She never tried to erase my blackness via the convenience of color blindness in order to justify my place in her life.

One of the first things that cemented our friendship was that not only was she a white girl who recognized racism, but one who dared to speak about it. A math teacher who was white insisted on using my name interchangeably with the names of two other girls who were in our class. One day when she called me Ophelia—a sister with matte skin and narrow features who was also about half a foot shorter than I was—I once again told her that was not my name. She made no attempt to apologize, only stated that we looked alike. "No we don't," I said, echoed by Ophelia. "Yes you do," the teacher responded. "You both have the same nose." We screwed up our faces, Ophelia contorting her aquiline nose and me twisting my much broader and flatter one with contempt. We said nothing else, for we had no doubt been randomly confused with other black people before. It was Tara who cut through the politeness and respect we had reserved for this authority figure and blurted out, "No they don't; you just called her that because they're both black."

Of course all of us knew this was the truth. But never had I expected a white person to bother to understand and recognize the truth of a racist act, much less speak up about it. In this act, in my regard for Tara, "underhand" became solely the color of the palm of my hand. If Tara had been present when I chased down that boy who called me nigger, I don't think she would have turned around and gone home. In fact, she might even have joined in with me.

In addition to being the product of two open-minded parents, Tara had understanding and principles around race that were no doubt largely influenced by the fact that her brother is the only child of her mother's marriage to a black man years after her own parents divorced. She spoke to me about watching the way people responded to him when they walked down the street and the way her own Irish-Catholic family had trouble dealing with his existence for quite some time. For a time I naïvely reasoned that although the Irish were not enslaved, black people and Irish people should be able to relate to each other because they were both products of British colonialism. I found out mostly through experience and confirmation from Tara that this would never be the case, as many members of her family were bigoted in the worst way.

Tara did not talk much about her family's attitudes toward black people, and I never shared my instructions to be especially careful about trusting white people, nor did I share my experiences with other friendships with white girls. I wanted to keep the friendship untainted by the painful experiences of the past. And as I was evolving into adulthood I was no longer so fearful of choosing the wrong person to befriend. Tara and I were linked, and the bond we created was based on things that were so important to us that we chose not to make race an issue because we were so grateful we had found someone who could understand. Understand our love of words, the way they got under our skin and became flesh of our flesh, and our desire to use them. Our secret bulimia was something that we dared not tell anyone before our friendship lest they think we were insane. Our depression was fueled by a hatred of our bodies that would not conform to an oppressive standard of beauty except through the unhealthy methods we employed. We muddled through this period together, though helping each other out of it was like the blind leading the blind. We knew at least that we were not alone, and the wonderful qualities we admired about each other but could not see in ourselves gave us reason to believe that things would be better, that we each had much to live for.

Almost as soon as I began to need this intense friendship, we were separated by a letter of acceptance Tara received to attend college early. Here began her roaming. I missed her terribly and was afraid that she would make new college friendships and abandon ours. But when we reentered each other's lives during her school breaks, and later my own, the same intensity was there. In fact, at times our lives paralleled each other in ways that were eerie; we seemed to be having crises and breakthroughs at the same time. We even joked that we were the same person who came back to this life splintered to encounter life as both a black woman and a white woman simultaneously.

No one ever came up to me and told me not to tell Tara certain things. Within the closeness of our friendship I shared things with her that I never told anyone else regardless of race, and she divulged family secrets to me as we both struggled to figure out who we were and separate the part of us that was us out of our family histories and expectations. But often when I spoke I began to feel increasingly as though I were betraying my family by allowing a white person into the matrix of its very being. And I questioned my obligation to my race. Was I guilty of airing dirty laundry? Did she think what I told her was true of all black families?

Although it was painful for me, I told her these things but along with this admission came her own admission that she sometimes used me and another friend who was also black as a barometer of her own racism. Her "judges," she called us. If we were friends of hers then she must be okay. She admitted what black people talk about, but rarely in mixed company: that white liberals often idealize the experience of the African-American as the "real" experience in America and feel tremendous guilt about their part in the American legacy of racism. Tara and others like her hold us in esteem for being clean and unsoiled by the position of oppressor, and at the same time resent us because we are a reminder of a legacy they cannot escape. Somehow, to this Irish-Catholic girl we played the role of a priest to whom she could confess her sins and be granted absolution by our friendship.

By this time I had developed friendships with young black women and begun to tire of being perceived as a minority and thus insignificant voice solely because I was often one of the only black faces in an otherwise white classroom. After a trip to Kenya, where I merged with crowds in a comforting and empowering way, I was even less tolerant of the ignorance and insensitivity on the part of many peers and teachers when I returned to face my senior year. At Howard University I became a woman without a label explaining her existence. I was simply one of many African-American students who were bright and smart and driven. While we had our internal problems, no one was being cut down on the basis of their race. To a certain extent, being at Howard was an extension of my trip to Kenya. Like the continent of Africa, Howard—nicknamed the Mecca of Black intellect—was a homeland both illusory and real. I was able to put down my warrior shield. I no longer had to explain to white students why their words offended me, and if someone confused me with someone else it was because we really did resemble each other.

As I continued to create bonds with many other women of African descent, I began to feel I no longer needed Tara's friendship. In addition to realizing I would never be the outsider in the same way, I became less tolerant of having to explain things. At times when I was with Tara, I was translating the details of my life and, as with any translation into another language, there were certain words in my language that were not in hers; this resulted in the loss of nuances, subtleties about my existence she would never fully understand.

I became active in a nationalist organization that functioned under the assumption that because of the backlash against the civil rights movement, we were slowly sliding back. I read a lot about the Black Panther party and other nationalist writings and even considered becoming a Muslim for about a week before concluding that I could not tolerate the sexism. As the decade-long party of the eighties drew to a close, it became evident who was going to bear the brunt of all that was to be lost. As in all times of economic hardship, people looked for someone to blame, and once again as so often in history, fingers pointed toward the darker Americans. One day when we met at her stepmother's house I announced that change was coming and that sometimes in revolution people lose each other. She told me she thought our friendship was worth trying to keep. I silently stared at her. "Maybe it's only worth it to me," she said, teary-eyed. I still said nothing and soon after that left. Years later I apologized for hurting her, but she claimed she did not remember this happening.

One of the things I have admired about Tara is her fearlessness and wanderlust. While I was interning during summers and semesters in addition to carrying a full course load, Tara took a cross-country trip or waitressed in towns on both coasts because she had never been there. She was in London struggling for a job while I was beginning a career. Once during a phone conversation while she was living in California I mentioned that I wanted to see what it was like out there, I had also been dreaming of Seattle. She encouraged me to do it. To throw caution to the winds and travel while I was still young. These days she was thinking of spending time in Africa.

I was envious and angry at the same time. In this friendship, Tara is the one who travels and I am the one who stays put and plods away, always building. But how can I say this to her without offending her? "It's different for me," was all I could say, but the truth was that she could probably return to the United States and the job market and explain her splotchy employment history by saying she had been traveling or out finding herself and have a better chance of being believed. As a young, creative person in the working world, despite my achievements I am starting out behind my white colleagues and there is no time for diversions if I expect to succeed.

I have an advertisement card that was printed circa the 1930s. It features two popular characters, Topsy and Missy, who appeared in advertisements for J. P. Coats thread. On this card Missy, a white woman dressed in finery, is standing on the porch of a store while Topsy, a black woman clad in a dress that is mostly apron, is standing below in the rain. The copy reads: "Come in Topsy out of the rain. You'll get wet." "Oh! —it won't hurt me Missy I'm like Coats' Black Thread. De color won't come off by wettin." Topsy and Missy appear in various scenes in all of J. P. Coats's advertisements, Topsy ever the sidekick. I wonder if Missy thought they were friends. For a long time my friendships with white women made me feel like either Topsy or an emblem of liberal-mindedness or chic until I met Tara. But her ignorance about the ways race made our seemingly parallel lives cease to be parallel made it clear that there would always be a gap.

Despite our best efforts to avoid it, as Tara and I have made the journey from adolescence to adulthood, each of us has adopted the rules of silence and dishonesty around matters of race that our parents' generation accepted and which led to the end of the dialogue begun by the civil rights movement. The civil rights movement brought things out into the open that those willing are largely afraid to discuss today, and racism exists not in law anymore but in truth. As one of Lorraine Hansberry's characters in her play *Les Blancs* put it, race is an economic device, and once you introduce such a device it is not easily taken away.

What I have learned most in my friendships with white women including Tara is that race is too powerful to ignore. But I believe that at the core of everything between us is a love so deep that we will do anything to keep it from dying. So in our attempts to keep our friendship alive Tara and I dance around tricky and painful subjects, afraid that if we tell the truth our friendship will be too fragile and crumble beneath our words. The words we love that brought us together we now find difficult to utter. When we do talk to each other, we are always eager to hear the other's voice and thoughts. Mostly we talk about writing. But if writing is at its very essence the peeling away of layers and the champion of truth, then as it exists now our friendship is a lie.

Tara wrote me a letter from a new city she calls home. I treasured the beauty of this gifted writer's words and found I missed her. We are each other's history. Tara knows me from a time and place of my person that no one else can access. It is for this sense of anchoring and illumination that we love our friends. But I want our love to be honest, not half-assed and pale but full and robust, fearless as it once was. In this letter Tara confessed that she was jealous of my closer friendship with a black woman who is my best friend. This friend and I once called ourselves "The Two Fridas" after Frida Kahlo's self-portrait of dual selves linked by an umbilical cord, and it is so. Tara wrote that she was jealous of the fact that my new friend and I shared something as black women, a black woman friendship, she called it. But this twin-spiritedness is not based on race alone.

Black women and white women can be friends. However, it is different, and this friendship cannot allow the painful history of race in this country to force it toward dishonesty. In the words of Audre Lorde, our silences will not protect us.

Negative

A Play by

Joyce Carol Oates

CHARACTERS

MARY,
a young Caucasian woman

VERONICA,
a young black woman

In this encounter, racial stereotypes are reversed, as in a photograph negative. The mood and pacing should suggest a comedy of which the participants are unaware.

LIGHTS UP. *Mary has just entered the college dormitory room she will be sharing with another freshman woman. She is moderately attractive and modestly dressed; may wear glasses; wears a yellow freshman beanie and a shiny yellow identification button with* HI! *in black letters. The room is sparely furnished: two beds at opposite corners, two desks (one near a window), lamps, chairs, bureaus; two closets, doors shut. Clothes have been laid in neat piles across suitcases and cartons of books, shoes, etc. in the center of the room. Veronica's possessions are considerably more lavish than Mary's; included is a hefty trunk.*

MARY: *(A naïve childlike tone)* So—this is it! At last! My freshman room! Oh God I'm so excited I can't stand it! The college of my choice—my dreams! And I'm here on a scholarship—*they want me! (Pause, hugs herself)* For months I've been dreaming of this moment and now I'm here—alone. My roommate's been here—and gone out again—we haven't met—my folks are driving back to Davenport and I'm—here—alone. *(A touch of panic)* For the first time in my life I will be—*living away from home.* A thousand miles away where no one knows me. Gosh, I'm scared. *(Thumb to mouth)* Oh Mom!—Mommy! Daddy!—come back! *(Pause)* No. I am not scared. I am Mary Strep, Class of 1998. Whooeee! *(Tiptoes over to examine her roommate's things.)* Oh, God!—my roommate must be rich. *(Holds a stylish leather miniskirt against herself; stares into a mirror on a wall)* Wow. *(Holds up a dressier costume; sighs)* Oh! —so *pretty. (She discovers a framed photograph of Veronica and her family which she stares at appalled.)* Oh!—oh *no.* Oh *no.* The college has matched me with one of *them.*

(Veronica strides into the room with a dazzling smile. Very attractive, self-assured. She too is wearing a freshman beanie but wears it with style; also a tight colorful college T-shirt, an eye-catching skirt. The HI! *button is prominent on her breast.)*

(A beat as Mary and Veronica stare at each other.)

VERONICA: *(Recovering first, exuding "personality")* Well, hi! I'm Veronica Scott, your roommate!

MARY: Oh!—h-hi! *(She has almost dropped the photograph; stammers guiltily)* I was j-just admiring your f-family—

VERONICA: *(Warmly extending her hand to shake Mary's)* Please call me "Ronnie"—all my friends do.

MARY: *(Shyly and awkwardly shaking hands, as if it's a new thing for her)* "R-Ronnie"—

VERONICA: "Veronica" is a nice enough name but far too formal, don't you think? *I* believe in informality.

MARY: *(Nervous)* Oh, yes—

VERONICA: *I* believe in egalitarianism.

MARY: "Egali—?" Oh, yes—

VERONICA: And what is *your* name?

MARY: *My* n-name?

VERONICA: Maybe it's on your name tag?

MARY: *(Squinting down at the button)* Oh yes—"Mary Strep."

VERONICA: "Mary Step."

MARY: "Strep."

VERONICA: "Step"?—that's what I said.

MARY: *"Strep."*

VERONICA: With your accent I'm having trouble hearing it. "Mary *Strep*"—?

MARY: Yes.

VERONICA: Hmmm!—"Mary Strep." I *like* it.

MARY: *(Faintly incredulous)* You do?

VERONICA: Oh, yes! You don't hear many names like that. So—exotic. Musical. Is it a name with a legend?

MARY: I guess it's just a, a—name. Like in the telephone directory.

VERONICA: Oooooh no, it isn't just a *name*, it's a—an *aura*. It has its own history, I bet.

MARY: My mother's name is "Mary," and so is my grandmother's—"Mary." Back through my father's family everybody is named "Strep."

VERONICA: *(Wide-eyed)* Ooooh, see what I mean?

MARY: *(A bit too eagerly)* People call me "Mary"—for short.

VERONICA: Fascinating! And where are all these people?

MARY: Huh?

VERONICA: Sorry, I mean where are you from, Mary?

MARY: Davenport, Iowa.

VERONICA: Ooooh no! You aren't! *(Enunciates words sensuously)* "Davenport, Iowa"!

MARY: What's wrong?

VERONICA: Nothing's *wrong,* it's just you're the first person from Davenport, Iowa, I've ever met.

MARY: Gosh, I'm sorry . . .

VERONICA: Oh, no—it's *fabulous.* "Davenport, Iowa." Such a wholesome *cereal*-sounding kind of place! *(Pause, sighs) I'm* from Greenwich, Connecticut: quintessence of American suburbia.

MARY: "Greenwich, Connecticut"—I've heard of it, I think. It sounds beautiful. So—green?

VERONICA: And where did you go to high school, Mary?

MARY: *(Surprised)* In Davenport, Iowa.

VERONICA: Oh—there's a school there?

MARY: *(Puzzled)* Sure. Davenport High School.

VERONICA: *(Catching on)* Oh, I see!—public school. You went to public school—of course.

MARY: Where—did you go?

VERONICA: *(Airily)* Oh, Exeter. Eight members of our graduating class are here as freshmen; must be twenty-five Exeter grads on campus. Can't escape us!

MARY: Exeter must be an—exclusive school?

VERONICA: Oooooh no! Not really. We had lots of scholarship students. Exeter is racially mixed, and balanced; two of my closest friends—*and* a roommate, junior year—were white girls. Really.

MARY: That's . . . nice.

VERONICA: *(Proudly)* The president of our senior class was a white boy.

MARY: Oh that's . . . nice . . .

VERONICA: *And* he was gay; *and* he had multiple sclerosis. We all loved him.

MARY: . . . Nice . . .

VERONICA: At least, *he's* not here. *(Pause; rubbing hands together briskly)* Well! Which corner of the room would you prefer, Mary? I was here earlier but I deliberately didn't choose, I thought I'd leave the choice to you.

MARY: To me?

VERONICA: Why, yes!—to you. That corner has the window, and that corner has the, um, corner.

MARY: *(Shyly)* Gosh, I—just don't know.

VERONICA: A view of the bell tower and the historic green where a climactic battle of the Revolutionary War was fought—or a view of the, um, corner?

MARY: *(Very hesitantly pointing toward the window)* Well— maybe—if you don't m-mind—

VERONICA: My, thanks! *(As if Mary has pointed in the reverse direction, Veronica takes the bed near the window; she speaks sincerely)* Now, you're sure, Mary? You don't mind not having the view, or any natural light?

MARY: *(Swallowing)* I guess not . . . Veronica.

VERONICA: *(Shaking forefinger, big smile)* Now, now—"Ronnie"!

MARY: "R-Ronnie."

VERONICA: I'll call you "Mary,"—I *adore* that name!—if you'll call me "Ronnie." *(Places a quilted spread on her bed as if to claim it)* Now: the closets. Which is your preference, Mary?

MARY: *(Squinting and groping about)* It's sort of . . . dark . . . over here. I don't see a closet.

VERONICA: The big, spacious one is back beyond your desk; the absurdly cramped one is over here by mine. But please feel free to choose whichever you wish.

MARY: Oh, now I see it! *(Opens closet door)* Gee, it *is* spacious.

VERONICA: Obviously, I have many more clothes and suitcases than you do, Mary, but—it's your choice.

MARY: *(Apologetically)* It probably makes sense for me to take this one, Ronnie, doesn't it?—since it's—

VERONICA: *(Sharply)* What'd you call me, girl?

MARY: "R-Ronnie"—

VERONICA: Oh, right—I guess I told you to call me "Ronnie." *(Slightly forced smile)* If we're going to be roommates I suppose it's best to be—informal. *(Tapping foot impatiently)* Take your time choosing, Mary. We've got all afternoon.

MARY: *(Shyly)* Well, like I said it probably makes sense for me to take this closet, since it's right beside my—

VERONICA: *(Now a sincere dazzling smile)* Oh, that's sweet of you, Mary!—thanks.

(Again Veronica behaves as if Mary has said exactly the reverse of what she has said. Veronica begins to hang up her clothes in the larger closet; Mary has no choice but to hang up her clothes in the other closet.)

VERONICA: We'll have dinner together, Mary, okay? You can join me and my friends from Exeter—and these really cool guys I just met. Unless you have other plans?

MARY: *(Quickly)* Oh no, no—I don't know anyone here. It's such a big place and I—I don't know anyone here.

VERONICA: *(Squeezing Mary's hand)* Well, you know *me*. *(As Mary goes to hang up a dress, Veronica pauses to admire it effusively. It is a quite ordinary plaid wool dress with a white bow, white cuffs.)*

VERONICA: Ooooh! What is *this?*

MARY: *(Shyly)* My good wool dress . . .

VERONICA: Where'd you find such a style?

MARY: My grandmother sewed it for me. For my eighteenth birthday in June.

VERONICA: No! Your grandmother *sewed* it—*(She makes a sewing gesture as if plying a needle)*—by *hand?*

MARY: Oh no, Grandma uses a sewing machine—a Singer. She's had the same identical machine since 1938.

VERONICA: No! You don't say!

MARY: Grandma sewed my senior prom gown, too—sixty yards of pink taffeta and chiffon, and strapless! *(A bit daringly)*

VERONICA: *My* grandmothers, they insist us grandchildren call them "Meredith" and "Tracey"—their first names. They look as young as my mother. *(Laughs)* They'd as soon run a sewing machine as a—butter churn; or one of those quaint old rural practices where the farmer yokes up a—mule, is it?—and plugs the soil.

MARY: "Plows."

VERONICA: "Plows"—what?

MARY: "Plows the soil." Farmers "plow" the soil.

VERONICA: So what?

MARY: You said "plugs the soil." But it's—"plow." At least in Iowa.

VERONICA: I thought you said Indiana.

MARY: I did?

VERONICA: I swear I heard Indiana! *(Chuckles)* With your accent, though, I might've heard wrong. *(Holding Mary's dress against herself, admiring)* So your grandmother sewed this!

MARY: *(Proudly)* Actually, Grandma sews all my clothes. She sewed these. *(Indicating the nondescript outfit she is wearing)*

VERONICA: Isn't that sweet! Soooo caring! Must be a folkway, or something? In Indiana?

MARY: What's a folkway?

VERONICA: *(Airily intellectual)* Oh, just some species of unexamined ethnic, religious, or regional custom aborigines persist in practicing over the centuries without a clue as to *why*. Claude Lévi-Strauss is still the most helpful analyst of the phenomenon. Your high school anthropology class probably studied *The Raw and the Cooked?*—the classic *Tristes Tropiques?*

MARY: *(Helpless, cowed)* Anthro-p-pology? We didn't get that far I guess—We did a lot of reading—of books; and writing—learning grammar.

VERONICA: *(Staring)* You didn't deconstruct texts—you *read* them?

MARY: Then we wrote about them, or tried to.

VERONICA: On your mainline, I assume!

MARY: Main—?

VERONICA: Word processors?

MARY: N-no, we *wrote*. By hand. *(Makes a handwriting gesture)* Some of us had typewriters—but not me.

VERONICA: *(Incredulous)* The state of Indiana is not computer literate? And our President comes from there?

MARY: —Iowa. I'm from Iowa.

VERONICA: I'd wonder how you can keep them straight—there's Nebraska, too, isn't there?—and Arkansas— *(She pronounces it "Ar-kansas" rather than "Arkansaw")*

MARY: "Arkansas."

VERONICA: *(A bit sharply)* From thirty thousand feet in the air you all look alike: "Midwestern."

(Mary makes a timid gesture to retrieve her dress, but Veronica retains it, preening before the mirror.)

VERONICA: This *is* charming! You see, Mary, a folkway creates a spurious bond between people; gives the illusion of permanence in a universe of transience; makes unreflective people *happy*. Like, when you wear this, um, most original dress your grandmother sewed for you, you feel *happy* because you feel *loved*.

MARY: I guess so. I mean, I never thought of it like that . . .

(Mary would take the dress back, but still Veronica keeps it.)

VERONICA: Well, your grandmother loves you, probably?—and you love her?

MARY: Sure. *(Suddenly wipes at eyes)* I'm g-going to miss her—so far away!

VERONICA: That's why it's a quaint ethnic folkway. Emotion of a primitive, visceral nature is generated out of . . . not much. *(Examining dress inside, turning a sleeve roughly inside-out)* How's this sewed together?—Oh!— *(She has ripped a seam)*

MARY: *(As if feeling pain)* Oh!—

VERONICA: Gee, I'm sorry.

MARY: *(Taking dress back)* You ripped the seam, Veronica . . .

VERONICA: It was an accident, Mary. I'm sorry.

MARY: You *tugged* at it . . .

VERONICA: I did—what?

MARY: You *tugged* at it.

VERONICA: I did not *tug*, I possibly *pulled*. The thread is rotted or something—see? *(Tugs at another seam, which comes apart)* Substandard.

MARY: *(Further hurt)* Oh! Grandma—!

(Mary staggers to her side of the room contemplating the dress; Veronica locates a camera amid her possessions, and approaches Mary.)

VERONICA: Mary?—turn here!

(Mary turns, and Veronica takes a quick flash photo.)

VERONICA: Thanks, Mary! That's cool.

MARY: W-What did you take that for?

VERONICA: *(A bit evasively)* Um—just wanted to. I'm one of these camera freaks, I improvise. *(Takes another quick flash; Mary shields her eyes)* Sorry! *Thanks!*

MARY: I don't like my picture taken without my—permission. It makes me n-nervous.

VERONICA: *(Immediately sympathetic)* Oh I *know!*—I feel the exact same way. I *hate* it!

MARY: Then why do you do it, Veronica?

VERONICA: *(Putting on the charm, shaking forefinger)* Now, now, Mary—I'm "Ronnie." Your roomie—"Ronnie." Remember!

(Mary sighs, hangs up the dress.)

VERONICA: *(Snapping fingers)* Mary, here's what: I'll have your dress mended by a tailor. A professional. He can replace all that rotted old thread with good thread. And, um, maybe straighten out the hem—it's a little crooked, I noticed.

MARY: *(Quickly)* No, thanks—I'll take the dress home at Thanksgiving, and Grandma can mend it herself. She'd want to.

VERONICA: I just hope these quaint old Midwestern folkways don't die out before Thanksgiving!

MARY: *(Coolly)* If you mean my Grandma Crockett, she's only eighty-three years old. *Her* mother is still alive and going strong with *her* Singer sewing machine—*(Proudly)*—at the age of one hundred and four.

VERONICA: No! You actually have a great-grandmother, Mary? —one hundred and four years old?

MARY: Great-grandma Quantril is my *younger* great-grandmother, in fact.

VERONICA: Oooooh! I just have to record this! *(She has located a tape recorder amid her possessions; slips in a cassette, sets the machine going)* You say, Mary, you have *two* great-grandmothers?—and how many grandmothers?

MARY: *(Staring at recorder)* W-What is that?

VERONICA: Oh probably you don't have these in Nebraska— don't pay the slightest heed.

MARY: You're—recording what I say? R-Right now?

VERONICA: No, no, it's nothing! Just a little hobby of mine. Like say a guy calls me, I have the recorder hooked up to the phone, I set it going—just for fun.

MARY: But why?

VERONICA: Well goodness, why not?—*I'm* not technology-illiterate.

MARY: It makes me n-nervous . . . Please don't.

VERONICA: *(Playfully)* Now Mary, you wouldn't be n-nervous if you weren't obsessing over a detail.

MARY: But—

VERONICA: Never mind me, *you're* the fascinating one of the two of us, Mary! *(Mysteriously)* I see I have much, much to learn this freshman year. More than I'd guessed! Now, about the grandmothers—

(Mary has been hanging up her clothes, unpacking possessions including shoes, books, etc. Moving stiffly and self-consciously as Veronica observes her.)

MARY: I'd rather not discuss my grandmothers any more right now, thanks. "Ronnie."

VERONICA: *(Positioning the tape recorder more advantageously)* Oh I know, I know!—*I* never talk about mine even to friends, I just *loathe* the subject. Every time it comes up I stop my ears and hum as loud as I can. *(Stops ears, hums loudly)* But: *your* grandmothers are special, Mary. Think of these old pioneer women out there on the great cereal plains of America—*sewing away*. Gives me shivers!

MARY: Actually, Davenport is a city.

VERONICA: "Davenport"—what's that?

MARY: Where I'm from—Davenport, Ohio. I mean—Iowa.

VERONICA: You said you were from Step, Nebraska.

MARY: No, "Step" is my name. I mean—"Strep" is my name.

VERONICA: Well, goodness, you don't need to get excited. *I* didn't name you "Step."

MARY: My point is, Davenport is a city, not a cereal field. *(A bit boastful)* We have a population of over one hundred thousand.

VERONICA: *(Skeptical)* People?

MARY: Yes . . .

(Veronica stares at Mary for a beat; then snaps fingers dismissively.)

VERONICA: Oh, you mean *white* people.

MARY: *(Weakly protesting)* Is that—thing still on? It makes me—

VERONICA: I know: "n-nervous." *(Pretends to be switching the recorder off)* There we are! Off. *(Teasing, joking)* My, we're a little thin-skinned, aren't we?

MARY: I'm s-sorry, it just makes me—

VERONICA: You know, Mary, your accent is so *interesting*. I've never heard one quite like it before.

MARY: My accent?

VERONICA: *(Laughs)* Hear? The way you say "accent . . ."

MARY: How is it supposed to sound?

VERONICA: *(An English intonation)* "Ac-cent."

MARY: *(Tries to imitate her but cannot)* "Ac-cent." "AC-CENT."

(Veronica positions herself close in front of Mary.)

VERONICA: First, take a deep breath—deep!

(Mary tries to comply.)

VERONICA: Deep down in the diaphragm!

MARY: *(Expelling air)* Like this—?

VERONICA: Fill your lungs, clear your larynx, let your tongue rest *lightly* against the roof of your mouth—

(Mary tries, choking.)

VERONICA: Now repeat after me: "Ac-cent."

MARY: "Ac-cent"—

VERONICA: Not through your nose, through your *mouth.*

MARY: "Not through your n-nose, through your *m-mouth.*"

(Veronica laughs.)

MARY: What's so f-funny?

VERONICA: Not a thing. I *adore* the way you talk, Mary!

MARY: *(Perplexed)* Up until a few days ago, when we left home to drive East, I never had the slightest accent. Nobody did! I don't know how on earth I got one *here.*

VERONICA: *(Hands to mouth but snorting with laughter)* Oh! there you go again!

MARY: What? What?

(Veronica squeals with laughter as if she's being tickled; then forces herself to become sober.)

VERONICA: Mary, look: America is a mosaic of many, many different ways of speech—local customs—"ac-cents"—*(She cruelly imitates Mary's "accent")*—it's a democracy and *we're all equal.*

MARY: We are?

(Veronica stifles laughter again.)

MARY: *(Miserably)* Everybody's going to laugh at me here—I know it. My professors, my classmates, my r-roommate—In my dreams, all summer, I'd hear strangers laughing at me—but I didn't know *why.*

VERONICA: *(Practicably)* Well, now you know. That's a gain.

MARY: Maybe you could h-help me, Ronnie? I could learn to talk like you?

VERONICA: *(Graciously)* I have no objections if you try to model yourself after me, certainly. My little, um, white-girl roommate at Exeter tried that, too. It was such *fun.*

MARY: What happened?

VERONICA: Oh, I don't know. We were just roommates a few weeks before she, um, dropped out of school. Vanished without a trace.

MARY: *(Grimly)* That's what I'm afraid of. Scared to death. I'll fail my subjects—drop out—vanish without a trace. Oh gosh-golly!

VERONICA: *(Enunciating in the direction of the recorder)* "Gosh-golly!"

MARY: *(Hurt, upset)* Is that thing still *on?*

VERONICA: *(Hurt, stiffly)* It is *not.* I told you I turned it off, didn't I?

MARY: Why is this wheel still going round?

VERONICA: It's unwinding, that's why. Don't you know how recorders work?

MARY: I guess not . . .

(Veronica has been gazing at Mary closely.)

VERONICA: Mary, now we've broken the ice and we're getting along so well—can I ask you something personal?

MARY: *(Guardedly)* What?

VERONICA: Your hair.

MARY: *(Touching hair, alarmed)* My hair? That's a question?

VERONICA: Promise, now, you won't be miffed?—you're kind of thin-skinned, I've discovered.

MARY: I won't . . . be miffed.

VERONICA: Promise!

MARY: *(With dread)* I promise.

VERONICA: I've always wanted to ask one of you: is your hair naturally that way?

MARY: What way?

VERONICA: Or do you do something to it?

MARY: How—is it?

(Veronica touches Mary's hair with cautious fingers; her expression is one of someone touching an insect.)

VERONICA: So sort of—fine. Dry. Ooooh!—sort of *shivery.*

MARY: *(Backing off)* I d-don't do anything to my hair except shampoo it.

VERONICA: Don't you brush it? Comb it?

MARY: *(Hotly)* Of course I brush and comb it! I just don't *think* about it.

VERONICA: But your hair is—lovely, Mary. It suits *you.*

MARY: I—I'd better finish unpacking . . . *(She picks up a toiletry kit but is so rattled she drops it, and its contents spill on the floor. Veronica doesn't notice.)*

VERONICA: *(Cheerfully)* I'd better finish unpacking! We have a date for dinner, remember?—a big table of us. You'll love my friends, Mary. And these two guys I just met—are they *cool.*

(Mary and Veronica are busily hanging up clothes, unpacking suitcases and boxes, etc.)

MARY: *(Worried)* These guys, um—are they—?

VERONICA: Seniors. Real hunks!

MARY: Are they, er—?

VERONICA: Good-looking? You bet!

MARY: I mean, um—

VERONICA: Tall? For sure. *I* don't go out with dwarfs!

MARY: *(Miserably nervous)* I, er, was wondering what— r-r-race—

VERONICA: *(Surprised)* "Race"—?

MARY: I mean, you know—what c-c-color—their skin—

VERONICA: "Color"?—"skin"? *(A beat)* I didn't notice.

MARY: Oh.

VERONICA: I never notice such superfluities. Race—skin—color: America is a *mosaic,* we're all absolutely *equal,* we're beyond primitive divisions of *us* and *them.*

MARY: Yes, but I—I get n-nervous, if—I mean, I don't feel comfortable if—I had this feeling, when my folks and I crossed the quad, and came into the dorm here—p-people were watching us.

VERONICA: What kind of people?

MARY: The, uh—majority people. *Your* people.

VERONICA: *(Warmly)* Oh Mary! That isn't so! People like you are one hundred percent welcome here—this college has been integrated since 1877! Wasn't that a stirring speech the Chancellor made this morning?—"Giving a Hand to Those in Need." And you "Deficiency Scholars" aren't tagged in any evident way; it's like you scored high SATS and your folks can pay full tuition like the rest of us. Really.

MARY: *(Thumb to mouth)* R-Really?

VERONICA: Roommates are warned—I mean, notified—but only so we can help tutor you, if necessary. *I* volunteered to room with one of you, for that purpose.

MARY: Gee, you did?

VERONICA: Well, it fits in with my Freshman Honors Seminar thesis.

MARY: *(Stunned)* You've chosen your topic already? What is it?

VERONICA: Um . . . a photo-journal account. Kind of a personal diary. With anthropological and psychological dimensions, of course.

MARY: You're going to write about . . . me?

VERONICA: Oh no, oh no!—don't be silly, Mary. Not *you*. Not you *personally*.

MARY: Now I feel kind of . . . funny.

VERONICA: Well, you wouldn't, if you didn't take everything so personally! *(Pause)* Just be yourself. Be your natural self. That's *my* philosophy of life.

MARY: *(Swallowing hard)* "Just be yourself." I'll try, Ver—, Ronnie. Can I model myself after you?

VERONICA: Oooooh is that sweet! *(Gives Mary a quick kiss on the cheek, which quite dazes Mary)* But you should just be *you*, if you know who that is. That's what growing up in America in these enlightened times is all about.

(Mary and Veronica continue unpacking, etc. Veronica removes her beanie and tosses it onto her bed; Mary, watching her, imitates her —but Mary's beanie misses her bed. Veronica whistles and moves to suggestive dance music; Mary imitates her, unable to do more than hiss, and moving about most clumsily.)

VERONICA: Um—Mary?

MARY: *(Eagerly yet in dread)* Y-Yes, Ronnie?

VERONICA: Could you carry this damn old trunk downstairs to the storage room for me?—I'll be happy to pay you.

MARY: *(Stunned)* Now?

VERONICA: Well, whenever. Is five dollars enough?

MARY: I . . .

VERONICA: Okay, then—ten dollars.

MARY: But I . . .

VERONICA: These suitcases, I think they can fit into your closet. Let's see.

MARY: S-Suitcases? Gosh, I don't think so—

VERONICA: *(Peering into Mary's closet, shoving clothes on hangers aside)* Well, we can *try*.

MARY: But, R-Ronnie—

VERONICA: C'mon, give me a hand! *(They push several suitcases into the closet; some of Mary's shoes are squeezed out)* Tight fit, but the damn things are *in*.

(Mary picks up her shoes, not knowing what to do with them; puts them beneath her bed.)

MARY: But I have my own s-suitcases—

VERONICA: You're going down to the storage room, you can take them with you. They're made of cardboard, not leather—they won't scratch. What's the problem? *(She seems genuinely puzzled)*

(Mary covers her face with her hands; during this speech of Veronica's she goes trancelike to sit heavily on her bed and stares off into space, as if catatonic.)

VERONICA: *(Proudly)* I should inform you, Mary—my father is Byron T. Scott. *(Pause; no response from Mary)* Now in a lucrative private practice in Manhattan but, in the sixties, a renowned civil rights attorney. You know his name I'm sure— a personal friend of John F. Kennedy?—and, now, Bill and Hillary? *(Pause; no response from Mary)* Daddy was a champion of integration from the first. In his law firm he always hired whites—not by quota, either. *And* the handicapped. *(Pause)* Physically and mentally challenged—Daddy doesn't discrimi- nate. *(Pause; has tiptoed over to get her camera)* And *I* don't discriminate. *(Lyrical voice)* One of my earliest memories is of Nellie Fay Cotton, the kindly, obese, diabetic Ozark woman my parents hired at the minimum wage to take care of me when I was a baby. Ooooh did I love Nellie Fay! Ugly as sin—but she had a beautiful soul inside. Imagine!—Nellie Fay had nine- teen children of her own, and her husband was an ex-miner with black lung who had nothing to do all day but drink and beat up on her till finally she escaped and came North—but Nellie Fay never lost her faith in God, or in mankind. Never! "He sees into our hearts, He loves us each and every one"— Nellie Fay used to tell me, when I was still in my crib. *(Wiping at eyes, maudlin)* Then, one summer, these sort of snooty relatives of Mother's were visiting, from Boston, and my aunt's sapphire choker was missing from the guest room, and Nellie Fay was the suspect, and oh! it was so, so sad!—Nellie Fay was scared and nervous and acted guilty—poor thing! She loved us so, loved me so, it was like I was her own baby—truly! Well, the Greenwich police came—interrogated Nellie Fay—did a thorough body check, I guess—didn't find the damn sapphire choker—Nellie Fay was dismissed and went away and a few days later guess what!—

(Veronica dramatically turns to Mary, who sits as before, staring glassily into space.)

VERONICA: You guessed it!—the choker was discovered in the deep end of our swimming pool, when the maintenance man came to clean it. Oh were my parents apologetic! oh were they chagrined! Right away they called Nellie Fay—I was just a baby but remember, clearly—they failed to reach her—finally got one of her daughters—but it was too late. Poor dear Nellie Fay had killed herself in shame—swallowed a full can of Drano. Oh! the sorrow in our household! the regret! It took Mom and Dad weeks and weeks to find a replacement. *(Pause; she has the camera ready)* Excuse me, Mary?—would you mind?—I'd like an intimate shot of both of us. To commemorate our first day together as roommates. The frontispiece of my photo-journal . . .

(Telephone rings. Veronica answers it.)

VERONICA: *(Exuding "personality")* Hi! Yeah! *(Listens wide-eyed; big smile; unconsciously strokes herself)* What?—oh, wow! Tonight? DeWitt, Evander, Jacey?—and Buchanan? Who's driving? How many cars? All the way to Manhattan—that's an hour and a half. Okay, but when? *(Checks watch)* Wow, that's in half an hour. *(Listens)* Okay, sure. Count me in. *(Listens)*

Buchanan's got his Jaguar? Cool! *(Listens)* No, no—what other plans would I have for tonight? Bye! *(Hangs up)*

(Veronica approaches Mary, who sits unmoving as before.)

VERONICA: *(Fussing with camera, positions it on a desk facing Mary)* Now!—I'm going to set this here—set the timer— Okay! *(She hurries to get into the picture, sitting beside Mary on the bed; her arm around Mary's shoulders and her head close beside Mary's)* One-two-three *smile!* We're going to have a terrific freshman year!

(Veronica smiles her dazzling smile; Mary remains catatonic but smiles, a ghastly wide blank smile.)

(Camera flashes.)

(Immediate LIGHTS OUT.*)*

Commissioned by the Philadelphia Festival Theatre for New Plays (production spring 1995, Annenberg Theatre, Philadelphia)

Recitatif

Toni Morrison

My mother danced all night and Roberta's was sick. That's why we were taken to St. Bonny's. People want to put their arms around you when you tell them you were in a shelter, but it really wasn't bad. No big long room with one hundred beds like Bellevue. There were four to a room, and when Roberta and me came, there was a shortage of state kids, so we were the only ones assigned to 406 and could go from bed to bed if we wanted to. And we wanted to, too. We changed beds every night and for the whole four months we were there we never picked one out as our own permanent bed.

It didn't start out that way. The minute I walked in and the Big Bozo introduced us, I got sick to my stomach. It was one thing to be taken out of your own bed early in the morning—it was something else to be stuck in a strange place with a girl from a whole other race. And Mary, that's my mother, she was

right. Every now and then she would stop dancing long
enough to tell me something important and one of the things
she said was that they never washed their hair and they smelled
funny. Roberta sure did. Smell funny, I mean. So when the Big
Bozo (nobody ever called her Mrs. Itkin, just like nobody ever
said St. Bonaventure)—when she said, "Twyla, this is Roberta.
Roberta, this is Twyla. Make each other welcome," I said, "My
mother won't like you putting me in here."

"Good," said Bozo. "Maybe then she'll come and take you
home."

How's that for mean? If Roberta had laughed I would have
killed her, but she didn't. She just walked over to the window
and stood with her back to us.

"Turn around," said the Bozo. "Don't be rude. Now
Twyla. Roberta. When you hear a loud buzzer, that's the call
for dinner. Come down to the first floor. Any fights and no
movie." And then, just to make sure we knew what we would
be missing, *"The Wizard of Oz."*

Roberta must have thought I meant that my mother would
be mad about my being put in the shelter. Not about rooming
with her, because as soon as Bozo left she came over to me and
said, "Is your mother sick too?"

"No," I said. "She just likes to dance all night."

"Oh." She nodded her head and I liked the way she understood things so fast. So for the moment it didn't matter that we
looked like salt and pepper standing there and that's what the
other kids called us sometimes. We were eight years old and
got F's all the time. Me because I couldn't remember what I
read or what the teacher said. And Roberta because she
couldn't read at all and didn't even listen to the teacher. She
wasn't good at anything except jacks, at which she was a killer:
pow scoop pow scoop pow scoop.

We didn't like each other all that much at first, but nobody
else wanted to play with us because we weren't real orphans

with beautiful dead parents in the sky. We were dumped. Even the New York City Puerto Ricans and the upstate Indians ignored us. All kinds of kids were in there, black ones, white ones, even two Koreans. The food was good, though. At least I thought so. Roberta hated it and left whole pieces of things on her plate: Spam, Salisbury steak—even Jell-O with fruit cocktail in it, and she didn't care if I ate what she wouldn't. Mary's idea of supper was popcorn and a can of Yoo-Hoo. Hot mashed potatoes and two weenies was like Thanksgiving for me.

It really wasn't bad, St. Bonny's. The big girls on the second floor pushed us around now and then. But that was all. They wore lipstick and eyebrow pencil and wobbled their knees while they watched TV. Fifteen, sixteen, even, some of them were. They were put-out girls, scared runaways most of them. Poor little girls who fought their uncles off but looked tough to us, and mean. God, did they look mean. The staff tried to keep them separate from the younger children, but sometimes they caught us watching them in the orchard where they played radios and danced with each other. They'd light out after us and pull our hair or twist our arms. We were scared of them, Roberta and me, but neither of us wanted the other one to know it. So we got a good list of dirty names we could shout back when we ran from them through the orchard. I used to dream a lot and almost always the orchard was there. Two acres, four maybe, of these little apple trees. Hundreds of them. Empty and crooked like beggar women when I first came to St. Bonny's but fat with flowers when I left. I don't know why I dreamed about that orchard so much. Nothing really happened there. Nothing all that important, I mean. Just the big girls dancing and playing the radio. Roberta and me watching. Maggie fell down there once. The kitchen woman with legs like parentheses. And the big girls laughed at her. We should have helped her up, I know, but we were scared of those girls with lipstick and eyebrow pencil. Maggie couldn't talk. The kids said she had her tongue cut out, but I think she was just born that way: mute. She was old and sandy-colored and she worked in the kitchen. I don't know if she was nice or not. I just remember her legs like parentheses and how she rocked when she walked. She worked from early in the morning till two o'clock, and if she was late, if she had too much cleaning and didn't get out till two-fifteen or so, she'd cut through the orchard so she wouldn't miss her bus and have to wait another hour. She wore this really stupid little hat—a kid's hat with ear flaps—and she wasn't much taller than we were. A really awful little hat. Even for a mute, it was dumb—dressing like a kid and never saying anything at all.

"But what about if somebody tries to kill her?" I used to wonder about that. "Or what if she wants to cry? Can she cry?"

"Sure," Roberta said. "But just tears. No sounds come out."

"She can't scream?"

"Nope. Nothing."

"Can she hear?"

"I guess."

"Let's call her," I said. And we did.

"Dummy! Dummy!" She never turned her head.

"Bow legs! Bow legs!" Nothing. She just rocked on, the chin straps of her baby-boy hat swaying from side to side. I think we were wrong. I think she could hear and didn't let on. And it shames me even now to think there was somebody in there after all who heard us call her those names and couldn't tell on us.

We got along all right, Roberta and me. Changed beds every night, got F's in civics and communication skills and gym. The Bozo was disappointed in us, she said. Out of 130 of us state cases, 90 were under twelve. Almost all were real orphans with beautiful dead parents in the sky. We were the only ones dumped and the only ones with F's in three classes including gym. So we got along—what with her leaving whole pieces of things on her plate and being nice about not asking questions.

I think it was the day before Maggie fell down that we found out our mothers were coming to visit us on the same Sunday. We had been at the shelter twenty-eight days (Roberta twenty-eight and a half) and this was their first visit with us. Our mothers would come at ten o'clock in time for chapel, then lunch with us in the teachers' lounge. I thought if my dancing mother met her sick mother it might be good for her. And Roberta thought her sick mother would get a big bang out of a dancing one. We got excited about it and curled each other's hair. After breakfast we sat on the bed watching the road from the window. Roberta's socks were still wet. She washed them the night before and put them on the radiator to dry. They hadn't, but she put them on anyway because their tops were so pretty—scalloped in pink. Each of us had a purple construction-paper basket that we had made in craft class. Mine had a yellow crayon rabbit on it. Roberta's had eggs with wiggly lines of color. Inside were cellophane grass and just the jelly beans because I'd eaten the two marshmallow eggs they gave us. The Big Bozo came herself to get us. Smiling, she told us we looked very nice and to come downstairs. We were so surprised by the smile we'd never seen before, neither of us moved.

"Don't you want to see your mommies?"

I stood up first and spilled the jelly beans all over the floor. Bozo's smile disappeared while we scrambled to get the candy up off the floor and put it back in the grass.

She escorted us downstairs to the first floor, where the other girls were lining up to file into the chapel. A bunch of grown-ups stood to one side. Viewers mostly. The old biddies

who wanted servants and the fags who wanted company looking for children they might want to adopt. Once in a while a
grandmother. Almost never anybody young or anybody whose
face wouldn't scare you in the night. Because if any of the real
orphans had young relatives they wouldn't be real orphans. I
saw Mary right away. She had on those green slacks I hated
and hated even more now because didn't she know we were
going to chapel? And that fur jacket with the pocket linings so
ripped she had to pull to get her hands out of them. But her
face was pretty—like always—and she smiled and waved like
she was the little girl looking for her mother, not me.

I walked slowly, trying not to drop the jelly beans and
hoping the paper handle would hold. I had to use my last
Chiclet because by the time I finished cutting everything out,
all the Elmer's was gone. I am left-handed and the scissors
never worked for me. It didn't matter, though; I might just as
well have chewed the gum. Mary dropped to her knees and
grabbed me, mashing the basket, the jelly beans, and the grass
into her ratty fur jacket.

"Twyla, baby. Twyla, baby!"

I could have killed her. Already I heard the big girls in the
orchard the next time saying, "Twyyyyyla, baby!" But I
couldn't stay mad at Mary while she was smiling and hugging
me and smelling of Lady Esther dusting powder. I wanted to
stay buried in her fur all day.

To tell the truth I forgot about Roberta. Mary and I got in
line for the traipse into chapel and I was feeling proud because
she looked so beautiful even in those ugly green slacks that
made her behind stick out. A pretty mother on earth is better
than a beautiful dead one in the sky even if she did leave you
all alone to go dancing.

I felt a tap on my shoulder, turned, and saw Roberta smiling. I smiled back, but not too much lest somebody think this

visit was the biggest thing that ever happened in my life. Then Roberta said, "Mother, I want you to meet my roommate, Twyla. And that's Twyla's mother."

I looked up it seemed for miles. She was big. Bigger than any man and on her chest was the biggest cross I'd ever seen. I swear it was six inches long each way. And in the crook of her arm was the biggest Bible ever made.

Mary, simpleminded as ever, grinned and tried to yank her hand out of the pocket with the raggedy lining—to shake hands, I guess. Roberta's mother looked down at me and then looked down at Mary too. She didn't say anything, just grabbed Roberta with her Bible-free hand and stepped out of line, walking quickly to the rear of it. Mary was still grinning because she's not too swift when it comes to what's really going on. Then this light bulb goes off in her head and she says, "That bitch!" really loud and us almost in the chapel now. Organ music whining, the Bonny Angels singing sweetly. Everybody in the world turned around to look. And Mary would have kept it up—kept calling names if I hadn't squeezed her hands as hard as I could. That helped a little, but she still twitched and crossed and uncrossed her legs all through service. Even groaned a couple of times. Why did I think she would come there and act right? Slacks. No hat like the grand-mothers and viewers, and groaning all the while. When we stood for hymns she kept her mouth shut. Wouldn't even look at the words on the page. She actually reached in her purse for a mirror to check her lipstick. All I could think of was that she really needed to be killed. The sermon lasted a year, and I knew the real orphans were looking smug again.

We were supposed to have lunch in the teachers' lounge, but Mary didn't bring anything, so we picked fur and cello-phane grass off the mashed jelly beans and ate them. I could have killed her. I sneaked a look at Roberta. Her mother had brought chicken legs and ham sandwiches and oranges and a whole box of chocolate-covered grahams. Roberta drank milk from a thermos while her mother read the Bible to her.

Things are not right. The wrong food is always with the wrong people. Maybe that's why I got into waitress work later —to match up the right people with the right food. Roberta just let those chicken legs sit there, but she did bring a stack of grahams up to me later when the visit was over. I think she was sorry that her mother would not shake my mother's hand. And I liked that and I liked the fact that she didn't say a word about Mary groaning all the way through the service and not bringing any lunch.

Roberta left in May when the apple trees were heavy and white. On her last day we went to the orchard to watch the big girls smoke and dance by the radio. It didn't matter that they said, "Twyyyyyla, baby." We sat on the ground and breathed. Lady Esther. Apple blossoms. I still go soft when I smell one or the other. Roberta was going home. The big cross and the big Bible was coming to get her and she seemed sort of glad and sort of not. I thought I would die in that room of four beds without her and I knew Bozo had plans to move some other dumped kid in there with me. Roberta promised to write every day, which was really sweet of her because she couldn't read a lick so how could she write anybody? I would have drawn pictures and sent them to her but she never gave me her address. Little by little she faded. Her wet socks with the pink scalloped tops and her big serious-looking eyes—that's all I could catch when I tried to bring her to mind.

I was working behind the counter at the Howard Johnson's on the Thruway just before the Kingston exit. Not a bad job. Kind of a long ride from Newburgh, but okay once I got there. Mine

was the second night shift, eleven to seven. Very light until a
Greyhound checked in for breakfast around six-thirty. At that
hour the sun was all the way clear of the hills behind the
restaurant. The place looked better at night—more like shelter
—but I loved it when the sun broke in, even if it did show all
the cracks in the vinyl and the speckled floor looked dirty no
matter what the mop boy did.

It was August and a bus crowd was just unloading. They
would stand around a long while: going to the john, and looking at gifts and junk-for-sale machines, reluctant to sit down so
soon. Even to eat. I was trying to fill the coffeepots and get
them all situated on the electric burners when I saw her. She
was sitting in a booth smoking a cigarette with two guys
smothered in head and facial hair. Her own hair was so big and
wild I could hardly see her face. But the eyes. I would know
them anywhere. She had on a powder-blue halter and shorts
outfit and earrings the size of bracelets. Talk about lipstick and
eyebrow pencil. She made the big girls look like nuns. I
couldn't get off the counter until seven o'clock, but I kept
watching the booth in case they got up to leave before that. My
replacement was on time for a change, so I counted and stacked
my receipts as fast as I could and signed off. I walked over to
the booth, smiling and wondering if she would remember me.
Or even if she wanted to remember me. Maybe she didn't want
to be reminded of St. Bonny's or to have anybody know she
was ever there. I know I never talked about it to anybody.

I put my hands in my apron pockets and leaned against the
back of the booth facing them.

"Roberta? Roberta Fisk?"

She looked up. "Yeah?"

"Twyla."

She squinted for a second and then said, "Wow."

"Remember me?"

"Sure. Hey. Wow."

"It's been a while," I said, and gave a smile to the two hairy guys.

"Yeah. Wow. You work here?"

"Yeah," I said. "I live in Newburgh."

"Newburgh? No kidding?" She laughed then, a private laugh that included the guys but only the guys, and they laughed with her. What could I do but laugh too and wonder why I was standing there with my knees showing out from under that uniform. Without looking I could see the blue-and-white triangle on my head, my hair shapeless in a net, my ankles thick in white oxfords. Nothing could have been less sheer than my stockings. There was this silence that came down right after I laughed. A silence it was her turn to fill up. With introductions, maybe, to her boyfriends or an invitation to sit down and have a Coke. Instead she lit a cigarette off the one she'd just finished and said, "We're on our way to the Coast. He's got an appointment with Hendrix." She gestured casually toward the boy next to her.

"Hendrix? Fantastic," I said. "Really fantastic. What's she doing now?"

Roberta coughed on her cigarette and the two guys rolled their eyes up at the ceiling.

"Hendrix. Jimi Hendrix, asshole. He's only the biggest— Oh, wow. Forget it."

I was dismissed without anyone saying good-bye, so I thought I would do it for her.

"How's your mother?" I asked. Her grin cracked her whole face. She swallowed. "Fine," she said. "How's yours?"

"Pretty as a picture," I said and turned away. The backs of my knees were damp. Howard Johnson's really was a dump in the sunlight.

.   .   .

James is as comfortable as a house slipper. He liked my cooking and I liked his big loud family. They have lived in Newburgh all of their lives and talk about it the way people do who have always known a home. His grandmother has a porch swing older than his father and when they talk about streets and avenues and buildings they call them names they no longer have. They still call the A&P Rico's because it stands on property once a mom-and-pop store owned by Mr. Rico. And they call the new community college Town Hall because it once was. My mother-in-law puts up jelly and cucumbers and buys butter wrapped in cloth from a dairy. James and his father talk about fishing and baseball and I can see them all together on the Hudson in a raggedy skiff. Half the population of Newburgh is on welfare now, but to my husband's family it was still some upstate paradise of a time long past. A time of ice houses and vegetable wagons, coal furnaces and children weeding gardens. When our son was born my mother-in-law gave me the crib blanket that had been hers.

But the town they remembered had changed. Something quick was in the air. Magnificent old houses, so ruined they had become shelter for squatters and rent risks, were bought and renovated. Smart IBM people moved out of their suburbs back into the city and put shutters up and herb gardens in their backyards. A brochure came in the mail announcing the opening of a Food Emporium. Gourmet food, it said—and listed items the rich IBM crowd would want. It was located in a new mall at the edge of town and I drove out to shop there one day —just to see. It was late in June. After the tulips were gone and the Queen Elizabeth roses were open everywhere. I trailed my cart along the aisle, tossing in smoked oysters and Robert's sauce and things I knew would sit in my cupboard for years. Only when I found some Klondike ice cream bars did I feel less guilty about spending James's fireman's salary so foolishly. My father-in-law ate them with the same gusto little Joseph did.

Waiting in the checkout line I heard a voice say, "Twyla!"

The classical music piped over the aisles had affected me and the woman leaning toward me was dressed to kill. Diamonds on her hand, a smart white summer dress. "I'm Mrs. Benson," I said.

"Ho. Ho. The Big Bozo," she sang.

For a split second I didn't know what she was talking about. She had a bunch of asparagus and two cartons of fancy water.

"Roberta!"

"Right."

"For heaven's sake. Roberta."

"You look great," she said.

"So do you. Where are you? Here? In Newburgh?"

"Yes. Over in Annandale."

I was opening my mouth to say more when the cashier called my attention to her empty counter.

"Meet you outside." Roberta pointed her finger and went into the express line.

I placed the groceries and kept myself from glancing around to check Roberta's progress. I remembered Howard Johnson's and looking for a chance to speak only to be greeted with a stingy "wow." But she was waiting for me and her huge hair was sleek now, smooth around a small, nicely shaped head. Shoes, dress, everything lovely and summery and rich. I was dying to know what happened to her, how she got from Jimi Hendrix to Annandale, a neighborhood full of doctors and IBM executives. Easy, I thought. Everything is so easy for them. They think they own the world.

"How long," I asked her. "How long have you been here?"

"A year. I got married to a man who lives here. And you, you're married too, right? Benson, you said."

"Yeah. James Benson."

"And is he nice?"

"Oh, is he nice?"

"Well, is he?" Roberta's eyes were steady as though she really meant the question and wanted an answer.

"He's wonderful, Roberta. Wonderful."

"So you're happy."

"Very."

"That's good," she said and nodded her head. "I always hoped you'd be happy. Any kids? I know you have kids."

"One. A boy. How about you?"

"Four."

"Four?"

She laughed. "Step kids. He's a widower."

"Oh."

"Got a minute? Let's have a coffee."

I thought about the Klondikes melting and the inconvenience of going all the way to my car and putting the bags in the trunk. Served me right for buying all that stuff I didn't need. Roberta was ahead of me.

"Put them in my car. It's right here."

And then I saw the dark blue limousine.

"You married a Chinaman?"

"No." She laughed. "He's the driver."

"Oh, my. If the Big Bozo could see you now."

We both giggled. Really giggled. Suddenly, in just a pulse beat, twenty years disappeared and all of it came rushing back. The big girls (whom we called gar girls—Roberta's misheard word for the evil stone faces described in a civics class) there dancing in the orchard, the ploppy mashed potatoes, the double weenies, the Spam with pineapple. We went into the coffee shop holding on to one another and I tried to think why we were glad to see each other this time and not before. Once, twelve years ago, we passed like strangers. A black girl and a white girl meeting in a Howard Johnson's on the road and having nothing to say. One in a blue-and-white-triangle waitress hat, the other on her way to see Hendrix. Now we were behaving like sisters separated for much too long. Those four short months were nothing in time. Maybe it was the thing itself. Just being there, together. Two little girls who knew what nobody else in the world knew—how not to ask questions. How to believe what had to be believed. There was politeness in that reluctance and generosity as well. Is your mother sick too? No, she dances all night. Oh—and an understanding nod.

We sat in a booth by the window and fell into recollection like veterans.

"Did you ever learn to read?"

"Watch." She picked up the menu. "Special of the day. Cream of corn soup. Entrées. Two dots and a wriggly line. Quiche. Chef salad, scallops. . . ."

I was laughing and applauding when the waitress came up.

"Remember the Easter baskets?"

"And how we tried to *introduce* them?"

"Your mother with that cross like two telephone poles."

"And yours with those tight slacks."

We laughed so loudly heads turned and made the laughter hard to suppress.

"What happened to the Jimi Hendrix date?"

Roberta made a blow-out sound with her lips.

"When he died I thought about you."

"Oh, you heard about him finally?"

"Finally. Come on, I was a small-town country waitress."

"And I was a small-town country dropout. God, were we wild. I still don't know how I got out of there alive."

"But you did."

"I did. I really did. Now I'm Mrs. Kenneth Norton."

"Sounds like a mouthful."

"It is."

"Servants and all?"

Roberta held up two fingers.

"Ow! What does he do?"

"Computers and stuff. What do I know?"

"I don't remember a hell of a lot from those days, but Lord, St. Bonny's is as clear as daylight. Remember Maggie? The day she fell down and those gar girls laughed at her?"

Roberta looked up from her salad and stared at me. "Maggie didn't fall," she said.

"Yes, she did. You remember."

"No, Twyla. They knocked her down. Those girls pushed her down and tore her clothes. In the orchard."

"I don't—that's not what happened."

"Sure it is. In the orchard. Remember how scared we were?"

"Wait a minute. I don't remember any of that."

"And Bozo was fired."

"You're crazy. She was there when I left. You left before me."

"I went back. You weren't there when they fired Bozo."

"What?"

"Twice. Once for a year when I was about ten, another for two months when I was fourteen. That's when I ran away."

"You ran away from St. Bonny's?"

"I had to. What do you want? Me dancing in that orchard?"

"Are you sure about Maggie?"

"Of course I'm sure. You've blocked it, Twyla. It happened. Those girls had behavior problems, you know."

"Didn't they, though. But why can't I remember the Maggie thing?"

"Believe me. It happened. And we were there."

"Who did you room with when you went back?" I asked her as if I would know her. The Maggie thing was troubling me.

"Creeps. They tickled themselves in the night."

My ears were itching and I wanted to go home suddenly. This was all very well but she couldn't just comb her hair, wash her face, and pretend everything was hunky-dory. After the Howard Johnson's snub. And no apology. Nothing.

"Were you on dope or what that time at Howard Johnson's?" I tried to make my voice sound friendlier than I felt.

"Maybe, a little. I never did drugs much. Why?"

"I don't know, you acted sort of like you didn't want to know me then."

"Oh, Twyla, you know how it was in those days: black—white. You know how everything was."

But I didn't know. I thought it was just the opposite. Busloads of blacks and whites came into Howard Johnson's together. They roamed together then: students, musicians, lovers, protesters. You got to see everything at Howard Johnson's, and blacks were very friendly with whites in those days. But sitting there with nothing on my plate but two hard tomato wedges wondering about the melting Klondikes it seemed childish remembering the slight. We went to her car and, with the help of the driver, got my stuff into my station wagon.

"We'll keep in touch this time," she said.

"Sure," I said. "Sure. Give me a call."

"I will," she said, and then, just as I was sliding behind the wheel, she leaned into the window. "By the way. Your mother. Did she ever stop dancing?"

I shook my head. "No. Never."

Roberta nodded.

"And yours? Did she ever get well?"

She smiled a tiny sad smile. "No. She never did. Look, call me, okay?"

"Okay," I said, but I knew I wouldn't. Roberta had messed up my past somehow with that business about Maggie. I wouldn't forget a thing like that. Would I?

Strife came to us that fall. At least that's what the paper called it. Strife. Racial strife. The word made me think of a bird—a big shrieking bird out of 1,000,000,000 B.C. Flapping its wings and cawing. Its eye with no lid always bearing down on you. All day it screeched and at night it slept on the rooftops. It woke you in the morning, and from the "Today" show to the eleven o'clock news it kept you an awful company. I couldn't figure it out from one day to the next. I knew I was supposed to feel something strong, but I didn't know what, and James wasn't any help. Joseph was on the list of kids to be transferred from the junior high school to another one at some far-out-of-the-way place and I thought it was a good thing until I heard it was a bad thing. I mean I didn't know. All the schools seemed dumps to me, and the fact that one was nicer looking didn't hold much weight. But the papers were full of it and then the kids began to get jumpy. In August, mind you. Schools weren't even open yet. I thought Joseph might be frightened to go over there, but he didn't seem scared so I forgot about it, until I found myself driving along Hudson Street out there by the school they were trying to integrate and saw a line of women marching. And who do you suppose was in line, big as life, holding a sign in front of her bigger than her mother's cross? MOTHERS HAVE RIGHTS TOO! it said.

I drove on and then changed my mind. I circled the block, slowed down, and honked my horn.

Roberta looked over and when she saw me she waved. I didn't wave back, but I didn't move either. She handed her sign to another woman and came over to where I was parked.

"Hi."

"What are you doing?"

"Picketing. What's it look like?"

"What for?"

"What do you mean, 'What for?' They want to take my kids and send them out of the neighborhood. They don't want to go."

"So what if they go to another school? My boy's being bussed too, and I don't mind. Why should you?"

"It's not about us, Twyla. Me and you. It's about our kids."

"What's more *us* than that?"

"Well, it is a free country."

"Not yet, but it will be."

"What the hell does that mean? I'm not doing anything to you."

"You really think that?"

"I know it."

"I wonder what made me think you were different."

"I wonder what made me think you were different."

"Look at them," I said. "Just look. Who do they think they are? Swarming all over the place like they own it. And now they think they can decide where my child goes to school. Look at them, Roberta. They're Bozos."

Roberta turned around and looked at the women. Almost all of them were standing still now, waiting. Some were even edging toward us. Roberta looked at me out of some refrigerator behind her eyes. "No, they're not. They're just mothers."

"And what am I? Swiss cheese?"

"I used to curl your hair."

"I hated your hands in my hair."

The women were moving. Our faces looked mean to them of course and they looked as though they could not wait to throw themselves in front of a police car or, better yet, into my car and drag me away by my ankles. Now they surrounded my car and gently, gently began to rock it. I swayed back and forth like a sideways yo-yo. Automatically I reached for Roberta, like the old days in the orchard when they saw us watching them and we had to get out of there, and if one of us fell the other pulled her up and if one of us was caught the other stayed to kick and scratch, and neither would leave the other behind. My arm shot out of the car window but no receiving hand was there. Roberta was looking at me sway from side to side in the car and her face was still. My purse slid from the car seat down under the dashboard. The four policemen who had been drinking Tab in their car finally got the message and strolled over, forcing their way through the women. Quietly, firmly they spoke. "Okay, ladies. Back in line or off the streets."

Some of them went away willingly; others had to be urged away from the car doors and the hood. Roberta didn't move. She was looking steadily at me. I was fumbling to turn on the ignition, which wouldn't catch because the gearshift was still in drive. The seats of the car were a mess because the swaying had thrown my grocery coupons all over and my purse was sprawled on the floor.

"Maybe I am different now, Twyla. But you're not. You're the same little state kid who kicked a poor old black lady when she was down on the ground. You kicked a black lady and you have the nerve to call me a bigot."

The coupons were everywhere and the guts of my purse were bunched under the dashboard. What was she saying? Black? Maggie wasn't black.

"She wasn't black," I said.

"Like hell she wasn't, and you kicked her. We both did. You kicked a black lady who couldn't even scream."

"Liar!"

"You're the liar! Why don't you just go on home and leave us alone, huh?"

She turned away and I skidded away from the curb.

The next morning I went into the garage and cut the side

out of the carton our portable TV had come in. It wasn't nearly big enough, but after a while I had a decent sign: red spray-painted letters on a white background—AND SO DO CHILDREN****. I meant just to go down to the school and tack it up somewhere so those cows on the picket line across the street could see it, but when I got there, some ten or so others had already assembled—protesting the cows across the street. Police permits and everything. I got in line and we strutted in time on our side while Roberta's group strutted on theirs. That first day we were all dignified, pretending the other side didn't exist. The second day there was name calling and finger gestures. But that was about all. People changed signs from time to time, but Roberta never did and neither did I. Actually my sign didn't make sense without Roberta's. "And so do children what?" one of the women on my side asked me. Have rights, I said, as though it was obvious.

Roberta didn't acknowledge my presence in any way, and I got to thinking maybe she didn't know I was there. I began to pace myself in the line, jostling people one minute and lagging behind the next, so Roberta and I could reach the end of our respective lines at the same time and there would be a moment in our turn when we would face each other. Still, I couldn't tell whether she saw me and knew my sign was for her. The next day I went early before we were scheduled to assemble. I waited until she got there before I exposed my new creation. As soon as she hoisted her MOTHERS HAVE RIGHTS TOO I began to wave my new one, which said, HOW WOULD YOU KNOW? I know she saw that one, but I had gotten addicted now. My signs got crazier each day, and the women on my side decided that I was a kook. They couldn't make heads or tails out of my brilliant screaming posters.

I brought a painted sign in queenly red with huge black letters that said, IS YOUR MOTHER WELL? Roberta took her lunch break and didn't come back for the rest of the day or any day after. Two days later I stopped going too and couldn't have been missed because nobody understood my signs anyway.

It was a nasty six weeks. Classes were suspended and Joseph didn't go to anybody's school until October. The children —everybody's children—soon got bored with that extended vacation they thought was going to be so great. They looked at TV until their eyes flattened. I spent a couple of mornings tutoring my son, as the other mothers said we should. Twice I opened a text from last year that he had never turned in. Twice he yawned in my face. Other mothers organized living room sessions so the kids would keep up. None of the kids could concentrate, so they drifted back to "The Price Is Right" and "The Brady Bunch." When the school finally opened there were fights once or twice and some sirens roared through the streets every once in a while. There were a lot of photographers from Albany. And just when ABC was about to send up a news crew, the kids settled down like nothing in the world had happened. Joseph hung my HOW WOULD YOU KNOW? sign in his bedroom. I don't know what became of AND SO DO CHILDREN****. I think my father-in-law cleaned some fish on it. He was always puttering around in our garage. Each of his five children lived in Newburgh, and he acted as though he had five extra homes.

I couldn't help looking for Roberta when Joseph graduated from high school, but I didn't see her. It didn't trouble me much what she had said to me in the car. I mean the kicking part. I know I didn't do that, I couldn't do that. But I was puzzled by her telling me Maggie was black. When I thought about it I actually couldn't be certain. She wasn't pitch-black, I knew, or I would have remembered that. What I remember was the kiddie hat and the semicircle legs. I tried to reassure myself about the race thing for a long time until it dawned on me that the truth was already there, and Roberta knew it. I didn't kick her; I didn't join in with the gar girls and kick that lady, but I sure did want to. We watched and never tried to help her and never called for help. Maggie was my dancing mother. Deaf, I thought, and dumb. Nobody inside. Nobody who would hear you if you cried in the night. Nobody who could tell you anything important that you could use. Rocking, dancing, swaying as she walked. And when the gar girls pushed her down and started roughhousing, I knew she wouldn't scream, couldn't—just like me—and I was glad about that.

We decided not to have a tree, because Christmas would be at my mother-in-law's house, so why have a tree at both places? Joseph was at SUNY New Paltz and we had to economize, we said. But at the last minute, I changed my mind. Nothing could be that bad. So I rushed around town looking for a tree, something small but wide. By the time I found a place, it was snowing and very late. I dawdled like it was the most important purchase in the world and the tree man was fed up with me. Finally I chose one and had it tied onto the trunk of the car. I drove away slowly because the sand trucks were not out yet and the streets could be murder at the beginning of a snowfall. Downtown the streets were wide and rather empty except for a cluster of people coming out of the Newburgh Hotel. The one hotel in town that wasn't built out of cardboard and Plexiglas. A party, probably. The men huddled in the snow were dressed in tails and the women had on furs. Shiny things glittered from underneath their coats. It made me tired to look at them. Tired, tired, tired. On the next corner was a small diner with loops and loops of paper bells in the window. I stopped the car and went in. Just for a cup of coffee and twenty minutes of peace before I went home and tried to finish everything before Christmas Eve.

"Twyla?"

There she was. In a silvery evening gown and dark fur coat. A man and another woman were with her, the man fumbling for change to put in the cigarette machine. The woman was humming and tapping on the counter with her fingernails. They all looked a little bit drunk.

"Well. It's you."

"How are you?"

I shrugged. "Pretty good. Frazzled. Christmas and all."

"Regular?" called the woman from the counter.

"Fine," Roberta called back and then, "Wait for me in the car."

She slipped into the booth beside me. "I have to tell you something, Twyla. I made up my mind if I ever saw you again, I'd tell you."

"I'd just as soon not hear anything, Roberta. It doesn't matter now, anyway."

"No," she said. "Not about that."

"Don't be long," said the woman. She carried two regulars to go and the man peeled his cigarette pack as they left.

"It's about St. Bonny's and Maggie."

"Oh, please."

"Listen to me. I really did think she was black. I didn't make that up. I really thought so. But now I can't be sure. I just remember her as old, so old. And because she couldn't talk—well, you know, I thought she was crazy. She'd been brought up in an institution like my mother was and like I thought I would be too. And you were right. We didn't kick her. It was the gar girls. Only them. But, well, I wanted to. I really wanted them to hurt her. I said we did it, too. You and me, but that's not true. And I don't want you to carry that around. It was just that I wanted to do it so bad that day—wanting to is doing it."

Her eyes were watery from the drinks she'd had, I guess. I

know it's that way with me. One glass of wine and I start bawling over the littlest thing.

"We were kids, Roberta."

"Yeah. Yeah. I know, just kids."

"Eight."

"Eight."

"And lonely."

"Scared, too."

She wiped her cheeks with the heel of her hand and smiled. "Well, that's all I wanted to say."

I nodded and couldn't think of any way to fill the silence that went from the diner past the paper bells on out into the snow. It was heavy now. I thought I'd better wait for the sand trucks before starting home.

"Thanks, Roberta."

"Sure."

"Did I tell you? My mother, she never did stop dancing."

"Yes. You told me. And mine, she never got well." Roberta lifted her hands from the tabletop and covered her face with her palms. When she took them away she really was crying. "Oh, shit, Twyla. Shit, shit, shit. What the hell happened to Maggie?"

What Tina Has to Do with It

Beverly Lowry

The first time I saw Tina Turner in concert was in the Houston Astrodome, back in the middle seventies. A temple to size and ticket sales, the Astrodome's a fine place for watching football or a tractor pull, not so great for music. The sound was thin and blurry. Smoking was still allowed and so a steady cloud of blue haze hung between us and the performers. I had binoculars but the stage seemed miles away. In her groin-high leather cavewoman tunic doing "Proud Mary," Tina might have been dancing her heart out in the parking lot out by the chain-link fence, for all I could see.

People thrive on secret dreams: the single Hershey's kiss bought for a nickel on the way out of the convenience store, melted surreptitiously on the back of the tongue long before we arrive home, mysteriously chocolate-breathed; the fantasies movie and rock stars cook up in us all, from Tarzan to Madonna. I left the Astrodome that night lit up like a young girl with a hot new crush. Tina was, of course, still with Ike then. Ike ran the show. Back then, who had the nerve to think she could do without him? They were a team. Ike and Tina. The Ikettes.

For a couple of years in there I got through a lot of blank spaces in my life cooking up my own secret dream, of becoming—wildly, improbably—an Ikette. Driving the interstate, nothing to do but keep the speed down and steer, I would stare off into distances, make a certain mental adjustment and suddenly, magically, I would just *be* there, down on the stage hard by Tina, mouth puckered doing oo-doo's, hips bumping and grinding, making the fringe of my short short dress jump and shiver. I was in my thirties at the time, understand, two young sons, a book about to be published. If I was going to accomplish anything in this life, I knew I was going to have to depend on pure, selfish stubbornness, and on being *smart.*

What do dreams care about intellect or accomplishment? In my shameless I-10 fantasy, I lifted my strappy stilettos and pranced like a brainless happy show pony, to "River Deep, Mountain High" and "Nutbush."

I grew up in Mississippi, the fifties. For a white girl back then, identification took a while to sink in. So much was kept under wraps. We, my girl friends and I, knew how to get by. We were not fools; we would take advantage of every subterfuge and ploy handed down to us through generations of Southern white women. But there was starting to be the slightest edge to things, the faintest glimmer of change. We were different from our mothers, bolder, with higher aspirations. We would live lives that included a family but which were not restricted exclusively to the concerns of that, would live in the world, even move away. We would not relive our mothers' lives. To make this great leap, however, we needed a model, methods, examples.

In the opening vamp to "Proud Mary," Tina used to do that famous line about liking to do something for us "nice and easy." I am trying to distinguish the difference as we perceived it then, between "nice" and "good." Nice had to do with behavior—manners—while good was deeper set and had a moral equivalent. Nice was or could be sensory; good was not. A nice girl was expected to be pleasant to other people—polite, at any rate; a good one didn't have to be. The difference was somewhat like that between faith by works and being saved. Like a heaven-blessed religious fundamentalist, a good girl was among the chosen few, and beyond reproach. Virginal, in other words: white as the steamy aura around a candle flame.

White girls in the fifties. Were we good? In our white piqué dickies and sterling-silver-spoon pins? Our pearls and pony tails? Talk about subterfuge. It was a show, all right. We fooled even ourselves, some of us for years and years.

Interesting how racial instruction is passed down. Because I remember very few spoken lessons, one in particular stands out. It came, surprisingly enough, from my mother. For a Southerner, my mother was not especially racist. She grew up in Arkansas, we lived in the Mississippi Delta, the usual attitudes had been hammered in. But at bottom my mother was a populist, uncomfortable with privilege and racial stereotyping. Nonetheless, the incident occurred in the car, downtown, when I was about ten years old. As my mother waited for a car to pull out of a parking place, I referred to a black woman walking down the sidewalk as a lady. "Don't say lady," my mother corrected. Her voice trembled. Puzzled, I waited, wondering what I was supposed to call the person in question if not a lady. My mother pulled into a parking place and, all but clipping the next car, gave me the rest of it. "Say woman."

Woman! My heart skipped a beat. And the lesson I received was far different from the one my mother intended.

Nutbush. One more time.

White Southern women of my generation, brought up to conciliate, caretake, negotiate and please, nurture a simmering need to be, one way or the other—in this we take what we can get—*bad*. Like a chronic illness, the need nags and hangs tough. Resisting cool cloths, aspirin, and home cures, the low-grade fever rises in the late afternoon, cools to clammy stillness upon waking. The need—urge, wild longing—shouldered us into dark corners of private back rooms where we fed our desire in stealthy doses, flushing the medicines away, making a life of secrets and shadows.

Sexuality, I thought, was for *them*. Sex meant the boy did it until he finished. My part was one of patience and, especially, of vigilance, against pregnancy, and shame. I thought that until I was twenty years old. What woman was there after all to look up to, who was both heroic *and* sexual?

Music expands our little worlds on the instant, in ways we may not understand but feel no need to articulate or question. In my hot-damn, boogey-down, bootlegger's-on-the-county-line-drive-down-a-dark-road-for-secret-half-pints-Mississippi Delta world, dancing was crucial. We bumped, we ground, we did the dirty bop. Dancing dirty did not necessarily carry over to the backseats of cars. Dancing was music, life, liveliness, fun. We bopped and twirled to "One Mint Julep," "Money, Honey," and "Hearts of Stone"; we studied new steps, and music gave us news of what was going on in other hearts and minds, beyond the Delta rivers and bootlegger's shack, beyond white dickies and don't-say-lady-say-woman lessons and endless cotton fields.

Dumb as a light-pole in matters of sexual innuendo, I used to lie in a half-slumbering swoon across the beds of my friends, playing the same song over until I had the lyrics down stone pat. And some of the time I heard what I wanted to, and pumped the words up until they were even more wicked than the singers intended, and I sang along with the records and wondered as I sang what working with Annie exactly meant and who the sixty-minute man in fact was and what he was precisely doing when he was blowing his top all that time, and just how dangerous these black men we were listening to really were and what the nature of the danger specifically was. The music of black men told us who else we might be, beneath the costumes.

When I first started writing, I bought the generally accepted notion that said if you wrote like a woman, and had as your subject the events and occasions of a woman's life, you were doomed to the ranks of the second-rate, outside the great line of history and literature, down among the no-counts, published only in women's magazines. I wanted, I assumed, to write like a man.

If it's not real, I do not wish to see. The heart knew what the mind did not have the courage to see. When I peek into the secret dreams of the young white girl I was, and later into the I-10 fantasies and daydreams of the woman I became, it is clear that my heartdeep mythical heroes—way beyond worldly accomplishments, or even my own use and understanding—were all women.

Imaginary heroes came first: Sheena, Queen of the Jungle, Nancy Drew, Wonder Woman. Then figures of biography: Clara Barton, Florence Nightingale, Amelia Earhart, Helen Keller. Biography was a comfort. It told us to hold on, it was okay, people grew into themselves in the strangest, most unpredictable ways. I tried to swim like Esther Williams, I wanted to be an Ikette. Eventually Tina told us what was going on with Ike. And I don't know one woman who does not admire her. Miraculously, she got away.

And all that time, with Ike or not, she was just so energetic and sexy, so vital and loving and angry. So many seeming contradictions. She had dignity and fire. The dignity acted as an agent for irony. In her cavewoman animal-skin costumes, she both played out the role of the primitive within us all— played out? milked is more like it—and laughed a little at herself, and us, at the same time—as if the whole time she was doing her impossible dances she was also making comments on what she was doing, as if to say, "Look at this, aren't I, aren't we, a flat riot?" And there was sweetness in that, and the sweetness provided us with a glorious example. A woman could be all of that, sexual *and* sweet, angry *and* loving. We did not have to divide ourselves into good and bad, we could be wholly who we were to the farthest extremes we dared venture, at whatever age, in whatever circumstances. And she would be out there on the thinnest branch of the farthest limb, showing us how . . . with grace, and fire, and even—this is the hard part—with humor.

I can't say exactly when I began listening more to the songs of black women than men—sometime, I think, around the time when I was about to become a published author, *after* I had read Doris Lessing and had come to understand that it was possible both to write about a woman's life *and* be a serious writer. Just before I went to see Tina at the Astrodome.

The first college writing class I ever taught, I walked in wearing a Tina Turner concert muscle T-shirt. Having never taken, much less taught, a writing class, I was nervous. The shirt was an in-your-face overcompensation, saying this is who I am: a woman of power—watch out, you may not know me but get used to it, I am in charge here. All these years later— after the autobiography, the movies, the prizes, Tina's new status as a folk hero—her effect on me has not changed. At the gym, I unpack my Walkman and plug her into my ears. She gets me through boring time on the Stairmaster, through jogs and crunches, lunges and push-ups. While others struggle through, earnestly frowning, I am in a Tina haze, laughing and prancing like a show pony.

What's black got to do with it? Black women in the South knew they were sexual creatures from day one, and even if they weren't as sexual as the white man's myth made them out to be—and how could they be?—they knew how to make use of that myth, just as white girls made use of theirs, suppressing sexuality, pretending to be Ivory-Flake pure. White men made the rules. White men wrote the books. White men defined the terms. Black women and white used what they had, exploited the myths, and no wonder. It was a way to get by. When asked the secret of her sex appeal, Mae West is supposed to have said, "First you've got to use what's lying around the house."

When she sings about not needing another hero, unlike a lot of us Tina doubtless doesn't consider herself a candidate. In times of trouble, she is mine. In dark times, I have a mantra I go by. It goes: *If Tina can get away from Ike, I can get through this*. If Tina can get away from Ike, I can do anything.

Legacies and Ghosts
Patricia Browning Griffith

ot long ago a student of mine was writing a novel in which
one of the three major characters in the book, all of them
white, was rumored to have been involved in a lynching
in the distant past. The lynching had been investigated by a
New York journalist but in this Southern locale charges were
never brought. The suspect was the protagonist's father and
the rumor of this past deed was presented as an element of his
psychological makeup as one might mention a past business
failing or an earlier drinking problem to render characteriza-
tion. The novel focused on the breakup of the marriage of a
young woman who was dominated by this same father. In the
manuscript the truth of the allegation was never determined.

"Look," I said to this writer, a pleasant young female
lawyer, "you can't just drop something like this into a novel
and not deal with it. To my mind this blows your story out of

the water. It renders every other event benign and insignificant."

The young lawyer nodded and assumed that patient look that says, rather than tangle with her I'll just hear her out. That wasn't the only time I discussed the issue with her, but whatever I said about this being an explosive and major element to her story, I never managed to convince her.

Since then I have wondered how someone writing fiction, where unlike in real life there are resolutions, could fail to explore such an incident. It has led me to wonder where are the stories of the ancestors of those who held the dogs in Selma, who stood under the trees in hundreds of little towns where black men and women's blood was spilled. After all, as I say to my students, it will be your obligation, as it is each writer's, to present honestly the story of your own time.

Picture a town in East Texas around 1930, the "north star of Texas" it is sometimes called, only a few miles below the Red River which separates northeast Texas from Oklahoma. It is the county seat and the commercial center to the many rural communities spread throughout that cotton-producing black-clay soil. The town is laid out around a square with a monument to the men who gave their lives in World War I. The major residential streets radiating from the square are lined with graceful elms and pecan trees and sprawling Victorian houses with side verandas and generous green lawns. At this time five railroads pass through the town. Both the Santa Fe to Dallas and the Texas and Pacific to Fort Worth passed through and on to neighboring Greenville, where for decades a sign near the railroad station and over the highway proclaimed "the blackest land and the whitest people."

On this particular day around 1930 a lovely white woman steps off the wide, wraparound veranda of a sprawling, ramshackle Victorian house in need of paint. The house seems too large for its lot and narrow yard. Some of the smaller houses up and down the block appear in better condition than this one, whose glory days have faded like the aging cherry tree by the front walk that will one day be hollow so that children can crawl into its decaying base and climb it from inside. The woman is nearing thirty. She has curly brown hair and blue eyes, a friendly smile, a soft voice, a ready laugh and often wears too much face powder. Her life has not been easy. Her own mother was widowed twice. She became an early telephone operator and there sits on my mantel today a photo of her from this time dressed in a loose smock and sitting before a switchboard. She was working as a telephone operator when she met the young man she would first marry, a handsome man with dark hair from a well-to-do farming family.

Five months after their marriage her young husband was playing sandlot baseball when a ball ricocheting off a bat struck him a hard blow in the temple. He walked a mile home and said to his wife, I think I'll lie down and take a nap. He never woke up. And so after only five months of marriage she was left alone and "expecting," as they called it, so that she moved back to her mother's old rambling Victorian house on Plumb Street.

It is several years later; her daughter has been born and she has remarried, but is still living with her mother in the old house where she makes braided rugs and embroiders pillow-cases and aprons, crochets doilies and makes quilts on the hooks that hang in the large and dark middle hall of the old house. It is the Depression now and times are hard, and some of the rooms are rented out to people who will live there for many years.

On this early spring day perhaps she wears a red hat, and a blue sailor dress with a wide white collar, and a light coat. She is cold natured all her life. When she is eighty her family will tease her for wearing a sweater by a pool near the Gulf Coast in July. But now she waves to neighbors as she moves up Plumb Street toward town. Perhaps she is not alone. Maybe some of the neighbors, hearing of the excitement—maybe the neighbor who runs a dry cleaner's that six days a week emits a hot chemical cloud onto the sidewalk—will join her.

She makes her way up the sidewalk and at the corner she turns right, heading toward the town square and the Plaza movie theater where years later I will see my first movie star signing autographs—a scowling, impatient cowboy star named Alan Rocky Lane. At the second corner she heads east. She passes the old granite courthouse surrounded by benches where some of the older men of this small town congregate daily to discuss their affairs. But the benches are empty as the young woman passes under the line of graceful elms, pale green in the early spring and past the broad Southern magnolia whose branches sweep the courthouse lawn. There is an excitement in the air as others too head toward the edge of town, toward trouble, as people do, past the old wagon yard which stood there long after its usefulness.

Finally they reach a place where a large crowd has gathered around men in white robes, their heads covered. In their midst is a black man they've pulled from the jail in the basement of the old granite courthouse. He is accused of rape. The young woman in the red hat stands back in the crowd. There are other women there, even some children. She sees the children and surely thinks they shouldn't be there. Probably she can't see all that is happening, though she can hear the speeches, the accusations, the inflammatory rhetoric. These people are not unaccustomed to such from the hell-and-damnation preachers who travel through town and set up tent revivals and stir crowds with their cries of doom and charges of original sin so that no one, not the least among them, is deemed innocent. Often their heroes are Pretty Boy Floyd, the Oklahoma outlaw who is said to have helped the poor farmers, and Bonnie and Clyde, whom many will claim to have helped evade the law. And Earle Mayfield, the gubernatorial candidate who supported the Ku Klux Klan, or governor James Ferguson, commonly called "Pa Ferguson," candidate of tenant farmers, who was impeached for corruption in 1917. Later his wife Miriam, or "Ma Ferguson" as she was commonly called, became governor. Her term is most remembered for the long weekly lists in agate type, published in newspapers throughout the state, of men released from prison. There is on that early spring late afternoon perhaps even a ceremony of sorts and the electric charge of a crowd stirred into a mob, stirred by the same emotion that even today brings us hatred, violence, and genocide.

Later the black man in the center of the crowd is hanged, his body left long enough for some to return home for their Brownie box cameras to record the occasion. Then the man's body, she told me when I was a child, was tied behind a car and dragged through what was called in this town, as in every town of any size in Texas by many members of the population, "niggertown."

Her husband—her second husband, a law officer—was probably there on that spring day. She will not know that, however, until he dies suddenly a few years later and she discovers his white robe among his personal effects. He was a man whose memory was not greatly admired. But she was beloved.

That day is a diagonal mark that makes one's history, the steady development of one's present consciousness, uncertain, unsteady, like quicksand on the banks of that Red River not far away. In my mind the new leaves fall suddenly, leaving the trees bare as winter. How did it feel to stand in such a crowd, feel the charge of that rhetoric amid the soft innocent breeze of an early spring? Who else was there and in how many hearts is this event hidden, tucked away to fester and gnaw at the soul? The events reverberate to this day in how many families? Like the town of Rosewood, Florida, where similar accusations of rape provoked a search-and-destroy mission in 1923 in which eight people were killed and every black home and business burned to the ground. A story so shameful it was hidden for seventy years and only then brought to light and reparations made.

My grandmother, the woman in the red hat, was the kindest person I ever knew. Widowed a second time, she took me to movies on Saturdays when I was a little girl, to Sunday school on Sundays, and later in church I'd draw during the sermon with the crayons she kept for me in her purse. She taught me to crochet and knit. I would sit beside her and try to follow with my smaller hands the motions of my grandmother with the red garnet birthstone ring on her right hand and her gold wedding band on the left. And sometimes she would take my hands and move them, and I remember how awkward it felt at first having her moving my fingers until I'd completely relax and give over to my grandmother's motion. And sometimes, looking at our hands together, she would say, "Don't ever pop your knuckles, darling." (She pronounced it "dawlin'.") "See how big it made my knuckles?" But I never saw that—only the wide, sturdy hands so much like my own only larger.

She taught me to play canasta and forty-two, and every Wednesday afternoon we'd walk across town to the library where she would check out novels like *Magnificent Obsession* or *Dr. Hudson's Secret Journal,* romantic novels that also preached the wisdom of secret acts of charity.

She was a great storyteller. She believed in fortune-telling, talking tables, and poltergeists. Every house on Plumb Street was a fascinating world, from the pretty little girl next door who'd auditioned for the Our Gang Comedies to her friends the identical twins who worked in a bakery and often brought her pastries, and who could only be distinguished one from the other by a neck scar from a thyroid operation.

She told me stories of movies, of Al Jolson in blackface in *The Jazz Singer* singing "Sonny Boy," of her favorite movie, *The Birth of a Nation,* when the young girl being pursued by a black man threw herself off the cliff rather than be captured. Of course when she told me that story I didn't understand it. That is how it works, those profound, resonant fears communicated early and instilled beyond and prior to intellectual understanding, so that one is haunted forever by those fears like the scary webs and dark, soughing innards of the old cherry tree we used to climb.

In my own family this day is still spoken of in a moment of family intimacy, still grappled with as it has been over the years. "How could she do that?" an aunt said to me not so long ago, meaning how could she have been there, how could she have borne witness, this woman we loved. And the question lingers on year after year, becomes more complicated and inexplicable. I think of the others there that day. The men in the robes, the others watching, holding the coats and equally guilty, as Paul said in the Bible. I think of the family of the victim and what spilling that man's blood means to that town, and how many others.

Just what led my grandmother on that day, down those streets and to that place? Her own grandmother who, legend has it, was something of a Southern belle, came from one of the Southern states to Texas after the Civil War. They brought with them cattle and a few slaves though Texas was not a slave state; when he was governor, Sam Houston resigned from office rather than join the Confederacy.

The first winter the cattle died. It's not known what happened to the former slaves. Perhaps they settled in that same area of East Texas which is, even in this last decade of the century, torn by racial tensions and sometimes violence. Her family eventually settled in a rural area of central Texas next to

Sam Houston's house, where a few years earlier the treasury of Texas had been kept in a trunk.

The head of the family became a stagecoach driver between Austin and Waco. His son became a prominent preacher, and his wife, this woman's mother, was an early college graduate from a school where a cornerstone on the woman's dormitory reads, "Dedicated to female education and piety."

It is important to say that the attitude, the prejudice— though that is not a strong enough word—did not go on. The television images of the civil rights movement, the instinctive fair-mindedness of her own children, and the fact that the world changed around her led her to change. Ironically, before she died we looked upon her insistence on a kind and benevolent view of the world as naïve and otherworldly. Our world was perhaps more just, but also leagues more cynical in the face of her Christian goodwill.

Now I ask myself why I didn't find out more about this event of that spring day before she died, which was only a few short years ago. She was always eager to talk about the past, to tell us the old stories of those people she looked back on with such fondness and benevolent recollection. Why did I wait until she was gone to pick up this jagged and painful particle of our past to try to deal with it? Somehow, I think, I couldn't reconcile the woman I knew and loved with this knowledge. It is a painful task to look back at the injustice of the past and assign a role to one you loved. It takes a period of time, of living, of garnering strength, to look a ghost in the face.

That area of East Texas, the "north star of Texas," is not too many miles as the crow flies from the area of Louisiana where Ernest Gaines lived and sets his novels. Gaines, author of *The Autobiography of Miss Jane Pittman* among others, was born on a plantation in Pointe Coupee Parish near New Roads, Louisiana. In Gaines's recent novel *A Lesson Before Dying*, the character wrongly accused of killing a white man listens in his jail cell to the same radio station I listened to as a teenager, a rhythm and blues station out of Gallatin, Tennessee. When I began to read Gaines's work I quickly realized his stories were the obverse of my own. There in his graceful prose was the painful recognition of the small and not so small cruelties and the subtle and consistent indignities I'd witnessed growing up. There in print was the other side of the coin, the whole truth perhaps as much as could be realized. It was as if my experience had been concave, and suddenly, reading his work, the empty spaces, the interior lives of those on the same canvas as I, were suddenly manifest, as if the hollow, rotted center of the old cherry tree were there whole again.

And I ask myself, is that any kind of a resolution to that spring day so many years ago, to at least fill in the blanks of the other's past? Is it possible that literature can perhaps make us whole after the fact? Is it possible our common stories, both black and white, might free us all from this past and lead us to some common gray truth?

Recently, around the time Ernest Gaines received a prestigious grant from the MacArthur foundation, he revealed that he was in the process of trying to preserve the burial ground on that plantation where he grew up. It was an attempt to honor the graves of those whose stories he'd told, those who went before him and who lie in unmarked graves.

Meanwhile my grandmother rests in the rolling green hills above the rich black clay of the Red River bottom, at the edge of that same town. On a wet day of a funeral that black clay attaches itself to the bottom of one's shoes like a second sole. "Perpetual care," the cemetery promises, unlike the unmarked graves in Pointe Coupee. But the markers are flat to the ground so that it's easy for the maintenance workers to mow around them, and from some of the promontories there's a view of an abandoned drive-in movie house that once charged a dollar a head, so that as teenagers we'd pack two or three in the trunk before driving inside. Now the old useless, deteriorating white screen stands there facing the cemetery, empty forevermore of images of the past. Maybe the idea of an afterlife, of the "peace that passeth understanding" as the Bible says, has to do with an honest confronting of the past, so that we can see the present whole and face our common ghosts. So we can all get past it and we and our children can rest in peace.

Adjustments
Mary Morris

We didn't know the chiropractor was moving in next door until after we bought the house. Actually we didn't know until the day we moved in. As the previous owners were leaving, they said, "By the way, you know the building where the law student committed suicide last winter? Well, we've heard that a chiropractor is moving in."

I wept but Mitchell, who looks on the bright side, said it wouldn't be a big deal; "It could be a lot worse," he said. "A methadone clinic could've moved in. Or a family with teenagers. It's just a chiropractor, a bone cracker, you know; how many people can hobble up to his door a day?"

The morning after we moved in, the construction began. Not ours, but his. Walls were ripped out, others put in. We sipped our morning coffee to the sound of hammers. The peace

I'd envisioned in our first house was shattered by the whir of saws and drills which punctuated our days.

I had fallen in love with this house the first time I saw it. I loved the stone steps that led up to it, the open parlor with the mahogany trim, the backyard with its brick patio and flowing rosebushes. I loved the staircase and the gaslight out front. I knew the moment I walked in that I would live here. I would have a home and a studio in which to do my graphic design. It was a house where we could raise a family, though in the end this would not happen. We had thought of everything when we bought the house. But we didn't think about who our neighbors might be.

For months I never saw the chiropractor, but we heard the sounds of hammers, saws, and drills. In the evening I'd stand on my deck and gaze down into the chiropractor's garden. It was filled with Coke cans and Styrofoam containers from fast-food restaurants which various tenants had left behind. The garden was populated with terrifying weeds—giant, mordant growths with barren branches that sprouted hideous blurts, but only at their tips. There was something perverse about those towering weeds which threatened my oak and loomed on the other side of the fence that separated our two yards. I wanted to pull them out by the roots.

The Monday after the construction stopped, we heard "The Star-Spangled Banner" for the first time. The opening refrain played over and over again in chimes. We heard it from early in the morning until late at night, reverberating through our house. Mitchell sang along with it, "Oh, say can you see . . ." After a day or two of this, I decided to phone next door. He had already hung out his shingle which read, "Dr. Henry Armand, Chiropractor." Dr. Armand's phone number was on the shingle so I wrote it down. I called and a woman with a distinctly island accent answered the phone. "Excuse me," I said, "but do you have some gadget that plays 'The Star-Spangled Banner'?"

"Yes, we do," she said, her voice huffy and defensive.

"And what's that?" I asked.

Without hesitating she said, "It's the national anthem."

"I know it's the national anthem," I told her, "but what is the gadget?"

"You'd better speak with the doctor," she said. "He's not here, but he can call you back."

When I got off the phone, I was screaming at Mitchell. "You see, I told you, you see what kind of people we're dealing with. A doorbell that plays that 'Star-Spangled Banner'."

Dr. Armand called in the evening. We introduced ourselves and I explained to him what the problem was. He was sorry that his doorbell disturbed me and promised to do what he could to change it. His voice was clear and in it I heard tropical breezes, Caribbean nights, the kinds of places Mitchell and I visited on package tours.

Mitchell said that because the subway is down the street from our house and most people will go to the chiropractor's from the subway, I probably wouldn't notice the traffic at all. This seemed to make sense, but neither of us had imagined that they would come in vans. People in wheelchairs. People with canes. Carloads full of bent, broken, decrepit people, most of whom seemed beyond repair. One morning a van of amputees arrived and they all lined up in front of my house.

All day long ambulettes filled with little old black ladies who bantered in secret tongues unloaded in front of my studio while women with clipboards called out their names. I'd hear the van pull up. I'd listen to the bang as the metal ramp came down and the old ladies or amputees or broken men in wheel-chairs were slowly rolled out. Sometimes they used walkers and I'd hear the clang as rows of crippled people stumbled by.

In a half hour or so they were done with their treatment—which, as their faces grew more familiar, never seemed to make them better. If it was a nice day and their driver had gone off for lunch and the van wasn't there, idling, they'd line up in front of my house and wait for the van to return. They'd sit back and raise their faces to the sun.

Black people talk in loud voices. I'd noticed that before but never as much as when they were in front of my house. I'd noticed it on the subway or on the street. But it is amazing how the sound can carry through brick walls. It's a kind of laughter that comes from somewhere deep inside, a place I've never laughed from. They laugh louder and harder than white people do. It's as if everything is funnier to them.

I work at home, in a studio on the ground floor, and I spend a lot of time looking outside. I have a small graphic design business, though since the recession it has been slow. Much of what I do is catalogues for museums. A graphic artist's work isn't mechanical the way some people think. A lot of what I do involves spatial relations—determining how things fit or don't fit next to one another.

Often I sit at my desk just staring straight ahead. One day as I sat there, I heard a knock at the window. I looked up and saw two black men with walkers and a woman smoking a cigarette. "Where's the doctor?" they shouted at me. "Why don't you answer? Isn't he in?"

"Go away," I shouted. "His office is next door."

From my garden as I prune my roses and turn the compost, as I mulch, getting ready for winter, I stare up and see patients on treadmills, exercise bikes, ebony men drenched in sweat and little ladies from the Caribbean who chant in strange tongues, all staring down at me, panting.

·   ·   ·

One night Mitchell and I go to an Italian restaurant around the corner and I tell him I want to discuss the chiropractor. He says, "Please," and I tell him I really want to talk about it. Because it bothers me, having people in front of my window, staring in. Ringing my doorbell, or standing outside.

Mitchell and I have been married for a long time. Over ten years. He works for the city in urban planning—roads, traffic, that kind of thing. We've been trying to have a child, but haven't really gone to any lengths to make it happen. We keep expecting it will, but we aren't that disappointed when it doesn't. Briefly we looked into adoption, but we both seem to accept that this is the hand fate has dealt us. This is what our lives are supposed to be.

"I'm not sure why this is, but the people next door, they bother me."

Mitchell clears his throat, stares at his wineglass. "Is it because they're black?"

This enrages me because we live in a mixed neighborhood and Mitchell knows I voted for Dinkins. "I don't care if they're green," I tell him. "They don't belong here."

In November the doorbell began playing "Santa Claus Is Coming to Town" and I invited the chiropractor over for tea. Mitchell didn't want me to. He said Lorna, what's the point. That's my name, Lorna, like the cookies. It was my mother's idea. Dr. Armand arrives on time at four o'clock sharp. He wears a gray suit and a white shirt. He is in fact a tall and rather striking man. He brings his associate with him. A physical therapist with a long ponytail and a Hawaiian shirt. They look like a team of detectives.

I offer them cheese and crackers, tea with honey, which

they sip politely. They pick at the cheese and crackers. I can tell they'd rather be somewhere else, but they are being polite. Mitchell smiles and keeps offering something to spice up their drinks. The chiropractor's fingers tap the edge of the chair and I know he is wondering what he's doing here.

I have never had a black person in my house before. Actually that isn't true. I've had black people in to deliver packages or fix the furnace. Once I had a black man laying carpet all day long. But I've never had one at my dinner table or sitting in my living room with a teacup in his lap. I'm not uncomfortable about this, but I am aware of it.

The chiropractor and I discuss the weather, business, the city going down the tubes. He recommends that we not park our car on Second Street, but we tell him it's okay because our car was stolen the year before. He nods understandingly. The physical therapist is restless.

I tell them as politely as I can that we've got a few issues. Some things we'd like to discuss. The vans idling in front of the house, the rows of old ladies who chatter away. Noise seeps into my studio. They offer to put up a tapestry on their side of the wall. They will tell the van drivers to unload farther down the street.

"And the doorbell?" I ask, as delicately as I can.

"Yes, we'll do something about that."

The next morning when we get up, it is playing Beethoven's Fifth.

That afternoon I call my best friend, Angela, who has just moved to Cleveland. I call from my studio as vans of crippled, frail black women struggle past my window. "I've got a problem," I tell her and Angela laughs, a loud cackle I've never heard from her before.

"Oh, that's nothing." She tells me that the state has purchased the property behind hers and turned it into a halfway house for men, several of whom have Tourette's syndrome. "There's one guy who stands out in the yard, shouting shit and fuck all day. My kids can't go in the yard because this guy shouts obscenities at them."

"Oh," I said, thinking that Mitchell was right; things could be worse.

During the day I place my ear to the wall of the kitchen, and I hear the whir of stationary bicycles, whirlpools. Exercise equipment. Laughter permeates the walls. It is loud laughter, without constraint. I wonder what they can be laughing about all the time. What can be so funny?

In dreams late at night I see strange people staring in at me. Black people, Hispanic people—people I don't know, though I think I do, sitting in cars, idling, waiting, watching my house, watching me.

I want to get rid of them, the people next door. I decide they are illegal. The neighborhood isn't zoned for this sort of thing. Mitchell says I am probably right, but the chiropractor's in-laws own the building. What am I going to do about that? he asks me. You blow the whistle on them, or soon you'll have a rock band next door.

Mitchell and I have this way of reading in bed. We prop our pillows side by side. Plant our feet just so. We stay that way until one of us starts to fall asleep. Then the other one turns out the light. We haven't made love at night since I can remember. Our pattern is to do it in the morning, then take a shower. I have gotten used to this; it is one of the many things I have gotten used to over the years.

But one night as we are still reading, I curl next to Mitchell, tell him to put his book down. He's reading some kind of financial how-to like how to be your own broker so I don't think he should mind. I reach for him, press my mouth to his chest; my finger touches his neck, his ears. But he pulls away. It has been a long day, he tells me. He's tired and needs his rest. In the morning, he says.

No, now, I tell him. I want you now. And suddenly I do, ferociously. I feel that now I could make a baby. Now I could make everything different.

But he says he really can't. He really doesn't want to.

I get out of bed and hear him calling to me. Lorna, for Pete's sake. But I go outside. I want to breathe the air. I want to sit under whatever stars shine where I live. I see our bedroom light on and I see it go out.

I'm not sure how long I sit there, but after a while I know I am not alone. I look up and I see Dr. Armand standing in the window of his gym, staring down at me. With his hand, he is parting the shade. When he sees me look up at him, he lets it go.

I go to the chiropractor's office to complain about what is on the other side of my wall. I do not want to stand on my deck and see the debris and hideous growths. I have never been inside the waiting room before, but I am surprised by its oily smell, the plaid carpeting. A giant fish with a big ugly mouth swims alone in a tank. Who would buy a fish like that?

The receptionist greets me. She has gold earrings the size of door knockers and long nails painted red with black tips and little jewels shining in the middle. She taps these fingernails on the counter. I tell her I want to speak to the doctor.

Dr. Armand comes out and smiles. He is polite and asks how I am feeling. I am aware that I am the only white person in the room. I tell him that spring is approaching and his garden needs work. It is filled with garbage and I see it when I am on my deck. I hate the weeds, the overgrowth. Dr. Armand nods. "You don't like the front and you don't like the back," he says. I'm not exactly clear what he means, but he says he will take care of the problem.

That evening I see him outside with plastic bags, a rake. I shovel and rake. He gathers Styrofoam and tin cans and dead leaves in his arms. I see him unearth a barbecue pit, a bed of tulip bulbs just starting to rise. He goes inside and comes out with a small ax with which he starts to chop down the weeds. He raises the ax high, bringing it down.

I begin gardening again with a vengeance. I pull up the leaf mulches and make room for the bulbs. I pull out what I don't want; though the garden looks dead, I know I can bring it back again. I bend down to remove some dead growth when I feel the twinge. Just a small one, but I am surprised by the pain.

At first I don't think I've done anything, but soon I am having trouble straightening up and sitting down. At first it doesn't bother me. I just assume it will get better, but soon I can't walk. I'm stooped, bent over like the women who wobble in front of my studio.

Then I take to my bed. Mitchell brings me hot soups and tea. He stands by the side of the bed, stroking my brow. It is only with great difficulty that I can rise.

The pain gets worse. Mitchell says you really should see someone. You can't stay like this anymore. The next day I find myself hobbling, stooped and aching, past my own house. I move like an old person with cautious, anguished steps until I reach the gate to the doctor's office. A gate I have heard clang dozens of times a day. Now it clangs as I pass through.

I go into the office and tell the secretary I need to see the doctor. I explain that I've injured my back and can't seem to get straight. She tells me, without looking up, to have a seat.

I sit in front of the huge fish tank with one ugly fish in it like a giant piranha, its mouth and teeth going all the time. Black people come into the waiting room. They talk in loud voices, wear earrings the size of doorknobs. Someone calls my name and says Room Two.

I do not wait long before the doctor appears. In his white coat he stares at me, runs his fingers along my spine. He checks my range of motion, asking me to lean left and right. He has me reach forward and try to touch my toes, but I can barely bend. Lower lumbar, he mutters.

You need an adjustment, he tells me and hands me a white gown. It is paper and I hate the feel as I slip into it. I shiver because it is winter and the paper gown is cold. If someone put a match to me, I'd go up in smoke. Dr. Armand returns at last and finds me shivering on a small stool. He looms above me and I feel as if I have shrunk, like a child. Then he comes to me, runs his fingers up and down my spine. My skin is cold and the fingers feel warm and rough. He has me bend at the waist one more time.

Then he lays me face down on the table. He straps my ankles in. I joke with him about ancient methods of torture, but he doesn't laugh. I lie perfectly still, not moving, hardly breathing as I feel the pressure of his dark hands.

Prudential Life Insurance

Susan Richards Shreve

I *was nine, with a reputation for creating domestic unrest, when* Lula came to live with us in a middle-class neighborhood in segregated Washington, D.C. She had two children in tow and in spite of a college education had failed the civil service exam. According to my father, the government had quotas and Lula was one too many colored women for the 1950s bureaucracy to take on.

I remember lying on my stomach halfway down the carpeted stairs, peering through the banister, the night she arrived to be interviewed by my mother and father for a job which would include, in the twenty years we knew her best, everything from secretarial for my father who was a self-employed writer to domestic to nurse, operating the complicated dialysis machine in the year after my father's kidneys shut down.

"Little Lulu," I said to my brother alluding to the 1950s comic-strip character "Little Lulu."

"She's not *little* Lulu," Jeff said in his earnest way. "She's a giant."

And when I think back to the force she was in my childhood, not only as a woman but as a symbol for all of the women I knew growing up, "giant" is the word that comes to mind.

She was tall, taller than my father, over six feet, willowy, fine-boned and very black, with a reserve and calm which remained intact, as far as we could see, throughout a life of some high drama, petty violence, even bloodshed.

I must have had a child's sense of desperation about the precarious oddness of our situation. Even now I can hear the litany I repeated as a prayer or on stars or birthday candles— "God bless my family of four with Grandma and Lula" as if I knew that in the galaxy of lives, ours was particularly fragile.

She moved next door to my grandmother in the bedroom on the third floor with her children Mac and Bessie, then about five and seven, and in those years that was our household. It was a curious household for a white neighborhood in a Southern town. I was aware that the way we lived was different, that my parents were not on a mission as liberal thinkers—they were from a small town in conservative Ohio—but were people who were outsiders themselves. My father was from a poor family in an Underground Railroad town in South Central Ohio where the segregation was economic. My Danish mother had lost her own mother when she was a little girl and was always looking to fill that large space which Lula, ten years younger than she, seemed in her quiet, stubborn, independent way, to do.

This is not to say that we lived equally. We did not. I grew up in the forties and fifties in a middle-class family in a segregated city. The parameters of my experience and my point of view are determined by these facts. But a sense of injustice is another thing. It is either in the marrow or it's not, whatever the dimensions of a particular history.

I do believe that inside the walls of our house, something went on fundamentally different from what went on in some other people's houses. I took baths with Bessie, played dolls, told stories half under the bed in Lula's sweet-smelling bedroom, just as Mac and Jeffrey played cars and cowboys in the back bedroom. We went on the streetcar or bus to visit Lula's relatives on the other side of town—Crosstown, it was called, with all the implications, moving to the back, sitting in the colored section. We went to the colored movie theater in Adams Morgan; we were the only white children at the cousins' birthday parties and we hung in the kitchen, listening to the women talking and laughing and singing and uh-uhing the night away.

When Lula told us she was moving out to marry Jimmy Dargon, I was heartbroken. In my mind, her leaving marks the beginning of a kind of invisible splintering of childhood.

As is true of most storytellers, the real secrets of my life, concealed or buried in childhood, a Pandora's box ready to fly open with a flood of unstoppable tears, are in my stories. I see what I have written and then I know what I feel. Not think. I *know* what I think. Most of us do. In principle, it was easy to support the civil rights movement in Mississippi or Washington or on the streets of Detroit. Of course, it was right. But feeling —now, there's a war zone full of land mines which could blow to smithereens any right-thinking individual. And that of course is the territory of race.

What I know about that territory is very small but I think it has to do with my love affair with black women—a romance with all the limitations romance implies.

As a small child, when my slate was clean and the marks

made were indelible, I had polio. It was not a terrible case of polio but I was "lame" and not, by temperament, given to resignation. When I first went to kindergarten, I was an "other," called "Gimp," a name whose meaning I didn't know, although its implication was clear, a name which held. I was "different," "unclean," "contagious," "untouchable." In the tribal community of kindergarten, I could have found a place to belong, I'm sure—the one who took care of others, put the toys away, cleaned up the spilled milk, got the last chair, the last choice of cookies. But that was not a place I wished to have.

My father, in what I believe was a gesture of protection, warned me about my future. He was a man raised in the era of "legs," and it was his assumption that a young woman with mismatched legs would not be likely to find a man worth marrying who was willing to take her on. The message was that I'd have to fend for myself—a situation certainly no news to a black girl then or now, but in my generation middle-class white girls expected something else.

So it is no wonder to me now that the role models of my childhood lay not in the soft chatter on the subject of husbands and recipes and women not in attendance in the living rooms of my neighborhood, but in the noisy kitchens full of high laughter and raucous stories of the women where Lula took me—women who understood the weight of the word "Gimp" and all its bedfellows and would not allow such a definition to describe their lives.

I look back now on the stories I have written and what I see is telling. In one book, I have a crippled white woman in a romantic relationship with a black woman. In another, I have a blind photographer whose black companion, a former servant, is her sight. And then there's Prudential Life Insurance.

Prudential Life Insurance came to me in the early eighties, the year my mother died unexpectedly and I was writing a book called *Dreaming of Heroes.* Prudential is a character in that book, a black woman in her thirties with a son called Victory, no husband, and the job as a high-grade civil servant in Washington, D.C., that Lula would have liked. In the book she plays a minor role—a young woman from Okrakan, South Carolina, named from a sign in front of a white man's house: Prudential Life Insurance: Inquire Within.

Inquiring within, this is what I find projected on the small screen of memory.

It is late evening, my parents out, I am sashaying undressed into Lula's room where she lies on the bed in a robe, her long legs crossed over the bedpost. She is listening to the radio.

"Get your clothes on, girl," she says to me, throwing me a towel. She turns up the sound. "You hear that?" she asks, holding her robe modestly closed, sitting up on the bed.

The newscaster is telling about an eleven-year-old girl whose mutilated body was found face-down behind a woodpile in Rock Creek Park. We listen to the story.

"You see," Lula says, turning the radio off.

"I don't go to Rock Creek Park by myself," I say.

"No," she says to me, "but you run around the house naked in front of the window, and who is to say there's not someone standing on the street looking up at you with nothing better to do than pester little girls?"

I climb across her and lie down on the inside, next to the wall.

"Tell me some murders," I say to Lula, drunk on the sweet scent of hair grease, of singed hair that comes of ironing the kinks, of her tropical perfume. The room is always a little dark, low wattage in the lamps, the blinds pulled shut, and neat but crowded with treasures, pictures, trinkets and magazines and the Bible and jewelry, and bright silk scarves covering the tops of tables. There's a drawer in her dresser with the things of dead people—her mother's handkerchief she was holding when she died, her brother's flannel shirt with the bullet hole going through the front and out the back, things from her aunt and her baby cousin who drowned. She calls it her "death drawer."

"See," she says, opening the drawer wide, "but don't touch."

I wouldn't dare.

"Do you touch?" I ask her.

Her face takes on a long sadness, her lips pucker.

"I don't go around touching if I can help it," she tells me. "You never know what's contagious."

She lies down on the bed next to me, her arm a pillow under her head.

"What murder do you want tonight?" she asks.

"An eleven-year-old girl is riding her bike along the path between her house and Mirch Elementary," I begin. "It's October and she's wearing red corduroys and a turtleneck."

"In the bushes just beyond the path," Lula goes on, "there's a man with a blue-and-white bandana across his nose and mouth and he is waiting patiently for a schoolgirl, no one in particular, just the first schoolgirl to come down the path alone . . ."

This was the fifties, when the dangers of living sprang out of desire much more connected to bad dreams than real life.

When Lula went to her church crosstown, I was taken by my parents to the Episcopal Sunday school on the grounds of the Washington Cathedral, which I did not attend. My parents were uninformed about my religious education, which actually was in the basement of the Cathedral at the Greek Orthodox services set up in the crypt with candles lit for the dead and incense and, most satisfactory of all, a priest in a long robe, a high hat, a long beard, who carried out his priestly duties behind a transparent screen so his projection was larger in shadow than in life.

I'd wave good-bye to my parents, head in the front door of the Sunday school, go through the building, out the back door, across the lawn, down the steps to the crypt, light my candle for the dead in Lula's dresser drawer and join the congregation of Greek believers.

In the evening, I'd tell Lula about my day at church and she'd tell me about hers.

"What kind of singing do the Greeks do?" she asks me.

"Lalalalalalala," I hum the monotone of the chanted prayers.

"Uh-uh-uh," Lula grunts, "what kind of singing is that?" And she dances around her room, swinging her long body like a sail. "Swing low, sweet char-i-o-t . . ."

"Someday," she says, "you come to my church where the Lord visits."

I stand at the end of the aisle at the Pentecostal Baptist Church. There's Lula and her sister Esteline and her cousin Aida and Cinderella and some other people and me and Jeff. It's winter, daytime dark outside and cold and these women are dancing in the pews, clap-clapping, tap-tapping, swinging back and forth in a near frenzy. "So the Lord says to me . . . Yes, sister . . . Let my people go."

Mind, Lula is a pole of a woman, so dignified, so self-contained, I never imagine a soul spilling out of that black skin like sweat but here she is swinging, her head flying around in a circle, faster and faster. I am not singing and Jeff is sitting in the pew with his small hands folded in his lap. The lights go out and Lula has fainted dead away in the pew and no one is paying attention.

"You almost died," I say to her on the streetcar ride home.

"That was not death, darling," she says to me. "That was ecstasy. You got to learn the difference."

I am fourteen on a Saturday night in my house in Northwest Washington and we, Lula, Jeff, and me, are standing in the living-room window peering through the drapes at the driveway where a man is crouched, carrying, Lula tells us, a knife. He can't see us because the lights are out in our house. The man, Lula tells us, is an old boyfriend.

"Why does he have a knife?" Jeff asks.

"Now, why do you think he'd have a knife?" Lula asks. "Not for slicing bread."

"I'd like to call my mother," Jeff says.

I don't want to call my mother. I think it's exciting beyond belief that a man with a knife is in our driveway.

"What did you do to him?" I ask Lula.

She shrugs.

"I told him I wouldn't dance with him because I'm married now to Jimmy Dargon," she says peering through the curtain. "And that aggravated him."

*I am at a dance club, twenty, barefoot, colored strobe lights hip-*hopping across the dance floor, a live swing band, strangers at the tables around us where I sit with the man I'm going to marry whose leg is in a cast.

There is a tap on my shoulder.

I have never danced with a black man. In the world in which I've grown up, there has been no occasion—mine has been a life led in the middle, neither rich nor poor, privileged nor disadvantaged.

I move into his long arms, swing into the arch of his lean

body, alert, my heart beating like mad against his chest, my hip leaning against the knife in his pocket.

"What do you think frightened me?" I ask Lula days later. "He was a perfectly nice man and a good dancer."

She shakes her head. "I think you ought to mind your own business," she says to me, "or else learn how to dance."

Years later, talking to a black friend about race, I say, "I think it's sex between us."

"And God," she says. "Sex, God, and death."

*Prudential Life Insurance is the only character I have ever imag-*ined who has appeared more than once in a book of mine, and always her role in the story is to witness the action with clear eyes that see the world for what it is. In *A Country of Strangers,* it is 1942 in the still rural farmland of Northern Virginia, and Prudential is carrying her father's baby, living out the term with her aunt and uncle.

"Prudential Dargon was thirteen, high-tempered and bone-thin with a gentle round belly that was a baby growing into its sixth month of incubation. Not that Prudential hadn't tried. She'd used coat hangers and ridden the pony bareback over the fences and drunk some terrible brew her grandmama con-cocted, but the baby stuck, and so she was sent out of South Carolina before she showed to stay the summer with her Aunt Miracle. And then she'd plans to leave the baby with Moses and Miracle, who couldn't seem to get a baby of their own started.

"I send you Prudential, Miracle sweetheart," her mother had written. "See if you can tame her."

"I can't be tamed ever," Prudential said, dancing through the house to the music on the Victrola, lifting her summer skirt high in the air, turning her bare feet so fast you couldn't tell one from the other, hugging and kissing the lamps and banis-ters and mantelpiece, pretending they were boyfriends.

·   ·   ·

In The Visiting Physician, *a book in progress,* Prudential *is* around again. A child has died and a visiting physician has arrived in the town where Prudential, almost seventy years old, is working although not trained as a nurse.

Prudential—she had no last name that she gave out; too many husbands over the years, she said—was blue-black with skin that glistened waxy and a large head with a broad forehead. Not a trace of a smile.

"I'm Dr. Helen Fielding," Helen said.

"I know who you are." Prudential folded her arms across her chest, refusing Helen's extended hand. "I can't touch you. I've got death on my hands."

"So do I," Helen said. "We both do."

This is probably my last book with Prudential, the giant "Little Lulu" who filled our lives when I was small. She's pretty old to come around again, and no doubt tired of playing the role of seer in my stories. But she has been exactly what her name implies—Life Insurance for the white women she knows. And I thank her for that, amongst other things. That has been a gift.

Across the Glittering Sea

Jewelle Gomez

My mother, *Dolores, used to visit me on holidays in Boston,* where I lived with my great-grandmother. She seemed glamorous and grand with her long hair, perfectly manicured nails and tall, handsome second husband. They always came with gifts appropriate to the particular occasion, listened enthusiastically as my inept piano playing filled our tenement apartment, then laughed and talked loudly about bygone adventures that I found thrilling. Peachy, my mother's husband, was genuinely happy to have a stepdaughter and reminded me somewhat of my own father, Duke—sharp wit, snappy dresser, a charmer. But Peachy was white. Of French-Canadian extraction to be precise. His adoration of my mother, which he'd sustained since before my birth, was always romantic to me, like the great loves in movies. My grandmother and great-grandmother clearly appreciated him—his generosity, humor and style, so his ethnicity went without comment for the most part. Except, of course, when he did something wrong, like disagree with my great-grandmother. Then after he and my mother swept elegantly out to their car and headed toward their home in Rhode Island, he became "that white man" to my great-grandmother. But overall, his membership in our family was generally accepted and went unremarked. Until my mother's son was born.

My mother, Dolores, was always the fairest-skinned of our family. She looked less like her mother, who favored the bronze-toned Ioway and Wampanoag branches of the family, and more like her father, who was part Black but with a very light complexion and pale eyes. When my half-brother, Phillip, was born (resembling more my mother's father than me) my grandmother, great-grandmother and I began to visit my mother and Peachy in Rhode Island for the first time. It was then that I realized that just because my mother's husband was white didn't mean they were rich. In fact they lived in a very tiny apartment in a working-class section of Pawtucket, a mill town. And by the early 1960s all the mills had stopped. Our arrival for family visits turned out to be the local equivalent of the desegregation of Ol' Miss.

Residents of her neighborhood, plagued by unemployment and unnerved by immigration, were shocked to realize that Dolores didn't simply have exquisite coloring, she was colored! This precipitated months of harassment: telephone threats on my mother's life, garbage dumped on their front steps and other cruelties. After months of tension, the construction of Interstate Highway 95 effectively defused the racist attacks simply by cutting the neighborhood in half, forcing a good number of the anonymous callers and threateners to relocate. I was about eleven at the time and only knew what was going on because I was a good listener. I pretended to read or watch television while soaking up the whispered information. At that age it was both exciting and emotional, like when I watched the news coverage of black and white students "sitting in" at Southern Woolworth lunch counters.

Twenty-five years later, at the funeral mass for Peachy, what I thought of most was the fierce pride in his eyes when he'd talked of protecting my mother. Their bond seemed impervious to whatever obstacles bigots might heave into their path. I don't know if this was true, or if they ever even talked about what loving across the color line meant to them or to the world. For me, at the same time as I exulted in the Black nationalism of the sixties, Dolores and Peachy were the symbol of romance triumphing over all. They were the happy ending we were always denied in movies like *Pinky* and *Imitation of Life*.

I like to think that in the nineties and in the lesbian/gay community an interracial union would not be as explosive as it was in the movies and in Pawtucket, Rhode Island. In some ways that's true. But white lesbians and gays are just as much a product of a racist society as their heterosexual counterparts. And most of us—lesbians and gays of any ethnicity—don't live in isolated, prosperous ghettos, but in average working-class and middle-class communities alongside the majority of U.S. citizens. So even when we do find a common ground as individuals from very different backgrounds we still have to face the neighbors, some of whom are no more progressive than the bigots who tried to scare my mother and Peachy out of their home.

I was one of the innocent few who mistakenly believed that the advent of the lesbian nation in the seventies meant that the issue of racism has been resolved. It seemed natural that women, having struggled through the patriarchy to ascend to feminism would never stoop to anything as petty as racism. Unfortunately what W. H. Auden said was true: "Those to whom Evil has been done will do Evil in return." More than evil with a capital "E," it's usually the small ones that trip you up. Like when white women automatically assume that Black women are always aggressive or butch. Or when editors of lesbian/gay publications only ask me to review books by Black people. But these are public/professional issues, each of which can be addressed from a solidly considered philosophical and political position. As a Black lesbian feminist I have a prepared lesson plan for situations like those. But what happens among friends, or in the home? How do we navigate those vast seas of difference that feminism neglected to tell us would be so choppy and turbulent?

I'm just settling down in my first monogamous, committed relationship, with a woman who is not Black, so I have more questions than answers. If I begin with simply the term "committed relationship," the genesis of many issues that will be raised is obvious. If Diane and I were heterosexual I'd be able to say "marriage." There would be a set of (sometimes tedious) social engagements which would have marked our rite of passage from single to couple.

These rites, like all such activities, help to ease the participants into their new status and help to cement the relationship. They provide a background of supportive voices, a net of experiences, a validation. In an interracial, heterosexual relationship they might be a difficult gauntlet that must be run before the couple gets on with life. But even in those trials, the relationship can be made stronger. When Sidney Poitier nobly endured the parental barbs of Katharine Hepburn and Spencer Tracy in *Guess Who's Coming to Dinner?* in 1967, the audience knew that in the end the family unit would ultimately expand to include him. The simple fact that there's a title for him—husband—means he has a role in the family, whatever his ethnicity.

For us there've been no similar social activities or titles to provide us with the security of acknowledgment, so we must explore these unknown waters on our own. Some interracial

lesbian couples try to avoid family contact altogether, fearing
that the fact of a partner's being a woman and the "wrong"
color might send the family over the edge. Diane and I have
not chosen that type of distance because we're both too committed to our families even when the gauntlets are unpredictable. When I attended Diane's sister's wedding this year it
didn't occur to us until we were almost at the ceremony that I
might be the only Black person there. In fact I wasn't the only
one. I spotted an elegantly dressed Black woman about my age
during the reception. We greeted each other with easy recognition but she moved away quickly. She was the new in-laws'
housekeeper. It's not the first social situation I've been in
where the only other person of color was service staff, and it
won't be the last. But I felt badly that she didn't feel comfortable talking to me, and that I couldn't be sure if it was because
of our differing "status" (which is rarely acknowledged in this
country) or because I was the lesbian in-law. I will probably
never know.

From past experience I've developed one approach to overcome the negative impact of family influences. Long ago I
decided not to hold anything the "in-laws" do to me against
my partner; after all, they raised her, she didn't raise them.
Several years ago I journeyed with another white girlfriend to
meet her parents and they served (from their favorite take-out
place) a spread of fried chicken, collard greens, potato salad
and cornbread. My girlfriend kept reassuring me that they
always ate this way, that they weren't feeding me "soul food"
as a way of condescending to me. I let her know that, conscious
or not, her parents were making a statement about me which
she should not remain naïve about. But I also let her know I
didn't care. Her parents had their own set of issues, which did
not have to be mine or hers if she didn't let them be. As long as
my lover recognized the complexity of the situation enough to

want to address it, I was satisfied. I think it was easier for me to do that because we're lesbians; we are outsiders together.

Heterosexism regularly forces us to see our lives as independent of and unlike that of our parents. I accepted my girlfriend as a separate entity, capable of making better choices than her parents. She needed to be able to see their racism and to see herself apart from them. I needed to not make everything "all right" for her.

Once the family is put in a proper perspective, it is more a question of how I place myself and my ego in relationship to my partner. Diane says that, given the nature of U.S. culture, it's not *if* she'll do or say something racist or at least insensitive, but *when*. That she's smart enough to understand this and still not be too afraid to engage with a woman of color means a lot to me. I don't worry so much about when she'll do something, as that I will be looking so hard for her to do it I'll be a nervous wreck. I don't think I could live a life in which I'm on my guard constantly, and a full, long-term relationship can't be built on anxiety. Yet I have to be realistic and acknowledge that we both grew up in a racist society and be prepared to deal with the question if/when it comes up. Diane might do or say something racist, just as a Black male relative sooner or later might say something sexist.

What I worry about is that we might not do the work to talk it through. I don't want ethnicity and racism to be an unspoken issue as they seemed to be for my mother and Peachy. I would like difference to be something we learn to be curious about and enjoy rather than fear and despise. I want to be able to love my partner because she has red hair and freckles, not in spite of them. And to do that without feeling that I devalue Black aesthetics of beauty. For a woman this is a complex and difficult set of ideas. Years of indoctrination tried to make me believe that white skin and long hair, preferably blond, should be favored over the natural black attributes of kinky hair and varying shades of brown.

The Black Power movement then reset the scales, making all things Black beautiful and designating white the symbol of only oppression. Yet even under the reign of Black Power my beauty was dependent on my pliancy. I was a Black queen, subject to her king. Today when I look at images on television, in films, in magazines, even those produced by Black people, it's like the Black Power movement never happened. Most of the Black women look nothing like me; they are thin, with translucent skin and long, straight hair. This video image haunts us at a time when born-again Black Nationalists rail against the struggle for anyone's rights but their own, and regard the idea of a multicultural perspective as an insult to their status as victim. The contradictions are startling and disheartening.

I taught a class in Black Popular Culture at a small Northern California college in which almost twenty of the thirty enrollees were African-American, most of them young men nineteen to twenty years old. Five or six of them tried to dominate all conversation, acting as if the purpose of the class was not to explore culture but simply to mouth off about white people in general and Jews in particular. Their level of bitterness, ignorance and insensitivity (to other Black students, people of color and their white peers) was astounding. Sometimes the fiery atmosphere resembled what I imagine a KKK rally would be, except that the participants were young Black men. I felt angry and vulnerable. If they knew I was a lesbian and that my partner was white and Jewish, I was certain that everything I'd tried to do in the class would be dismissed.

I sensed in Black youth a crisis in the sense of self-worth that I feel I myself have passed through and that the struggles of the sixties were supposed to have eliminated. Because I had the perspective of the women's movement, alongside the Black

Power movement, I don't feel like a victim. At least not twenty-four hours a day, seven days a week. I have been victimized historically and personally, but my strength comes not from that victimization but from the triumphs and insights I've gained through my family and continued participation in political struggles of all kinds. When I think about my grandmother working at C. Crawford Hollidge, a downtown Boston department store, I don't just remember the management's inability to see what an asset she would have been as a sales clerk. I also remember how distinguished she looked in her uniform, standing beside her elevator. As elegant and capable as any of the higher-paid, white sales staff. Everything she had shone out from within her. She didn't need the store's white management to validate her existence. It's that independent spirit rather than bitterness that fuels my work, and that was so difficult to find in my young students.

In order for change to happen we all have to give up something, even those of us who feel we've already been asked to give up too much. What we must give up is a psychological position that might reduce whites to individual guilt but that also hobbles us with a narrow vision of our own possibilities. Those young students felt comfortable placing wholesale blame with white people. In doing so they absolved themselves of any current responsibility for their own lives. They were not willing to let go of macho posturing (which really translated into "poor Black me") long enough to see or care about the other people of color in their class to explore the evolution of Black popular culture, or to get to know me. They were not able to let go of the role that racism had stuck them with.

In an interracial relationship there must be a mutual relinquishing of those traditional roles, oppressor and oppressed, and then we must still be willing to explore the remnants of those roles. Sometimes having difficult teaching experiences such as that class provided a non-threatening opportunity to raise the issues. After each session I would rave about some ignorant remark and we would strategize together about how to address it in the next class in a way that would acknowledge the pain of the Black students as well as white students. In doing so we aired our own deep feelings about the position of race in this society. Having a natural, intellectual realm in which to think through the issues has been helpful.

Sometimes it won't be so academic. Diane told me that her father once said that if he had his preference she would have married a Jewish doctor. My response was that this was the equivalent of the aspirations of Black parents in the fifties— that we marry someone who worked for the railroad. She didn't understand the connection, because all of its implications weren't immediately available to her. Working for the railroad didn't translate to mean a black man's job, the Brotherhood of Sleeping Car Porters, or security. At first I thought she was refusing to equate the two aspirations because she was denying the legitimacy of the prestige a service position can have. Then I didn't understand that she didn't see the porter's job as historically a black man's job, so the sense of racial solidarity it conveyed missed her. What was really going on was that she didn't have the cultural references to interpret the experience. For a moment we were two people speaking two different languages. It was like a Moynihan Report nightmare until we disentangled the statements and provided the missing narrative.

Sometimes I fear that before we have the chance to deconstruct and reinterpret I'll just get angry or be so hurt, or she'll be so upset, that we withdraw rather than look directly at incidents our historical roles engender. But there are reasons that might not happen to us. She's a talker. When I look back at early letters between us they are filled with talk about so many different aspects of living—race, class, music, friends, death, her profession, my writing. There was no topic she would not approach. We have a relationship built on probing, revealing, even difficult conversations. We knew each other for almost ten years before we decided to live together, so we have a sense of each other as individuals in the world. It's not just because we're lesbians—some women are as close-mouthed and withholding as any man. But being accustomed—as two women friends together—to having intimate conversations, as sisters or best friends do all the time, it helps to expect that behavior to be a part of the natural exchange. Add to that: we're both feminists, so we are familiar with "processing." It's a much-maligned term in the smug nineties, but the act of decoding and analyzing feelings and behavior has been a key to personal and political progress for many women in the past one hundred years.

Another reason that communication is free-flowing between us is that Diane is Jewish—New York Jewish. She certainly has white-skin privilege, but she also has her own experience of oppression, both historical and personal, and consequently her own wariness about authority. She and her family are aware of not just the tensions between Blacks and Jews, which the press makes money by exploiting, but also the history of cooperation and liberation work that is rarely mentioned anymore. And alongside all of that is a persistent verbal tradition that some other white-skinned people would find "pushy" or "demanding." She's conscious of the need to talk about where we are and what's going on, no matter how uncomfortable it might feel. She, her two sisters and her parents are never at a loss for words.

Our negotiations—some direct, some not—around what to do for the Christmas/Hanukkah/Kwanza season was a first for me. Neither of us is religious, which simplified it somewhat. And for years I've preferred to celebrate the eve of Emancipation Proclamation Day rather than New Year's Eve on December 31. But what to do about red and green lights and wreaths of evergreen? We both wanted our new home to have a festive spirit that evoked the anticipatory thrills of our childhoods without riding over each other's heritage. After some floundering around we identified the elements that were the most important to each of us. The result was a Solstice celebration with ecumenical decorations (blue and white lights and boughs rather than wreaths) that satisfied both our politics and the child inside who still thinks December means the smell of pine (me) and brightly wrapped gifts early in the morning (her).

It was not simply that we both understand the need to talk that made that first hurdle successful, but that we both understand how precious is the ability to listen and to accept that we are basically different. We worked to find not a middle ground, but a new ground that would support us both. In order for change to happen, everyone has to give up something and in letting go, create something else. The struggle remains to appreciate the difference without losing touch with my own uniqueness and value. There are those from the nationalist camp on either side who say that distinction is impossible. But they are probably the same ones who choose to ignore our history and say that my loving a woman is a rejection of my people.

In an article on representation of interracial relationships film critic B. Ruby Rich says: ". . . difference can become a new route back to the self, since nothing any longer is self-evident. The tangle of individual versus cultural, the dissection of that place where personality leaves off and social construction begins, where imagined stereotypes merge into actual habits or disappear into erroneous projections is one that must be confronted only when lovers of different races, cultures, religions or classes face the political in the personal. It is there that desire must be wrestled into the light of day."[1]

Because of the public, activist position I've held in the lesbian community, many young women see me as *Black les-*

bian personified. And to each of them it means many different things. But I can see it in their faces sometimes when I do readings from my work, or hear it in their questions afterward. They hold me to some standard they don't even fully understand. Once a young Black woman openly expressed her shock that my lover was white when she saw us at an event together. In her mind my blackness was pure only if I was partnered with another Black woman. In another situation I ended a six-month relationship with a Black woman who said that the break was because I had difficulty being with another Black woman. I insisted that the problem was my relationship specifically with her, but I'm sure nothing could convince her.

It is important for me to examine my relationships with other Black women because regardless of how I present myself I will be considered a role model for Black lesbians. Both of their questions forced me to think about exactly who I thought I was. I resorted to bean counting: How many of my lovers have been Black women? How many of my close friends are women of color? How do I count my two best friends—one is Black and Native American and the other is Puerto Rican and Italian? I finally decided that sincerity and clarity, not purity, were the point of my life and my work. Dogmatism doesn't encourage healthy relationships or facilitate change.

In the United States the public always exerts some kind of pressure on interracial couples, if only by refusing to accept their representation in advertising, television shows, or movies. Before the civil rights movement it was illegal in many states for Blacks and whites to marry. Now I find that almost without exception it has been when I've been with white women that I've been harassed, in public, as a lesbian. It seems that two women of color walking down a city street together are invisible or inconsequential, but a Black woman walking with a white woman sets off alarms in the minds of bigots. So I've been subject to scathing verbal attack by a well-dressed white woman on Fifth Avenue, threatened with a club by an irate white construction site guard, and shoved by a group of young white college boys. Each time my white companion was overcome with guilt and we both were filled with anger. But because the assault came from outside it strengthened our bond. We were able to be mad together rather than at each other.

In an intimate relationship, raising the issue of ethnicity then necessitates that we address the issue of class, which is the silent obstacle in all interactions. I grew up with my great-grandmother, living in a cold-water tenement, on welfare. Diane's family was upwardly mobile, assimilated, middle-class. No matter where we both are now, how we look at our lives and at each other is affected by those very different backgrounds. Class, in our case, reinforces the power dynamic society has constructed around us. But if we examine our overall relationship, each advantage and disadvantage has to be weighed against the present reality as well as the past. I'm not simply a colored girl who grew up poor, but also a woman with education and a national reputation as a professional writer and an activist. In some aspects of our life I have more status than Diane does. Yet it still works better if she tries to flag down the taxi. The layers of identity are legion and only seem more so when examined closely.

Our agreement is to wrestle with all of them but not expect the contest to produce a single winner. The successful resolution produces not a simple statement of right and wrong but a better understanding of each position. Sometimes the idea of juggling all these things makes me want to laugh out loud derisively; at other times I want to cry with relief that I have the luxury and ability to think about how I want my life to be. Our agreement to wrestle, to discuss, implies we agree to move, to travel, to come closer to each other and let go of the static position we may have held before. As in any union (sanctioned by the state or not), it is a commitment to see ourselves as both uniquely separate and ultimately bound together.

Muriel Rukeyser, in one of her poems, "Across a Glittering Sea," notes the mistaken belief held by most people—that islands are distinct and separate, like them. She insists the islands are, whether large or small, all connected beneath the sea. My mother, Dolores, and her husband, Peachy, appeared to have had a relationship sturdy enough to make the journey between islands, even when there were storms. Given the period in this country's history, I can only guess at the cost to each of them. I hardly expected to be setting off in the same direction when I entered my middle years. But I've always known that love is unpredictable, so I am not taken completely unaware. The expanse of difference, that glittering sea, is terrifying. And it can also be a thing of magnificent beauty.

[1] *"When Difference Is (More Than) Skin Deep" by B. Ruby Rich, from* Queer Looks: Perspectives on Lesbian and Gay Film and Video, *ed. Martha Gever, Pratibha Parmar, John Greyson. New York City: Routledge, 1993.*

Loving Across the Boundary

Ann Filemyr

Nubian, *our puppy, scratches and whines at the bedroom door.* Essie sits bolt upright in bed, crying out, "What time is it?" Groggy, I squint at the clock. "Almost seven."

"Granny was supposed to wake us up at six!"

"Maybe she forgot." I hustle into my bathrobe at the insistent scratching on the door. "I've got to let Nubi out."

"Granny never forgets to wake us," Essie mutters under her breath as she scrambles out of the tangled sheets.

I race down the stairs, "Granny! *Granny!*" No! I will not accept what I feel inside when I find her body on the cold kitchen floor. She is gone—her spirit lifting up and out into the golden morning light filtering through the grand old maples that surround the farmhouse. Despite the utter peace in the room, I panic.

"Essie! Essie Carol!" I scream up the stairs to my partner.

Granny's breath is gone, but her body remains. A line from

the book *Daughters of Copper Woman* circles through my mind: *"And she left her bag of bones on the beach . . ."* Sun crowds the kitchen and the golden maple leaves gleam with the morning light. Essie flies barefoot across cold linoleum to cradle Granny in her arms, the first sob rising in our throats.

Granny was wearing the T-shirt I had given her from my trip to Brazil. Beneath a little refrain in Portuguese about protecting the rainforest for all the forest creatures was a brown-skinned elf with a green leaf hat. It reminded me of Granny's love for the forest, for the "red-birds" (cardinals) and "loud-mouth crows," for the gentle deer. She would wait all day just to catch a glimpse of them, moving from one window to the next or taking the short trail up to Sunset Hill to sit on her bench, waiting, watching for the deer.

Granny had on the green stretch pants Essie had given her, and pinned to the inside of her pants were her house keys. She always carried her keys when she went out on the paths surrounding the wooded farmhouse where we lived. She loved to take her cane and her cat and go out for a morning walk before we left for work. When she didn't have pockets, she would pin her keys to the inside of her pants just in case in our morning rush to get to work we would leave and lock her out—of course we never did.

Granny had made her bed that morning. She had gotten up, gotten dressed, and was ready for her morning walk. But instead of the familiar stroll, Granny had traveled where we could not follow. We shared a long, sad look. Essie's face crumpled in pain.

Yesterday morning Essie had had one of her dreams— disturbing, potent, deceptively simple but laden with clues. She woke up heavy with knowledge from an unnamed source. I too believe in dreams, but Essie's dreams are unforgiving.

Saturday at the vet's we found out that Granny's big orange cat, Papa, has feline leukemia. Papa was a stray, one of those unwanted kittens people toss out of their cars in the countryside expecting some barn full of cats and milking cows to welcome them. This hungry, frightened orange ball spitting fire at us could only be taken in, tamed and held by Granny. She affectionately named him Papa for her deceased husband. And that was it. We certainly couldn't object, so Papa joined us as cat number four. Now we couldn't tell Granny her cat had to be put to sleep, so instead we bought him medicine and asked Granny to care for him. In Essie's dream, she was worrying about the orange cat, Granny's cat, Papa, when a voice said, "Don't worry about the cat. Be prepared for Granny." The dream gave us only one day's warning, and we were not prepared.

In the hospital emergency room we wept, our heads bent over Granny's body. Stroking back her wavy black hair—even at seventy-nine her hair had not turned white—we sighed and pleaded. Two years ago in ICU the doctors had told us that she was gone. Her heart would not hold a steady beat. They pointed to the monitor above her unconscious body to show us the erratic yellow line, the uneven blip across the screen. The machines kept her breathing. We said no. It was her second heart failure in three months, that winter of 1991. We had plans for our shared lives—Granny, Essie and me. We were anticipating spring.

From my experience among the Anishinabe, the Great Lakes people also called the Chippewa or Ojibwa, the Ottawa, and the Pottawatomi, I knew the drum was the great heartbeat of the Earth. At their annual powwow in the Richards Street Armory, the drum echoed off the walls as the dancers moved in a sunwise circle around the center. The drum brought everyone's heartbeat together; that was part of its medicine—to unify and sustain. If only we could keep a drumbeat going in the room.

Essie and I had stayed in Granny's room in ICU that night,

and we kept up the heartbeat with hand on metal chair or foot on tile floor. We took turns imitating the da-dum da-dum of the Four Winds powwow drum, tapping out a sleepless steady beat in the whir and automated hum of life support. We watched the monitor for signs. Her heart would return and then fade, come back, keep a steady beat, then wobble. By dawn, her heartbeat was faint but constant. Finally she opened her eyes and tried to sit up, tried to speak. We rushed to her side. We had won! Granny regained her strength that time.

But that was March 1991 and this was October 1993. The doctor nodded to us and spoke with a strong Pakistani accent, "She looks happy. She had a long life. She would die one day." Then she left us alone, but the nurse on duty asked us a million questions about "the body"—about funeral arrangements . . . about donating organs . . . about contacting "the family"—we could not respond.

We are the family—an elder with her two granddaughters. This is the body which carries us forward and backward through time and healing. This is our story of love and death. What makes us alive; what keeps us from dying? We are the body of women weeping. Granny was ours to care for; we had taken her into our daily lives because we loved her, and now she is sleeping, and we cannot wake her.

Skin color marked Essie as the one who belonged to Granny. The nurse nodded and smiled at me. "It's so nice of you to stand by your friend at a time like this."

Where else would I be? Granny was my grandmother, too. She loved me like no one else did in my life: she loved me fiercely. She knew I had stepped across the line in North America which is drawn across the center of our faces to keep us separate—to keep the great-grandchildren of slavekeepers from the great-grandchildren of slaves. When she met me as Essie's "friend" twelve years earlier, she watched me closely, but then she accepted me into her household and into her family. As the elder, her acceptance meant acceptance. She recognized my love for her granddaughter and would say to me, "People talk, but you hold your head up. You walk tall. The Lord sees what you doing for my granddaughter, how you help her with her son. He sees how you stick together and help each other out." As far as she was concerned it was the quality of our caring, not our sexuality that mattered. In this she was far wiser than most.

For the past three years we had lived together in Yellow Springs, sharing meals and dishes. She would sometimes pull out her old photo albums and tell her stories, laughing at memories of wild times out dancing with her friends in the juke joint or riding horses with her cousin on her father's ranch or traveling cross-country with her husband and his magical black cat in the rig he drove as a truck driver. Rich, warm memories, and I would sip my coffee and imagine her days and nights. What sustained her? Love—there is no doubt. Love and greens and cornbread—good food. That's what she craved. And the kitchen was her favorite room next to her bedroom.

She had been raised in the fields and farms of the South. When I was deciding whether or not to take the job in Ohio, Granny was part of the decision-making process. Moving back to the country after four decades in the city felt like coming full circle to her. She said she wanted to come with us. And it was here in Ohio that Granny and I had the luxury of time together to make our own relationship to each other. She would talk to me about "the things white folks do"—how they tend to "put themselves first like they better than other folks"; how foolish they looked on the TV talk shows, "tellin' all of their business," or how much she had enjoyed some of the white friends she and her husband once had.

She spoke her mind without embarrassment or apology. I listened. She had survived the Jim Crow laws of the South. She had survived segregation and desegregation. She kept a gun she called "Ol' Betsy" under her pillow in case someone would try to break in or "mess with" her. Granny paid attention to details as a matter of survival. She prided herself on the subtle things she observed in watching how people acted and how they treated one another. She would interpret everything: tone of voice, a simple gesture, the hunch of someone's shoulders. She always knew when someone felt sad or tired. You didn't have to say anything. She comforted. She sympathized. She was extremely skilled at making others feel loved, feel noticed, feel good about themselves. If Essie had not been in my life it is doubtful that I would ever have known this remarkable woman, her namesake, Essie (Granny) Hall.

When I moved in with Essie in 1982, she stated her priorities directly. My nomadic tendencies were pulling at me, urging me to convince Essie that it was a perfect time for us to relocate to another city. I had lived in Milwaukee for two and a half years; for me that was long enough. I'd found a new love, an important someone in my life. It seemed like the perfect time to move on with my new partner. But Essie's life was described and defined by different currents. She had roots. She had family. She told me, "I will be here as long as Granny needs me." I was shocked. My feet carried me freely; I fought against family attachments. Was this difference cultural? Personal? Both? I have grown to respect and appreciate this way of being, this way of belonging. Is it a middle-class white cultural tendency to break free, to move on, to move up, to move out? Certainly the bonds of family and of commitment were far stronger for Essie than for me. One of the greatest gifts in my life has been that she shared her son and grandmother with me.

I wanted to tell the emergency room nurse all of this. I held Essie Carol in my arms as she cried. I wanted to scream, "Here we are, can't you see us? Lovers and partners holding each other in a time of crisis—What do you need for proof?" I wanted to confide, "We married each other beneath an oak in Washington Park on a sunny afternoon with the robins and insects as our witnesses, the wind as our preacher, and the red and golden leaves clapping in wild applause." But my voice was choked by my tears. I said nothing.

The funeral was an experience. Granny had touched so many, and they surrounded us in the Unitarian Fellowship that we had rented to avoid the dreary funeral home: Doug and Jeff, Peter and Ed, Yolanda and Carol, Nancy and Felicia; many of our gay and lesbian friends who had become family filled the straight-back chairs in the sunlit room. Katie from Cincinnati played Sweet Honey in the Rock's *Wading in the Water* over the boom box. Two weeks earlier one of Granny's other newly adopted granddaughters, Bituba, had taken Granny to a Sweet Honey concert in Dayton. She had met them all, sitting in the front row calling out "Yes, Lord!" and "Sing it, sister!" and greeting our friends as they came up and spoke to her.

We had hired a Baptist preacher to please Granny, as if she were there watching and laughing, enjoying herself. He had no idea what to make of the assembled mourners. He had never met Granny or the family. He was kind enough to show up and do this service for a roomful of strangers. If we had been able to do it our way, we would have had a simple service, a circle of chairs, a photograph of Granny, and the tumbling stories of our times together, our precious moments and memories. But we were caught between fulfilling our own desires and meeting the expectations of family members who were traveling to attend the funeral. Essie tried to do the expected. She hired a local African-American funeral home to handle preparations. She contacted a local Baptist preacher.

Sunday mornings Granny listened to gospel preachers on her old radio, rocking and clapping to the music. When we weren't home, she'd get up and dance through the rooms of the house, tears flowing freely as she sang out loud. We'd catch her and tease her. Once Granny hung a plastic Jesus in the bathroom; he had his hands folded in prayer and flowing locks thrown back over his shoulders. Essie groaned, *"A white man on the bathroom wall!"* She took it down and tried to explain to Granny that everybody did not worship the same way she did.

We were not only a multiracial household, we were one that held different spiritual beliefs. Essie followed a path she had first been introduced to by Granny's mother, her great-grandmother, Caroline Kelly Wright, affectionately known as Ma. Ma wore her hair in long braids and had been called "the little Indian" most of her life. She had married a freed African slave, but she herself was Blackfoot. Ma smoked a pipe and prayed to the sun. Essie remembered that as a child the whole family would gather in Ma's bedroom facing east. The dawn's pale light would begin to appear through the open window only a few city blocks from the enormous freshwater ocean called Lake Michigan. Everyone listened as Ma prayed aloud over the family, telling all secrets, opening up all stories, praying to the Creator to provide answers, to help guide them to find their purpose in life and hold to it, to be strong. Everything was said on those Sunday mornings, and tears fell as Ma blew her smoke toward the light of the rising sun.

But that was a long time ago, and Granny had "found religion" with her second husband, Daddy Son. After Ma moved in, Granny persuaded her mother not to pray outside anymore as it would draw too much attention from the neighbors. But Essie was raised by Ma, who stayed at home while Granny and Daddy Son worked. Ma had delivered Essie during a wild January blizzard. Ma was a midwife, herbalist, neighborhood dream interpreter, the community sage and soothsayer. If the term had been as popular then as it is now, Ma would have been honored as a shaman. Essie remembers the Baptist preacher visiting their house and saying to Ma, "I'll pray for you," and Ma responding, "You can't pray for me, but I can pray for you."

At the age of eight after a preacher had singled her out to stand up and receive the Lord, Essie had told her great-grand-mother that she did not want to attend church anymore. Ma agreed. So Essie had little patience with Granny's Christianity. She was especially offended by refrains such as "the good master" and would try to point out to Granny how Black Christian faith was a result of slavery, the product of an en-forced cultural genocide. Essie would try to educate Granny about the ways slaves were punished for trying to hold on to older beliefs, such as the care and worship of the ancestors or relating to land and nature as an expression of the sacred. Of course this didn't work, and I would try to negotiate peace settlements between the two generations, between the two Essies, between the centuries, between the ancestors and the youth. Neither one of them really listened to me. I would take the younger Essie aside and tell her, "Leave Granny alone. You're not going to change her." And the younger Essie would retort, "But she's trying to change me!"

The primary influence I had growing up was from the Society of Friends. I officially joined the local Quaker Meeting when I was sixteen, but later I found another path which spoke to a deep need in me to feel connected to the Earth beneath my feet. At twenty I was initiated in midewiwin, an Anishinabe belief system and spiritual practice still followed in the north-ern Great Lakes region, my favorite part of the country. Essie and I share a profoundly similar belief in relation to the power of nature to teach, heal and guide.

So at the funeral the man in the black suit did his best. He tried to save us. He opened the doors of the church and urged us to enter. He forgot about the corpse in the casket behind him, and he called the stray flock home. White men and Black men held each other in the back row. White women held Black women in the front row. And in between were all shades of brown and pink, young and old, from four-week-old Jade, the last baby Granny had blessed, to Mrs. Cooper, Granny's phone buddy. They had spoken on the phone every day for a year. Granny adored "Cooper" as she called her, though they had never met in person. Here we sat in rows before an open casket: all colors, ages, sexualities, brought together by a mutual love for an exceptional person. As some of Essie's family members called out urgently, encouraging the preacher with amens and oh yes, others ignored the eulogy, attending to their own prayers.

At the funeral we sat side-by-side in the front row in dark blue dresses. Essie's sister and son sat on the other side of her. We wept and held each other's hands. If Granny loved us for who we were then we weren't going to hide our feelings here. Certainly there were disapproving glances from some family members, but not all. During the decade we lived in Milwaukee, we had shared child care and holidays, made it through illnesses and the deaths of other beloved family members— what else qualifies someone as family? Yet despite this, I knew there were those who despised my presence, for what I represented was the alien. I was the lesbian, and I was white. For some, my presence was an inexcusable reminder of Essie's betrayal. She had chosen to be different, and I was the visible reminder of her difference. For some, this was a mockery of all they valued, but she did not belong to them so that they could control her identity. Granny knew this, and Granny loved her because she had the strength to be herself.

My family is liberal Democrat, yet my mother once said to me that my choice to love other women would make my life more difficult. She wanted to discourage me from considering it. She said, *"I would tell you the same thing if you told me you loved a Black man."* I was then nineteen. It struck me as curious that to love someone of the same sex was to violate the same taboo as to love someone across the color line. In the end I chose to do both. Does this make me a rebel? Certainly if my attraction was based initially on the outlaw quality of it, that thrill would not have been enough to sustain the trauma of crossing the color line in order to share love. The rebellious young woman that I may have been could not make sense of the other story, the story of her darker-skinned sister, without a willingness to question everything I had been raised to accept as normal, without an active analysis of the politics of racial subjugation—i.e., institutionalized white male supremacy. And without personal determination, courage, a refusal to be shamed, a sheer stubbornness based on our assumption that our lives held unquestionable worth as women, as women together, as women of different colors together, despite the position of the dominant culture—and even at times the position of the women's community—to diminish and deny us, we would not have been able to make a life together.

I have participated in and been witness to a side of American life that I would never have glimpsed if Essie had not been my partner. The peculiar and systematic practice of racial division in this country has been brought into sharp focus through many painful but revealing experiences. By sharing our lives, our daily survival, our dreams and aspirations, I have been widened and deepened. It has made me much more conscious of the privileges most white people are completely unaware of having.

One of the first awakenings came near the beginning of our relationship when her son, then in the third grade, came home with a note from the school librarian that said something like, "Your overdue books will cost forty-five cents in fines. Irresponsible handling of school property can lead to problems later including prison." I was shocked—threatening a nine-year-old boy with prison because of overdue books? I couldn't imagine what the librarian was thinking. Did she send these letters home with little white boys and girls? I wanted to call the school and confront her. Essie stopped me by telling me a number of equally horrifying stories about this school, so we agreed to take Michael out.

We decided that Michael, who had been staying with Granny and Daddy Son and attending the school near their home during the week, should move in full-time with us. Essie worked first shift at the hospital, and I was a graduate student at the university. She left for work at 6 A.M., and I caught the North Avenue bus at 9:30. I would be able to help Michael get to school before I left for the day. We decided to enroll Michael in our neighborhood school.

The neighborhood we lived in was one of the few mixed neighborhoods in the city. It formed a border between the run-down urban center and the suburbs on the west side. The neighborhood school was across an invisible boundary, a line I did not see but would grow to understand. Somewhere between our house and this building, a distance of approximately six blocks, was a color line. A whites-only-no-Blacks-need-apply distinctly drawn and doggedly patrolled. We scheduled a visit with the principal, and when both of us appeared the next morning we observed a curious reaction. Though polite, she was absolutely flustered. She could not determine which of us to direct her comments to. She looked from Essie's closely cropped black hair to my long, loose, wavy hair, from chocolate skin to cream skin, and stammered, "Who—who is the mother?"

"I am," said Essie.

"I'm sorry," was the reply. "We have already reached our quota of Black students in this school."

"Quota? We live in this neighborhood," I replied. "This is not a question of bussing a child in. He lives here."

She peered at the form we had filled out with our address on it. Then responded coldly, "We are full."

"That's ridiculous," I objected.

"Are you telling me that my child is not welcome to attend the third grade in your school?" Essie asked icily.

"We simply don't have room."

Essie stood up and walked out of the room without another word. I wanted to scream. I wanted to force the principal to change her mind, her politics, her preoccupation with the boundaries defined by color. I sat there staring at her. She refused to meet my eyes. I said slowly, "This will be reported to the Superintendent and to the school board," and walked out, following Essie to the car.

We scheduled a meeting at the school administration to register a formal complaint and find Michael another school. I was furious. We were taxpayers. These are public schools. How can he be refused entrance? How can a child be denied because of some quota determined by an administrator somewhere? Maybe I was naïve in matters of race.

I would have to say that all white people are naïve about the persistence of the color line. We prefer naïveté—in fact we insist on it. If we as white people actually faced the entrenched injustice of our socioeconomic system and our cultural arrogance, we might suffer tears, we might suffer the enormous weight of history, we might face the iceberg of guilt which is the underside of privilege. We might begin to glimpse our losses, our estrangement from others, our intense fear as the result of a social system that places us in the precarious position of the top. We might be moved to call out and protest the cruelty that passes for normal behavior in our daily lives, in our cities, and on our streets.

I had thought of white supremacists as some fringe lunatic group of extremists, mostly Southern bigots, who had been brought into line by the civil rights movement. Racism had been addressed despite tremendous resistance, and now things were better for darker-skinned people, weren't they? This was my stereotype built on myths perpetuated by the mainstream media. The idea that justice had been done and now all the problems faced by people of color were simply things they brought on themselves removed responsibility from the power holders and decision makers. Those with status and wealth did not have to feel any kind of remorse or be moved by the need that surrounded them. This was the dominant mood characterized by the Reagan era.

Nothing in my life, my education, my reading, my upbringing, prepared me to straddle the color line under the Reagan years in a post-industrial city suffering economic decline and social collapse. The rigidly entrenched division of social power by race and the enormously draining limitations we faced on a daily basis began to tear at the fabric of daily survival. I began to experience a kind of rage that left me feeling as sharp as broken glass. I was in this inner state when we finally arrived in the long, quiet corridors of the central administration of Milwaukee public schools.

We were ushered into an office with a man in a suit sitting behind a desk. He could have been an insurance salesman, a loan officer, or any other type of briefcase-carrying decision-making tall white man in a position of power and control. We were two women of small build and modest dress, but we were carrying the larger presence—righteous anger. We sat down. I leaned across his desk and challenged him to explain to us why Michael had been refused admittance into the school of our choice. He backpedaled. He avoided. He dodged. Essie suddenly said, "I am finished. I am taking my child out of school," and stood up.

I snapped my notebook closed, signaling the end of the conversation. The man had never asked me who I was. Did he assume I was a social worker? A family member? A friend? A lawyer? A journalist? Had it even crossed his mind that he was looking at a pair of lovers, at a family, at the two acting parents of this child? For the first time he looked worried. "I am sure we can find an appropriate school for your son. Tell me his interests. We'll place him in one of our specialty schools." We hesitated. "I'll personally handle his registration." He seemed to be pleading with us. He looked from Essie to me, wondering which of us his appeal would reach first.

We settled on a school with a square of wild prairie, the environmental science specialty school. It was a half-hour bus ride from our home. Michael liked the school, but we did not feel completely victorious. How could we? Though we had challenged the system, policies and practices that place undue emphasis on the color of a child's skin had not been changed. The school system simply accommodated us, perhaps fearing our potential to cause widespread dissent by giving voice to the intense dissatisfaction of the African-American community with the public school system. We compromised—perhaps exhausted by the constant fight against feeling invisible and powerless. It was not just that Michael was Black. It was also that his family consisted of a white woman and a Black woman, and regardless of our commitment to him, we were not perceived as a valid family unit if we were seen as that at all.

Michael is twenty now, and I am not sure how he would explain the advantages and challenges of growing up with two moms—one light and one dark. Sometimes in the neighborhood kids would stop and ask me if I was Michael's mom. Essie later explained to me that Michael sometimes told them I was his mother to protect me, especially as racial friction continued to escalate in the neighborhood. Michael's father was Creole so he had honey skin with light brown eyes. Essie is darker, though in most ways their features are alike. Sometimes he was mistaken for Puerto Rican. There were numerous mixed families in the neighborhood at that time before the escalation of violence, the presence of crack houses, and the continuing economic decline. A friend of mine who still lives in Milwaukee recently said that the white/Black division continues to widen. The white community continues to deny that the city suffers under the weight of enormous injustice perpetuated by decades of entrenched white supremacist practices. Meanwhile the Black community is in total crisis.

It is heartbreaking to raise an African-American boy in the city. From an early age he is taught that others fear him. He is taught that he is less than. He is taught that his future is defined by certain streets in certain neighborhoods, or that the only way out is through musical or athletic achievement. Michael played basketball and football. He wrote raps and performed them to the punctuated beat of electronic keyboards and drum machines. When it was fashionable he would break-dance on the living-room floor. He had a few good years in school, but by and large school did not satisfy his quest for knowledge nor did it provide him with creative avenues for self-expression.

The public high school he attended had one of the highest dropout rates for students of color in the city. It was in an affluent neighborhood near the northern suburbs. There was a reported race riot in the school which was fueled by administrative practices that recognized white students as the norm and students of color as troublemakers. There was not one day in detention that the room was not crowded with young Black men sitting in rows, policed by security guards, without books or papers, bored. As far as Essie and I were concerned, this was prison. We took Michael out of public school for good.

There were so many things I could not do for Michael. I could not clothe him in transparent skin to prevent him from being pre-judged by color-conscious teachers who would label him inferior. I could not surround him with safety on the street corner where he waited for his school bus. One grisly morning in November he came home shaking. He and a small boy had been shot at while waiting on a familiar corner two blocks from the house. It was 7:30 A.M. While he was preparing to attend school, boys his age were shooting guns out of car windows, hoping to kill somebody in order to get into a gang so they could make money.

On that gray morning, the capitalist notion of success as solely the acquisition of material wealth appears for what it is: an absolute perversion of human dignity. Yet white American culture persists in holding material affluence as the highest symbol of achievement. The way this plays out in the lives of people of color and those who love them can be summed up in one word: cruelty. We suffer for a lack of basic resources because of the hoarding, the feverish consumerism, and the complete lack of concern by people who have more than they will ever possibly need. Fashion crimes, ganking, children beating and killing other children to acquire the stingy symbols of status in a society devoid of real meaning—this is what happens on the city streets of the richest nation in the world.

I could not keep Michael from the bullets. I could not move him out into the suburbs where another kind of violence would confront him daily, from those who would question his presence and limit his right to move freely from one house to the next. I could not close his eyes to the terror he would see in his friends when death visited among them. I could not hold him against the rage he held inside—a rage that thundered through the house, pulverizing everything in its path, terrifying me, tearing at his mother.

What could we say to him about how to live on the mean streets of a bully nation? We did not live on those same streets even though we lived in the same neighborhood. His experience, my experience, his mother's experience—we walked out of the front door into three separate worlds, worlds we did not define or control except in how we would respond to them. Michael watched the hours I spent typing, writing, scratching out, rewriting. He watched the transformations his mother carried out with color on canvas, making lumps of cold clay into warm red altar bowls with her naked hands. He saw that we took our pain and rage, our grinding frustration and radiant hope, and made something out of it that gave us strength. Michael is still writing, making music, performing in his own music videos. He sees himself as an artist as we see ourselves; this is the thing that has carried us through.

The West side, where we bought a home, had always been a working-class neighborhood where people invested in their sturdy brick and wood frame houses, planting roses in their green squares of grass. The neighborhood had been built in the teens and twenties by German immigrants who took a certain pride in quality. These homes had fireplaces and stained-glass windows, beautifully crafted built-in bookshelves and beveled mirrors. Only a few generations earlier, there was safety and prosperity here. Waves of immigrants—Greek, Polish, Hasidic Jews, African-Americans coming North to work in the factories—shared these streets. I can remember walking into the corner bakery and the Greek woman behind the counter asked Essie and me if we were sisters. It was possible there at that time. Blood was shared. Love between the races happened. We laughed and nodded, "Yes—yes, we're sisters." In these moments we utterly and joyfully belonged together.

My friends who lived on the East side of the city rarely came to visit after I moved in with Essie. It was as if I had moved to the other side of the world. I think the absolutely most difficult aspect of moving in with an African-American woman was the racism I had to see in my white friends, particularly in what was then called the women's community. One shocking incident underlined for me the racism that I didn't want to see but could no longer avoid staring at. It occurred during a training session for volunteers at the Rape Crisis Line. As an African-American speaker entered the room, another panelist said loud enough for the woman to hear it, "Who let the n——— in."

This ignorant remark was outrageous enough, but what followed was devastating. I often wrote freelance articles for the various papers in town and was asked to report on this event by someone present. I needed to schedule interviews with the various women, so I approached the editor of the East side feminist paper to confirm my deadline for the story.

"We have decided not to run it."

"Why not?"

"It's too divisive."

"I'd say—but to silence it doesn't solve anything. People know already. We need to make room for debate, discussion, apology—it's not going to go away. We need to report it."

"We've already discussed it, and we've agreed not to run the story."

I stared at the editor across her desk. We were both standing by now, eyes locked in confrontation. She folded her arms. I stood my ground with the door-slammed-in-my-face feeling. I had to catch myself: Why am I trying to save their integrity? If they are racist, they are going to look it. But these women had once been my allies. I had thought we were on the same side battling women's oppression. My sense of belonging among them was crumbling, and I was angry. I thought I needed them to be my community. Because of the refusal to address racism within the so-called women's community, suddenly they were no longer on my side.

The landmark book *This Bridge Called My Back* appeared about the same time. Many white women found the anger in it, the raw emotion of it, too much. Perhaps the intense reaction in this smug white-women's community was a result of the ripple of discomfort caused by the accusation by women of color that the current brand of feminism smacked of racism. Unfortunately, personal and political examples abound. Essie told me of attending a Women's Center Meeting when someone turned to ask her, "Oh, and who do you represent?" As if she could not be just herself like most of the other women there, as if she had to be an ambassador from some distant woman-of-color-land on the other side of the moon.

The woman who suffered the insult at the Rape Crisis Line was furious about the feminist paper refusing to cover the issue. In response she gathered other women of color in the community together and they co-founded *Woman of Color News*. I began to write for them. It felt like choosing sides, as if battle lines had been drawn and I had to cross to the "other" side to express what I understood to be the truth. I trusted white women less and less as friends because they could not be counted on when things got tough. They tended to retreat. Race issues are ugly and hard, but if white women who want to fight male supremacy can't stand up to their own fears around the issue of color and simultaneously fight white supremacy, how can they really undertake the work of women's liberation? Certainly without an analysis and willingness to deal with race, there is no depth to the commitment. It is simply a get-ahead strategy for a particular middle-class white female minority. Today I feel there is a greater commitment to address issues of racism within the feminist movement, but most of the voices I hear still belong to women of color.

In a popular restaurant on the East side during a Sunday brunch, three young white men walked past us and threw a lit match at Essie's back, catching her blue silk jacket on fire. We were offered a free meal by the management. No effort was made to apprehend the men. Another time, on a hot summer day in early August, we were walking along Lake Drive to catch a cool breeze from the blue-green waves that stretched all the way to an untroubled horizon when a car full of young black men passed us, throwing obscenities and empty beer bottles at us. What provoked these attacks? Was it the sight of two women together enjoying themselves? Or was it because one of us was white and one was Black?

We sometimes limited our time "in the world" as we came to call it—as in "Do you want to go out in the world today?"—because the energy and effort of being out there was so much more draining than staying inside our home. The social ambivalence in regard to mixed race couples/same sex couples is so prevalent that we learned to keep our lives quiet. We tried to appear inconspicuous. One of the things we observed was that when we attracted unwanted attention, Essie was more often made the victim of the attack than I was. Violence would be directed against her as if she had trespassed by being with a white woman as an equal. Though we both felt the effects of these attacks, our vulnerability, our oppression, were not the same. The result was that more and more often I attended events alone. We just wanted to enjoy ourselves like other couples. We never expected to be treated like a moving target. I mean, was it that obvious and that offensive that we loved each other?

Part of the problem was the time and the place that we shared. Milwaukee, Wisconsin, is among the most racially seg-regated cities in the nation. The division is historical and spe-cific and can be traced to political leadership that maintains white control over all resources. In a desperate plea for atten-tion to the issue of racial injustice, Alderman Michael McGee began a Black militia. Soon after, our neighborhood was papered with flyers promising protection from the "armed and dangerous Black militants." I called the number on the flyer to try and find out who wrote it—maybe I could infiltrate the local vigilante white supremacy group. Essie talked me out of it.

Then the sale signs went up. Some of us fought back with "THIS PROPERTY IS NOT FOR SALE!" signs, but it was too late. We no longer felt safe. Most of our women friends on the West side began to carry guns. Essie's brother took her out to buy one "that can kill if you have to."

I became very depressed about the condition of our lives, Americans who pride ourselves on abstract concepts of freedom and justice but refuse to confront our own racist thinking and the depth of our fears. White women are conditioned to stay put; even rebellious daughters who love other women rarely cross the road that divides the races. Any woman who engages in a serious relationship—as friend or family, as lover or mother to daughter—with a woman of a different shade of skin will find this relationship demanding a deeper vulnerability than any other as long as race relationships continue to be fraught with tension. But if we settle for a divided nation, we settle for social rigidity and police brutality; we settle for ignorance and stereotypes; we settle for emptiness and fear.

I am still learning how to confront racism when I see it, how to educate my friends without alienating them, how to ask for what I need in terms of support. It has been a rare occurrence, but a joyful one, for us to find other mixed-race lesbian couples. When we begin to talk about how difficult it is, we discover certain patterns and find solace that we are not alone. But why should we suffer for being ourselves and finding ourselves in the borderless culture between races, in the undefined space where wakefulness is necessary for survival, where honest communication and self-reflection must replace the simple recipes of romance?

Part of me rejects the language of borders and boundaries. What is between us and within us is not so easily divided, nor are we so easily defined. I want to reject the social mythology that over here is Black America and over there is white America, yet the different realities experienced by people of the two groups persist. How can we leap into another way of understanding our connection to each other?

Few of us born in the Americas can trace our bloodline with impunity. So many of our ancestors have been erased or invented as need be. I know very few family names that have

not gone without at least one attempt at revision—to anglicize
it, simplify it, discard the ethnic or cultural baggage of a *ski* or
stein or other marker of race/ethnic identity. One who is raised
as part of an unwanted people will shift the identity to become
acceptable. Note the number of Chippewa and Menominee
people in Wisconsin with French last names. One Chippewa
man said that in every neighborhood they changed identity—
to Mexican when living on the South side, French on the East
side. Only back up on the reservation could they say aloud
their true names.

Despite the complex genealogy common to many in the
New World, we have been simplified and flattened into racial
categories of white and black. In this confusing construct,
strange things happen. Jews in the U.S. are white. In Europe
they are not. My sister-in-law is Jewish, but as her parents
state, "It's cultural—not religious. We are like many New
York Jews—once active Communists." Both sets of parents
accepted this marriage without question or protest. My family
also did not have any difficulty accepting him as a family
member. My sister's children will be Asian-American, something neither of their parents is. The new generation will carry
a new identity. But despite these cultural/ethnic combinations
not uncommon in the States, the ferocious line between white
and Black persists.

How many of us are African? Slavery was challenged in
part because of the enormous outcry against the "white slave
children." Children of enslaved African women who were the
result of forced sex with slavemasters ended up on the auction
block. Some of these children looked just like the "free" children of "free" European-American mothers. Obviously there
was a tremendous outcry resulting from the confusion that the
rationale for chattel slavery was based on a strict hierarchy of
skin color as the basis of privilege. How could they justify
selling these children that by all appearances looked white even

if the mother was a light-skinned African-American slave? White men in the South parented children on both sides of the yard: with the women they took as wives, and with the women who worked the fields. The brown and pale children were half-brothers and half-sisters related by blood through the father. This simple truth was denied. Part of my work has been beginning to claim these unnamed ancestors as family.

The day after I wrote that paragraph, I visited my parents. It was a week before Christmas, and I was planning to spend the day with my two grandmothers and my parents for Mimi's birthday. While in my parents' home, I asked about an old photo album that I remembered from childhood. My mother commented that it had recently surfaced from the jumble of daily life and brought it into the kitchen. Tintypes and daguerreotypes, family photographs spanning half a century, 1850 to 1900. Fifty years of Walkers, my mother's father's family.

That night, back in the city, stretched across the guest bed at a friend's house, I slowly turned the pages. These are my ancestors, among the first generation here from the British Isles. Aunt Mary and Uncle Tom Walker. By pulling the photographs out and inspecting the little leather and brass book, I discovered they settled in Clinton and Seaforth, Ontario. I knew these relatives had lived in Canada, but hadn't known they lived between Lakes Huron, Erie and Ontario. All of the faces were unfamiliar, stiff, caught in frozen poses over a century ago. A few of the photographs I remembered from my childhood, especially the sad-faced child in the unusual robe with straight cropped black hair and Asian eyes. For the first time it occurred to me that this could be the face of a native child, not European at all! Who was this child? Then a particularly striking face caught my attention. A young woman gazed confidently, intently—at what? Her hair, hanging around her wide face and high cheekbones in thick black ringlets, her full lips barely open, her strong chin—this was a woman of African descent. Who is she to me? She wore a gold hoop earring and a checkered bow over a satin dress. With one arm resting against an upholstered pillow, she posed proudly. Why had I never heard of her before?

I live near Wilberforce College, one of the oldest historically Black colleges in the U.S., which was founded by slaveowners who wanted to train their half-white children in the trades. A friend who used to work there told me a story about a white male teacher at the college who became an important ally to his students. Rather than returning the African-American sons and daughters of slaveowners to the South to work for their fathers after graduation, he helped them escape slavery by relocating to Ontario, Canada. Was this woman the daughter of those students of Wilberforce? Is she my great-aunt or distant cousin or great-great-grandmother?

No one in my family seems to know much about these faces, these people, these lives, and how they relate to us. My grandmother has already slipped into the memoryless borderland between waking and sleeping—she doesn't even know me anymore. My grandfather, whose biological family these photos represent, died a few years ago. If I am supposed to be a proud daughter of the colonizing English and the migrating Irish, why can't I also be a proud daughter of the Anishinabe or Haudenausaunee, two of the indigenous peoples of this Great Lakes region, as well as a proud daughter of the African diaspora? In America the idea of Europe was created, as if my English ancestors weren't trying to dominate my Irish ancestors. Why can't we talk about our truly diverse heritages? Nothing has been passed down in my family of these darker-skinned faces in my family's picture album. Is the refusal to see ourselves as something other than Northern European based in a fearful grasping after shreds of white-skinned privilege?

What do we lose if we acknowledge our connection? What do we gain?

Granny kept a photo album. The pictures were important. Some were tattered and worn out, but they mattered. They held the faces of relatives—cousins, aunts, sisters, men in fine hats and women in silk dresses looking into the camera, into the future. In the album is a small square black-and-white snapshot of two plump white babies seated outdoors on a stuffed armchair. The Kelly boys. Irish. Part of the family. Essie remembers her great-grandmother telling her children, grandchildren, and great-grandchildren, "These are your cousins." I bet those white boys don't show the dark faces of their cousins to their kin.

We must face the ways we are separated and challenge the system of privilege which viciously reinforces social hierarchies. It goes beyond confronting in yourself or others the tired tirade of media-generated stereotypes. A more meaningful place to begin is by questioning and pushing the boundaries where you find them—in your neighborhood, your school, your workplace, in your home. A boundary policed by brutality limits our self-knowledge and erases our complex cross-racial history. The problem is not only that we must question social systems that insist on maintaining divisions for easy categorization and more efficient social control; it is the problem of what is left out when prepackaged identities are handed out at birth. How little is communicated about who we are when we are labeled: *Black/white, queer/straight, male/female.*

The tight little boxes of identity defined by our society keep the building blocks of political and economic power in place. How can we gender-bend, race-cross, nature-bond, and love ourselves in our plurality enough to rebel against the deadening crush of identity control? Sometimes I feel it is an overwhelming failure of the imagination that prevents us from extending compassion beyond the boundaries of limited personal experience to listen *and be moved to action by* stories of injustice others suffer. How can we extend the boundaries of our own identities so that they include the "other"? If we have any hope for the future of life, how can we expand our sense of self to include other people as well as beings in nature? The structure of our society is articulated by separation and difference. How do we challenge this by living according to a sense of connection, not alienation?

For us, for Essie and me, the greatest challenge has been inventing ourselves as we went along, for we could not find a path to follow. Where are our foremothers? Light and dark women who held each other's hands through childbirth and child-raising? Who stood side by side and loved each other, refusing to budge despite everybody's objections? Who pooled their measly resources together to make sure there was food and heat and light enough for everyone's needs? I want to know them. I want to hear their stories. I'll tell them mine. This is the first time anyone has asked me to write anything about the twelve years we have shared.

Despite the absence of specific role models, we have support. Our circle of friends has widened. Our sense of community has been reinvigorated by a delightful variety of people. We have love. We share certain specific ancestors, disembodied presences gliding through our lives like a sudden breeze teasing the candle flame on the altar; secret-keepers who come under guard of moonlight, carrying apple baskets full of fresh fruit which they drop into our sleeping; we wake up before dawn with the sweet taste on our lips of good dreams and lucky numbers. We have our shared ancestors to thank, and we are fortunate to count Granny among them.

The Revenge of
Hannah Kemhuff

Alice Walker

In grateful memory of Zora Neale Hurston

I

Two weeks after I became Tante Rosie's apprentice we were visited by a very old woman who was wrapped and contained, almost smothered, in a half-dozen skirts and shawls. Tante Rosie (pronounced Ro'zee) told the woman she could see her name, Hannah Kemhuff, written in the air. She told the woman further that she belonged to the Order of the Eastern Star.

The woman was amazed. (And I was, too! Though I learned later that Tante Rosie held extensive files on almost everybody in the country, which she kept in long cardboard boxes under her bed.) Mrs. Kemhuff quickly asked what else Tante Rosie could tell her.

Tante Rosie had a huge tank of water on a table in front of her, like an aquarium for fish, except there were no fish in it.

There was nothing but water and I never was able to see anything in it. Tante Rosie, of course, could. While the woman waited, Tante Rosie peered deep into the tank of water. Soon she said the water spoke to her and told her that although the woman looked old, she was not. Mrs. Kemhuff said that this was true, and wondered if Tante Rosie knew the reason she looked so old. Tante Rosie said she did not and asked if she would mind telling us about it. (At first Mrs. Kemhuff didn't seem to want me there, but Tante Rosie told her I was trying to learn the rootworking trade and she nodded that she under-stood and didn't mind. I scrooched down as small as I could at the corner of Tante Rosie's table, smiling at her so she wouldn't feel embarrassed or afraid.)

"It was during the Depression," she began, shifting in her seat and adjusting the shawls. She wore so many her back appeared to be humped!

"Of course," said Tante Rosie, "and you were young and pretty."

"How do you know that?" exclaimed Mrs. Kemhuff. "That is true. I had been married already five years and had four small children and a husband with a wandering eye. But since I married young—"

"Why, you were little more than a child," said Tante Rosie.

"Yes," said Mrs. Kemhuff. "I were not quite twenty years old. And it was hard times everywhere, all over the country and, I suspect, all over the world. Of course, no one had television in those days, so we didn't know. I don't even now know if it was invented. We had a radio before the Depression which my husband won in a poker game, but we sold it some-where along the line to buy a meal. Anyway, we lived for as long as we could on the money I brought in as a cook in a sawmill. I cooked cabbage and cornpone for twenty men for two dollars a week. But then the mill closed down, and my husband had already been out of work for some time. We were on the point of starvation. We was so hungry, and the children were getting so weak, that after I had crapped off the last leaves from the collard stalks I couldn't wait for new leaves to grow back. I dug up the collards, roots and all. After we ate that there was nothing else.

"As I said, there was no way of knowing whether hard times was existing around the world because we did not then have a television set. And we had sold the radio. However, as it happened, hard times hit everybody we knew in Cherokee County. And for that reason the government sent food stamps which you could get if you could prove you were starving. With a few of them stamps you could go into town to a place they had and get so much and so much fatback, so much and so much of cornmeal, and so much and so much of (I think it was) red beans. As I say, we was, by then, desperate. And my husband prevailed on me for us to go. I never wanted to do it, on account of I have always been proud. My father, you know, used to be one of the biggest colored peanut growers in Cherokee County and we never had to ask nobody for nothing.

"Well, what had happened in the meantime was this: My sister, Carrie Mae—"

"A tough girl, if I remember right," said Tante Rosie.

"Yes," said Mrs. Kemhuff, "bright, full of spunk. Well, she were at that time living in the North. In Chicago. And she were working for some good white people that give her they old clothes to send back down here. And I tell you they were good things. And I was glad to get them. So, as it was gitting to be real cold, I dressed myself and my husband and the children up in them clothes. For see, they was made up North to be worn up there where there's snow at and they were warm as toast."

"Wasn't Carrie Mae later killed by a gangster?" asked Tante Rosie.

"Yes, she were," said the woman, anxious to go on with her story. "He were her husband."

"Oh," said Tante Rosie quietly.

"Now, so I dresses us all up in our new finery and with our stomachs growling all together we goes marching off to ask for what the government said was due us as proud as ever we knew how to be. For even my husband, when he had on the right clothes, could show some pride, and me, whenever I remembered how fine my daddy's peanut crops had provided us, why there was nobody with stiffer backbone."

"I see a pale and evil shadow looming ahead of you in this journey," said Tante Rosie, looking into the water as if she'd lost a penny while we weren't looking.

"That shadow was sure pale and evil all right," said Mrs. Kemhuff. "When we got to the place there was a long line, and we saw all of our friends in this line. On one side of the big pile of food was the white line—and some rich peoples was in that line too—and on the other side there was the black line. I later heard, by the by, that the white folks in the white line got bacon and grits, as well as meal, but that is neither here nor there. What happened was this. As soon as our friends saw us all dressed up in our nice warm clothes, though used and cast-off they were, they began saying how crazy we was to have worn them. And that's when I began to notice that all the people in the black line had dressed themselves in tatters. Even people what had good things at home, and I knew some of them did. What does this mean? I asked my husband. But he didn't know. He was too busy strutting about to even pay much attention. But I began to be terribly afraid. The baby had begun to cry and the other little ones, knowing I was nervous, commenced to whine and gag. I had a time with them.

"Now, at this time my husband had been looking around at other women and I was scared to death I was going to lose him. He already made fun of me and said I was arrogant and proud. I said that was the way to be and that he should try to be that way. The last thing I wanted to happen was for him to see me embarrassed and made small in front of a lot of people because I knew if that happened he would quit me.

"So I was standing there hoping that the white folks what give out the food wouldn't notice that I was dressed nice and that if they did they would see how hungry the babies was and how pitiful we all was. I could see my husband over talking to the woman he was going with on the sly. She was dressed like a flysweep! Not only was she raggedy, she was dirty! Filthy dirty, and with her filthy slip showing. She looked so awful she disgusted me. And yet there was my husband hanging over her while I stood in the line holding on to all four of our children. I guess he knew as well as I did what that woman had in the line of clothes at home. She was always much better dressed than me and much better dressed than many of the white peoples. That was because, they say, she was a whore and took money. Seems like people want that and will pay for it even in a depression!"

There was a pause while Mrs. Kemhuff drew a deep breath. Then she continued.

"So soon I was next to get something from the young lady at the counter. All around her I could smell them red beans and my mouth was watering for a taste of freshwater cornpone. I was proud, but I wasn't fancy. I just wanted something for me and the children. Well, there I was, with the children hanging to my dresstails, and I drew myself up as best I could and made the oldest boy stand up straight, for I had come to ask for what was mine, not to beg. So I wasn't going to be acting like a beggar. Well, I want you to know that that little slip of a woman, all big blue eyes and yellow hair, that little *girl*, took my stamps and then took one long look at me and my children and across at my husband—all of us dressed to kill I guess she thought—and she took my stamps in her hand and looked at

them like they was dirty, and then she give them to an old
gambler who was next in line behind me! 'You don't need
nothing to eat from the way you all dressed up, Hannah Lou,'
she said to me. 'But Miss Sadler,' I said, 'my children is hungry.' 'They don't look hungry,' she said to me. 'Move along
now, somebody here may really need our help!' The whole line
behind me began to laugh and snigger, and that little white
moppet sort of grinned behind her hands. She give the old
gambler double what he would have got otherwise. And there
me and my children about to keel over from want.

"When my husband and his woman saw and heard what
happened they commenced to laugh, too, and he reached down
and got her stuff, piles and piles of it, it seemed to me then, and
helped her put it in somebody's car and they drove off together. And that was about the last I seen of him. Or her."

"Weren't they swept off a bridge together in the flood that
wiped out Tunica City?" asked Tante Rosie.

"Yes," said Mrs. Kemhuff. "Somebody like you might have
helped me then, too, though looks like I didn't need it."

"So—"

"So after that looks like my spirit just wilted. Me and my
children got a ride home with somebody and I tottered around
like a drunken woman and put them to bed. They was sweet
children and not much trouble, although they was about to go
out of their minds with hunger."

Now a deep sadness crept into her face, which until she
reached this point had been still and impassive.

"First one then the other of them took sick and died.
Though the old gambler came by the house three or four days
later and divided what he had left with us. He had been on his
way to gambling it all away. The Lord called him to have pity
on us and since he knew us and knew my husband had deserted
me he said he were right glad to help out. But it was mighty
late in the day when he thought about helping out and the

children were far gone. Nothing could save them except the Lord and he seemed to have other things on his mind, like the wedding that spring of the mean little moppet."

Mrs. Kemhuff now spoke through clenched teeth.

"My spirit never recovered from that insult, just like my heart never recovered from my husband's desertion, just like my body never recovered from being almost starved to death. I started to wither in that winter and each year found me more hacked and worn down than the year before. Somewhere along them years my pride just up and left altogether and I worked for a time in a whorehouse just to make some money, just like my husband's woman. Then I took to drinking to forget what I was doing, and soon I just broke down and got old all at once, just like you see me now. And I started about five years ago to go to church. I was converted again, 'cause I felt the first time had done got worn off. But I am not restful. I dream and have nightmares still about the little moppet, and always I feel the moment when my spirit was trampled down within me while they all stood and laughed and she stood there grinning behind her hands."

"Well," said Tante Rosie. "There are ways that the spirit can be mended just as there are ways that the spirit can be broken. But one such as I am cannot do both. If I am to take away the burden of shame which is upon you I must in some way inflict it on someone else."

"I do not care to be cured," said Mrs. Kemhuff. "It is enough that I have endured my shame all these years and that my children and my husband were taken from me by one who knew nothing about us. I can survive as long as I need with the bitterness that has laid every day in my soul. But I could die easier if I knew something, after all these years, had been done to the little moppet. God cannot be let to make her happy all these years and me miserable. What kind of justice would that be? It would be monstrous!"

"Don't worry about it, my sister," said Tante Rosie with
gentleness. "By the grace of the Man-God I have use of many
powers. Powers given me by the Great One Herself. If you can
no longer bear the eyes of the enemy that you see in your
dreams, the Man-God, who speaks to me from the Great
Mother of Us All, will see that those eyes are eaten away. If the
hands of your enemy have struck you they can be made useless." Tante Rosie held up a small piece of what was once
lustrous pewter. Now it was pockmarked and blackened and
deteriorating.

"Do you see this metal?" she asked.

"Yes, I see it," said Mrs. Kemhuff with interest. She took it
in her hands and rubbed it.

"The part of the moppet you want destroyed will rot away
in the same fashion."

Mrs. Kemhuff relinquished the piece of metal to Tante
Rosie.

"You are a true sister," she said.

"Is it enough?" Tante Rosie asked.

"I would give anything to stop her grinning behind her
hands," said the woman, drawing out a tattered billfold.

"Her hands or the grinning mouth?" asked Tante Rosie.

"The mouth grinned and the hands hit it," said Mrs.
Kemhuff.

"Ten dollars for one area, twenty for two," said Tante
Rosie.

"Make it the mouth," said Mrs. Kemhuff. "That is what I
see most vividly in my dreams." She laid a ten-dollar bill in the
lap of Tante Rosie.

"Let me explain what we will do," said Tante Rosie, coming near the woman and speaking softly to her, as a doctor
would speak to a patient. "First we will make a potion that has
a long history of use in our profession. It is a mixture of hair
and nail parings of the person in question, a bit of their water

and feces, a piece of their clothing heavy with their own scents, and I think in this case we might as well add a pinch of goober dust—that is, dust from the graveyard. This woman will not outlive you by more than six months."

I had thought the two women had forgotten about me, but now Tante Rosie turned to me and said, "You will have to go out to Mrs. Kemhuff's house. She will have to be instructed in the recitation of the curse-prayer. You will show her how to dress the black candles and how to pay Death for his interception in her behalf."

Then she moved over to the shelf that held her numerous supplies: oils of Bad and Good Luck Essence, dried herbs, creams, powders, and candles. She took two large black candles and placed them in Mrs. Kemhuff's hands. She also gave her a small bag of powder and told her to burn it on her table (as an altar) while she was praying the curse-prayer. I was to show Mrs. Kemhuff how to "dress" the candles in vinegar so they would be purified for her purpose.

She told Mrs. Kemhuff that each morning and evening for nine days she was to light the candles, burn the powder, recite the curse-prayer from her knees and concentrate all her powers on getting her message through to Death and the Man-God. As far as the Supreme Mother of Us All was concerned, she could only be moved by the pleas of the Man-God. Tante Rosie herself would recite the curse-prayer at the same time that Mrs. Kemhuff did, and together she thought the two prayers, prayed with respect, could not help but move the Man-God, who, in turn, would unchain Death, who would already be eager to come down on the little moppet. But her death would be slow in coming because first the man-God had to hear all of the prayers.

"We will take those parts of herself that we collect, the feces, water, nail parings, et cetera, and plant them where they will bring for you the best results. Within a year's time the

earth will be rid of the woman herself, even as almost immediately you will be rid of her grin. Do you want something else
for only two dollars that will make you feel happy even today?" asked Tante Rosie.

But Mrs. Kemhuff shook her head. "I'm carefree enough
already, knowing that her end will be before another year. As
for happiness, it is something that deserts you once you know it
can be bought and sold. I will not live to see the end result of
your work, Tante Rosie, but my grave will fit nicer, having
someone proud again who has righted a wrong and by so
doing live straight and proud throughout eternity."

And Mrs. Kemhuff turned and left, bearing herself grandly
out of the room. It was as if she had regained her youth; her
shawls were like a stately toga, her white hair seemed to
sparkle.

II

To the Man-God: O great One, I have been sorely
tried by my enemies and have been blasphemed and lied
against. My good thoughts and my honest actions have
been turned to bad actions and dishonest ideas. My home
has been disrespected, my children have been cursed and
ill-treated. My dear ones have been backbitten and their
virtue questioned. O Man-God, I beg that this that I ask
for my enemies shall come to pass:

That the South wind shall scorch their bodies and
make them wither and shall not be tempered to them.
That the North wind shall freeze their blood and numb
their muscles and that it shall not be tempered to them.
That the West wind shall blow away their life's breath and
will not leave their hair grow, and that their fingernails

shall fall off and their bones shall crumble. That the East wind shall make their minds grow dark, their sight shall fail and their seed dry up so that they shall not multiply.

I ask that their fathers and mothers from their furtherest generation will not intercede for them before the great throne, and the wombs of their women shall not bear fruit except for strangers, and that they shall become extinct. I pray that the children who may come shall be weak of mind and paralyzed of limb and that they themselves shall curse them in their turn for ever turning the breath of life into their bodies. I pray that disease and death shall be forever with them and that their worldly goods shall not prosper, and that their crops shall not multiply and that their cows, their sheep, and their hogs and all their living beasts shall die of starvation and thirst. I pray that their house shall be unroofed and that the rain, the thunder and lightning shall find the innermost recesses of their home and that the foundation shall crumble and the floods tear it asunder. I pray that the sun shall not shed its rays on them in benevolence, but instead it shall beat down on them and burn them and destroy them. I pray that the moon shall not give them peace, but instead shall deride them and decry them and cause their minds to shrivel. I pray that their friends shall betray them and cause them loss of power, of gold and of silver, and that their enemies shall smite them until they beg for mercy which shall not be given them. I pray that their tongue shall forget how to speak in sweet words; and that it shall be paralyzed and that all about them will be desolation, pestilence and death. O Man-God, I ask you for all these things because they have dragged me in the dust and destroyed my good name; broken my heart and caused me to curse the day that I was born. So be it.

This curse-prayer was regularly used and taught by root-workers, but since I did not know it by heart, as Tante Rosie did, I recited it straight from Zora Neale Hurston's book, *Mules and Men,* and Mrs. Kemhuff and I learned it on our knees together. We were soon dressing the candles in vinegar, lighting them, kneeling and praying—intoning the words rhythmically—as if we had been doing it this way for years. I was moved by the fervor with which Mrs. Kemhuff prayed. Often she would clench her fists before her closed eyes and bite the insides of her wrists as the women do in Greece.

III

According to courthouse records Sarah Marie Sadler, "the little moppet," was born in 1910. She was in her early twenties during the Depression. In 1932 she married Ben Jonathan Holley, who later inherited a small chain of grocery stores and owned a plantation and an impressive stand of timber. In the spring of 1963, Mrs. Holley was fifty-three years old. She was the mother of three children, a boy and two girls; the boy a floundering clothes salesman, the girls married and oblivious, mothers themselves.

The elder Holleys lived six miles out in the country, their house was large, and Mrs. Holley's hobbies were shopping for antiques, gossiping with colored women, discussing her husband's health and her children's babies, and making spoon bread. I was able to glean this much from the drunken ramblings of the Holleys' cook, a malevolent nanny with gout, who had raised, in her prime, at least one tan Holley, a preacher whom the Holleys had sent to Morehouse.

"I bet I could get the nanny to give us all the information and nail parings we could ever use," I said to Tante Rosie. For the grumpy woman drank muscatel like a sow and clearly hated Mrs. Holley. However, it was hard to get her tipsy enough for truly revealing talk and we were quickly running out of funds.

"That's not the way," Tante Rosie said one evening as she sat in her car and watched me lead the nanny out of the dreary but secret-evoking recesses of the Six Forks Bar. We had already spent six dollars on muscatel.

"You can't trust gossips or drunks," said Tante Rosie. "You let the woman we are working on give you everything you need, and from her own lips."

"But that is the craziest thing I have ever heard," I said. "How can I talk to her about putting a fix on her without making her mad, or maybe even scaring her to death?"

Tante Rosie merely grunted.

"Rule number one: OBSERVATION OF SUBJECT. Write that down among your crumpled notes."

"In other words—?"

"Be direct, but not blunt."

On my way to the Holley plantation I came up with the idea of pretending to be searching for a fictitious person. Then I had an even better idea. I parked Tante Rosie's Bonneville at the edge of the spacious yard, which was dotted with mimosas and camellias. Tante Rosie had insisted I wear a brilliant orange robe and as I walked it swished and blew about my legs. Mrs. Holley was on the back patio steps, engaged in conversation with a young and beautiful black girl. They stared in amazement at the length and brilliance of my attire.

"Mrs. Holley, I think it's time for me to go," said the girl.

"Don't be silly," said the matronly Mrs. Holley. "She is probably just a light-skinned African who is on her way somewhere and got lost." She nudged the black girl in the ribs and they both broke into giggles.

"How do you do?" I asked.

"Just fine, how you?" said Mrs. Holley, while the black girl looked on askance. They had been talking with their heads close together and stood up together when I spoke.

"I am looking for a Josiah Henson"—a runaway slave and the original Uncle Tom in Harriet Beecher Stowe's novel, I might have added. "Could you tell me if he lives on your place?"

"That name sounds awful familiar," said the black girl.

"Are you *the* Mrs. Holley?" I asked gratuitously, while Mrs. Holley was distracted. She was sure she had never heard the name.

"Of course," she said, and smiled, pleating the side of her dress. She was a grayish blonde with an ashen untanned face, and her hands were five blunt and pampered fingers each. "And this is my . . . ah . . . my friend, Caroline Williams."

Caroline nodded curtly.

"Somebody told me ole Josiah might be out this way . . ."

"Well, we hadn't seen him," said Mrs. Holley. "We were just here shelling some peas, enjoying this nice sunshine."

"Are you a light African?" asked Caroline.

"No," I said. "I work with Tante Rosie, the rootworker. I'm learning the profession."

"Whatever *for?*" asked Mrs. Holley. "I would have thought a nice-looking girl like yourself could find a better way to spend her time. I been hearing about Tante Rosie since I was a little bitty child, but everybody always said that rootworking was just a whole lot of n———, I mean colored foolishness. Of course we don't believe in that kind of thing, do we, Caroline?"

"Naw."

The younger woman put a hand on the older woman's arm, possessively, as if to say, "You get away from here, bending my white folks' ear with your crazy mess!" From the kitchen window a dark remorseful face worked itself into various messages of "Go away!" It was the drunken nanny.

"I wonder if you would care to prove you do not believe in rootworking?"

"Prove?" said the white woman indignantly.

"Prove?" asked the black woman with scorn.

"That is the word," I said.

"Why, not that I'm afraid of any of this nigger magic!" said Mrs. Holley staunchly, placing a reassuring hand on Caroline's shoulder. I was the nigger, not she.

"In that case won't you show us how much you don't have fear of it." With the word *us* I placed Caroline in the same nigger category with me. Let her smolder! Now Mrs. Holley stood alone, the great white innovator and scientific scourge, forced to man the Christian fort against heathen nigger paganism.

"Of course, if you like," she said immediately, drawing herself up in the best English manner. Stiff upper lip, what? and all that. She had been grinning throughout. Now she covered her teeth with her scant two lips and her face became flat and resolute. Like so many white women in sections of the country where the race was still "pure," her mouth could have been formed by the minute slash of a thin sword.

"Do you know a Mrs. Hannah Lou Kemhuff?" I asked.

"No I do not."

"She is not white, Mrs. Holley, she is black."

"Hannah Lou, Hannah Lou . . . do we know a Hannah Lou?" she asked, turning to Caroline.

"No ma'am, we don't!" said Caroline.

"Well, she knows you. Says she met you on the bread lines during the Depression and that because she was dressed up you wouldn't give her any cornmeal. Or red beans. Or something like that."

"Bread lines, Depression, dressed up, cornmeal . . . ? I don't know what you're talking about!" No shaft of remembrance probed the depth of what she had done to colored people more than twenty years ago.

"It doesn't really matter, since you don't believe . . . but she says you did her wrong, and being a good Christian, she believes all wrongs are eventually righted in the Lord's good time. She came to us for help only when she began to feel the Lord's good time might be too far away. Because we do not deal in the work of unmerited destruction, Tante Rosie and I did not see how we could take the case." I said this humbly, with as much pious intonation as I could muster.

"Well, I'm glad," said Mrs. Holley, who had been running through the back years on her fingers.

"But," I said, "we told her what she could do to bring about restitution of peaceful spirit, which she claimed you robbed her of in a moment during which, as is now evident, you were not concerned. You were getting married the following spring."

"That was thirty-two," said Mrs. Holley. "Hannah *Lou?*"

"The same."

"How black *was* she? Sometimes I can recall colored faces that way."

"That is not relevant," I said, "since you do not believe . . ."

"Well of *course* I don't believe!" said Mrs. Holley.

"I am nothing in this feud between you," I said. "Neither is Tante Rosie. Neither of us had any idea until after Mrs. Kemhuff left that you were the woman she spoke of. We are familiar with the deep and sincere interest you take in the poor colored children at Christmastime each year. We know you have gone out of your way to hire needy people to work on your farm. We know you have been an example of Christian charity and a beacon force of brotherly love. And right before my eyes I can see it is true you have Negro friends."

"Just what is it you want?" asked Mrs. Holley.

"What *Mrs. Kemhuff* wants are some nail parings, not many, just a few, some hair (that from a comb will do), some water and some feces—and if you don't feel like doing either number one or number two, I will wait—and a bit of clothing, something that you have worn in the last year. Something with some of your odor on it."

"What!" Mrs. Holley screeched.

"They say this combination, with the right prayers, can eat away part of a person just like the disease that ruins so much fine antique pewter."

Mrs. Holley blanched. With a motherly fluttering of hands Caroline helped her into a patio chair.

"Go get my medicine," said Mrs. Holley, and Caroline started from the spot like a gazelle.

"Git away from here! Git away!"

I spun around just in time to save my head from a whack with a gigantic dust mop. It was the drunken nanny, drunk no more, flying to the defense of her mistress.

"She's just a tramp and a phony!" she reassured Mrs. Holley, who was caught up in an authentic faint.

IV

Not long after I saw Mrs. Holley, Hannah Kemhuff was buried. Tante Rosie and I followed the casket to the cemetery, Tante Rosie most elegant in black. Then we made our way through briers and grass to the highway. Mrs. Kemhuff rested in a tangly grove, off to herself, though reasonably near her husband and babies. Few people came to the funeral, which made the faces of Mrs. Holley's nanny and husband stand out all the more plainly. They had come to verify the fact that this dead person was indeed *the* Hannah Lou Kemhuff whom Mr. Holley had initiated a search for, having the entire county militia at his disposal.

Several months later we read in the paper that Sarah Marie Sadler Holley had also passed away. The paper spoke of her former beauty and vivacity, as a young woman, and of her concern for those less fortunate than herself as a married woman and pillar of the community and her church. It spoke briefly of her harsh and lengthy illness. It said all who knew her were sure her soul would find peace in heaven, just as her shrunken body had endured so much pain and heartache here on earth.

Caroline had kept us up to date on the decline of Mrs. Holley. After my visit, relations between them became strained and Mrs. Holley eventually became too frightened of Caroline's darkness to allow her close to her. A week after I'd talked to them Mrs. Holley began having her meals in her bedroom upstairs. Then she started doing everything else there as well. She collected stray hairs from her head and comb with the greatest attention and consistency, not to say desperation. She ate her fingernails. But the most bizarre of all was her response to Mrs. Kemhuff's petition for a specimen of feces and water. Not trusting any longer the earthen secrecy of the water mains, she no longer flushed. Together with the nanny, Mrs. Holley preferred to store those relics of what she ate (which became almost nothing and then nothing, the nanny had told Caroline), and they kept it all in barrels and plastic bags in the upstairs closets. In a few weeks it became impossible for anyone to endure the smell of the house, even Mrs. Holley's husband, who loved her but during the weeks before her death slept in a spare room of the nanny's house.

The mouth that had grinned behind the hands grinned no

more. The constant anxiety lest a stray strand of hair be lost
and the foul odor of the house soon brought to the hands a
constant seeking motion, to the eyes a glazed and vacant stare,
and to the mouth a tightly puckered frown, one which only
death might smooth.

Tulsa, 1921

Susan Straight

(An excerpt from a novel in progress.
The Gettin Place)

His mother's voice was silver-thin through the open front door, and without opening his eyes Hosea knew she was leaning against the front porch railing, talking to Miss Letitia next door. "He call hisself takin me out tonight," she said. "To the Dreamland, see a picture."

"You know you ain't walkin up there, Sophia," Miss Letitia said. "Big as you is. Close to your time."

"Two weeks off," Hosea's mother said, and he blinked, felt the morning on his knuckles. The women kept asking his mother, telling her: Your time. He listened closely, but all his mother said was, "And my back hurtin this mornin."

"You bet *not* talk like that," Miss Letitia said. "You don't want no back labor. No."

Hosea heard her door slam, and he rolled off the sharp iron rim of his new bed in the front room. He dangled his feet for a minute, the metal cold against his legs. He'd slept in the big bed while his father was gone to France, but now he was a little man, his father said. "You done turned six while I was gone? You ain't even waited for me?" he teased Hosea when he came back.

His mother would frown, but Hosea always jerked his head from under her dry fingertips when she said, "He still a baby, Robert."

Hosea heard his father's feet on the porch then, and his soft laugh, a gravel-rush of breath that came up his throat and through his nose. Edging toward the door to see his father's eyes, Hosea held his spit in his throat carefully. Sometimes the pain from his father's arm, where the France bullet had left worm-twisted scars all around his shoulder, would get up into his father's eyes; the blood would rise up there to the white part, like rusty screens covering the shine, and he stayed with his friends in the choc joint across the street. Even his teeth would look darker then, coated with a muddy film.

"You gon dulge me this one time, huh?" his father said now, taking the thick-edged plate with the huge slice of sweet-potato pie. All Hosea could see was the gold pie and his father's jaw, shining with the sweet oil he rubbed in after he shaved, and his father laughed again, long fingers already bent around the coffee cup. "Cause it's the last day a May, or cause it's Monday?"

"Cause my back hurt," his mother murmured. "Y'all can eat what you want this mornin." Hosea stared at the wedge of pie. His mother made them eat eggs, bacon and biscuits every morning, saying she couldn't catch them again till dark and they needed to fill up them bird legs. Hosea waited for his father to turn in the wooden chair and look up.

"Cause your friend comin today, and you look . . ." His mother stopped. "You in good shape today?"

"Better shape than you." Hosea saw that his mother's dress

had lost nearly every pleat from the push of her belly. "Hell, you sit here. I'ma go get more coffee."

When his father stood, Hosea saw the long slashes of white, nearly blue as milk-bottle edges, around the brown of his eyes, and he saw the corner of his father's grin.

He ran to the bedroom to look in his mother's hand mirror. The narrow, tilted stare that the other boys teased him about, calling him "Chinee eye, Injun nose, nigger face." His father had his eyes this morning.

"You gon come with us to pick up the wash from Retha's lady?" his mother asked, emptying the small pan of dishwater into the dirt yard between houses, and Hosea watched his father stop buttoning.

"Where Fred?" he asked sharply. "Send him—he love to visit with the white folks. I ain't in the mood to cross the tracks today."

Hosea sat on the back two steps, the kitchen behind him, smelling the hair irons heating up in Miss Letitia's, the sooty-sweet vapor that rose from her stove all day. Front room, bedroom, kitchen—all four shotgun houses on their street were the same, each pair of steps like a tiny tongue leading to the yard. Hosea tied his shoes, hoping his father would take him to the garage on Greenwood. Greenwood. The street was lined with brick buildings edged in white-stone icing: candy stores, groceries, barber shops, chili parlors, and the Dreamland Theater.

But his mother said, "I guess Hosea can carry it." She sat the pan on a tree stump and pushed the heels of her hands into her back. "But you know that lady still want to talk to you about the yard job. She offerin steady money, Robert. And half the time Milton ain't got enough for you to do at the garage." Hosea's father opened his mouth, but she went on. "Now your friend Maceo comin up here lookin for work, too. Maybe he want that yard job." Hosea heard the glitter in her voice.

His father spat into the dirt near the narrow street, grinning, his feet wide. "Me and Maceo should put on our uniforms and parade down there to her house—oh, her husband love that, now. Like red to a goddamn bull." He smiled wider at her. "Don't give me that evil eye. We livin better than the farm. Greenwood got plenty of work, got two more cabs need fixin, and that's where I'ma step to now." His shoes raised tiny breaths of dust when he crossed the yard to kiss her, his four long fingers in a tight row on the back of her neck under her rolled hair. And his father's hand came down looser, cupping Hosea's skull, tickling. "Carry your mama's things," he said. "When me and Maceo come back, we gon take you somewhere, boy." The warmth left Hosea's forehead, and his father said, "Here come trouble. Let me go."

Retha came out of Letitia's back door, saying, "He don't even realize, girl." She looked at them, her hair stiff and shined, and said, "Y'all ready? We been late, and you know Mrs. Hefferon ain't happy I done spent the night down here steada up over the damn garage." She blew out her breath. "Monday."

The big brick house had a long driveway, and Hosea saw the curtains tremble when the women clicked the back gate. "She done had a dinner Saturday night, so you know what you lookin at," Retha said softly.

"French lace," Hosea's mother murmured.

"She call herself givin me a dollar less that night when she paid me, talkin bout that big plate of food she want me to take. All that nasty sauce, I couldn't even eat it." Retha sucked at her teeth, and Hosea saw the back door open.

"Good *morning*," the white woman said, her face slanting down the wide steps, and Hosea saw her hair, white and nested as goosefeathers. He dropped his eyes, remembering what his mother said. Don't be starin in them people face. They don't like that.

The kitchen floor was shiny as tears. The woman said to Retha, "I trust you had a nice breakfast, as we've had to get ours. The longer you wait, the more there is, right, dear?" Her voice was curly as the tendrils of a pea vine, the green strings that licked tight around a wire.

Hosea kept his eyes on the heels of his mother's shoes. They were thick and rounded. There was no smell of men in the kitchen, no cigar or leather or sweet oil, but the man who hated red like a bull was somewhere in the house, he thought. "Your husband hasn't come about the yard," the woman said, and his mother shook her head. The woman puffed out air like a sneezing puppy. "Some people in Tulsa are too good for yard work. That's what Mr. Hefferon says." She waited. Hosea held still. "Well. You've done this once before, remember? You do remember the French lace? The table runner, the doilies, these cloths, the napkins. Mr. Hefferon's mother brought them from France."

Hosea stared at the froth in his mother's hands, froth folded into squares. French. Like the bullet, and the shell his father had sent them from France, the dull-nosed brass thing Hosea could hold. The metal was engraved with dotted letters, stuttered into the brass. "For my love Sophia—Saracen, France 1919."

"Retha has no patience for fine wash, and she'll ruin them." The woman went to the back window and stretched her neck to look out. Hosea saw the pink skin under her throat, cloudy and swirled with lines. Then she dropped her chin and looked at his mother again. "Mr. Hefferon's mother will be here tomorrow morning, and I'll need things arranged. She's terrifying. And Retha drives me to distraction." She paused, staring at Hosea's mother. "I'll need those by this afternoon. They're so thin they shouldn't be long drying."

His mother turned, her fingers in his shoulder like the tips of a fork when he forgot to move.

On the sidewalk, he heard her say, "She know that much about em, why she don't wash em herself?"

The French lace looked like foam in the washtub, and his mother's fingers swirled through the bubbles over and over, trailing and turning. When the creamy patterns were flat, she hung them on one of the lines stretching between two trees, and she began to wash all the white clothes from Miss Letitia's house and theirs. His father's white shirts gaped and turned on the line, and Miss Letitia's towels and cloths and blouses, and last, Hosea saw his socks like tiny worms. One of Miss Letitia's blouses and two of his father's white T-shirts lay on a clean board in the sun; the rust stains where sweat and car parts and hair irons had touched were sprinkled with lemon juice and salt.

His mother's fingers raked softly through the bowl of beans now, and she dropped a pebble on the dirt near his foot. "Your daddy loves beans and ham hock," she said. "He and Maceo probably be back in a few hours. Go on see if Miss Letitia need you. I'ma rest after I put these on the stove. Go on, Hosea."

He didn't run, because that might make her sad, that he didn't want to be there with her in the yard, sitting idly under the stiffening, waving white, but when he reached Miss Letitia's doorway, breathing perfume and laughter, his chest rang with hope that she might give him a quarter. And she shook her head, looking up from the dripping hair under her wrist.

"Didn't I say it was about time somebody come over here and got us some barbecue?" she laughed. "This boy live for Greenwood Avenue and lookin for his daddy. Here." She pressed damp money into his hand.

Greenwood was crowded with people doing afternoon errands, and Hosea wove through the sidewalks, heading to the

cab garage. The man in the folding chair shook his head when
Hosea reached the doorway. "Your daddy out fixin a car, boy.
Go on, now, before you get in the way."

Hosea walked back toward the barbecue place that Miss
Letitia liked best, smelling the way afternoon changed the air,
thickened it with sauces and hurrying and exhaust. But inside
the restaurant, people were arguing, yelling, gesturing at newspapers. He sat in the corner to wait for the plates, and the men
said, "You see this shit? They gon talk about lynchin that boy?
He ain't done a damn thing but bump into that girl in the
elevator. White girl want to make a fuss. White girls love
trouble."

A short, light-skinned man near the door had a long, deep
voice. "Tulsa ain't the place for that. They gon find out this
time." The bell on the door clanked hard when he went out.

Hosea stared at the faces chewing, talking, the tongues and
fingers and elbows close to him. Between the arguing were
quiet gashes, not like the usual thread of laugh and murmur
that rocked him half asleep while he waited for Miss Letitia's
order. He sat on the round stool, stiff, hearing the short spat
words. Kill. Hush. Stop. Now.

The dark corners in the house pooled over the floor, and his mother
still slept. She had taken in the French lace, dampened it for
ironing, and laid it in a basket, but she still lay in the bedroom,
her arm high on her stomach. Miss Letitia had come to say she
heard there was trouble with a white woman, but she didn't
know exactly what. She and her friend were going to do hair
for two girls on Detroit Avenue, because tonight was the
spring prom for Booker T. Washington High.

Hosea sat in the front room, waiting for his father and
Maceo. Maceo had been friends with his father in France, and

he'd come last year from Mississippi to visit. He'd brought Hosea a slingshot.

When he heard a car door slam, he ran to the window, wondering if they'd borrowed a cab. But he saw a black car, and the goosefeather hair of the white woman. Retha's lady. She wore a dark coat, and her hands were blinding white. Gloves. He saw her eyes fix on the house, and his throat clenched in fear. Trouble. White women made trouble. When he heard another car door, he ran to the bedroom and closed the door.

The house was sifting darkness now, and he sat on the floor near his mother's bed, hearing her husks of breath. He heard the knocking on the front door, and a softer voice than the wire call, "Sophia?" It was Retha's voice, but Hosea knew the gloves were there on the porch, too, and he covered his ears.

His mother's shoulders rustled on the bed, and she twisted her head to look up. "Who at the door, Hosea?" she said faintly.

"The white lady," he whispered, hearing the voices move toward the back.

"White lady?" She sat up. "Oh! The lace." She raised herself up on the pillows, her hand almost disappearing in the cleft between her belly and her chest. "Hosea, baby, go out there and tell her I'll have Robert bring it up there early in the morning. Tell her early."

He walked toward the kitchen door, hearing them talk through the cracks. "Look at these clothes! Where's the lace?" the tendril voice said. "What's wrong with everyone?"

Retha's murmur was only dust he couldn't hear. He pressed his cheek against the wooden door, and his mother said, "Hosea?"

The white woman's face filled the tiny window in the door, her cheeks gray and heavy as wrung cloth, her mouth stretching open when she reached to look inside. She saw him, and he froze while her face moved, her lips making sucking movements near the glass when she spoke.

She was angry, pulling the meat from the softened ham hocks, but his father made a fuss about the food, reaching for his favorite pieces, the long pink splinters that his mother pried from between the narrow bones. The foot, Hosea thought suddenly. We eating the toes. The meat between the leg bones. He lifted his pants leg and touched his shin. "You get hurt runnin around?" his father asked. "That why you got your mama mad?"

His father's eyes were still wide and clear as rain caught in a jar. He gave Maceo a plate, and Maceo stood to put his hand deep into his pocket, pulling out copper-bright BB's, a palmful. Hosea had to claw his fingers to scoop them from Maceo's broad hand. "Pretty soon you gon be old enough for your first gun," Maceo said, and Hosea closed the cool metal balls into his own hand.

"Don't be angry at the boy," his father said to his mother.

"I had to get up and tell her you'd bring it in the mornin," she said. "She was mad by then cause he wouldn't open the door. I don't know why he actin foolish."

"Daddy," Hosea said. "They was talkin about killin in the restaurant."

"Who?" his mother said, her voice sliding high. "Who talkin about that?"

Hosea watched his father's mustache, heavy and thick as a broom's edge, cloak his lips, and his father stared at him hard. "Talkin about killin a pig, probably," he said, standing up. "Come on outside, now. Show Maceo what you can do with that ax."

But they had enough wood already. His father crouched on

the ground in front of Hosea. "I know you been heard about some people gon kill a boy. But that ain't gon happen, and you ain't gon talk about it in front of your mama. She don't need to worry right now." When he stood, Hosea looked at Maceo, who stared across the street.

"Can I come with you?" he asked his father. "They got candy, too."

His mother spoke from the doorway, and he could see the half-moon of plump under her chin, glistening at her neck. "He need to be in bed."

"Take him off your hands for a minute," his father said, catching Hosea by the side of his face with careless fingers.

They walked across Archer and through a lot to the house where men went in and out all day and night for a shot. The two sisters who owned the house were thin and reddish-skinned, with fine freckles like sand at their temples, and they grinned at Hosea. "Look who call himself grown now," they called.

"Give him some a that pecan candy he like," his father said, and Hosea stared at the pointed hooves of pigsfeet, suspended in cloudy liquid.

The men each dropped a spoonful of sugar into the glasses of choctaw beer, so the thick drink bubbled milky as liquid clouds before they drank it. "I missed this stuff, man, when we was over there," Hosea's father said. "Remember that wine, Maceo? Didn't sit on my teeth. Wash right through you like acid."

Maceo said, "The white folks over there wasn't as tiresome, though. Came back to the same crackers here."

Hosea's father stared at the wood wall, and Hosea could see his lips wet under the mustache. He could smell the sweet beer floating down to his face. "I came back to Greenwood, man. Ain't no place like it, I'ma tell you. I met cats from Georgia over there, from Maryland and everywhere else, and nobody had nothin close to Greenwood. Negro Wall Street. Don't have to see no white folks if you don't want to."

Maceo said, "These white folks talkin about niggers got too many ideas over there."

Hosea knew they were talking about France. The French bullet. The French lace. He wondered if his mother would be angry when she smelled moist smoke on his head. She always bent to smell his hair and tell him where he'd been.

Two men burst into the room. "They gatherin up at the courthouse, crowd of em, say they gon bust that boy loose."

Hosea felt his chest fill with spiderwebs. The other men in the place began to talk louder, some arguing, some leaving, but his father put a hand on Hosea's elbow to draw him back down. He didn't know his legs had pushed him up.

The fatter sister said, "Ain't no need to go with them ruffians. They always courtin trouble." She frowned at the door.

But Hosea's father said slowly, "*Court* somethin take a plan. Don't need a plan to find trouble tonight."

"They kill that boy they got in jail, they might kill somebody for breathin." He paused. "Anybody."

"Over a foolish white girl," the sister said. "You take that boy home." She nodded toward Hosea.

Hosea's father drank again, and Hosea watched his eyes, the way they slanted toward him and then fixed on Maceo. "I ain't lookin for trouble," he said. "But if trouble get lost downtown and he find me, I'ma have to kick his ass a bit and send him on his way, now."

Maceo stretched his hands on the table. "Trouble got a whole lotta relatives," he said.

Hosea's father stood, pulling Hosea up with him. "Don't he?" he said.

.   .   .

She was ironing the French lace, patting it light and fast, and her face was wreathed with wet, her hair curling over her forehead like tiny vines. "You done forgot about that movie so quick, huh?" she said, barely looking up.

"Ain't nobody goin to the movies tonight," Hosea's father said, and then her face swiveled up like a sunflower.

"Robert?" she said. "Hosea?"

He stood in the space between the rooms—the kitchen, where the smell of heat and cloth and, somehow, milk rose from her, and the bedroom, where his father sat on the bed, loading the gun he'd brought home from France. Metal and oil and smoke—that was what Hosea smelled from his father's hands. But she thumped down the iron and came to clutch his shoulders. Her stomach against his back was hard and damp, but her fingers held him until the door was closed.

He twisted away and went through the kitchen door, among the shirts suddenly, smelling the clean nothing of cloth and feeling the air at his fingers when he tried to reach his socks. He heard the men shouting, and he ran out to the street, where he could barely see his father's back crossing the tracks.

Running after them, silent, he could feel the copper balls sliding in his pocket. He stayed behind them like his father had told him to stay close and far from the animal you were hunting. On the farm, he'd followed rabbits like this. But his father and Hosea began shifting in a swarm of other dark coats and square backs. The gun metal tucked into their elbows and palms gleamed dull. After three blocks, Hosea knew they were downtown, and the mass of men narrowed into a black river, his father's head above the crowd he was so tall. Hosea fixed his eyes on his father's ear, his collar, his forehead.

The white voices from across the street were hard and flat as shovels. The white man who hated bulls—was he here? Did he see Hosea's father? Hosea saw the feather hair of the white woman, her wire words. He watched his father's head bob and move, waiting for the eyes, but the shouting rose up like crows from a field, and then the river of men parted in streams flowing too many ways. And when the gully cleared, he saw his father and Maceo, and a white man angling toward them like a fish. Hosea froze, his back against coarse brick, and he heard the white man harsh and hollow.

"Nigger, what you doin with that gun?" The white man cut in front of Hosea's father.

"I'ma use it if I have to," his father said.

"No, you ain't. You givin it to me." The hand shone in the streetlight, reaching for the France gun in his father's fingers.

"Like hell," his father said, the wind roaring from his throat, and the river closed again before Hosea heard the shot that rang out to echo in the tall buildings above him.

He pressed himself into the deep doorway, hearing the gunfire pock the dark loud as hail on a tin roof, louder than the screaming inside his forehead. A shadow filled the doorway, and Maceo said, "Come on, boy."

The gunfire and shattering glass were jagged everywhere, and when Maceo lifted him to this shoulder and began to run down the sidewalk, close to the buildings, Hosea could see dark-humped forms in the street. "My daddy," he said, but the thump of Maceo's shoulder into his chin knocked the words back down his throat.

His mother was in the front doorway, screaming his name, when Maceo dumped him onto the porch. "I don't know, Sophia," he shouted. "I'ma wait for him. He'll make it back here. Take that boy inside and stay down, on the floor."

Maceo ran to the corner, peering back at them, and his mother's fingers raked Hosea's head, pulling his eyes so close to hers that he felt her eyelashes brush his when she asked him the questions. He understood nothing she said.

.　　.　　.

They pulled the mattress from the big bed to the floor. His mother's wrists scissored him softly, one over his chest, one behind his back. Hosea stared at the black walls, hearing shots and answers like distant conversation. He looked at the spidery iron bedstead. You a little man now, his father said; you still my baby 'til this one come, his mother said. After a long time, he heard her sleep-breath.

When he closed his eyes, he saw the men lying in the street, no faces, just coats and one hand knuckles down on the black, the fingers curled to receive something from the sky.

When he heard the airplanes overhead, Hosea realized that he had slept, because his face was tight to his mother's back, and he felt the soft pads of flesh that stretched around even to her spine, where his cheek lay. The floor was gray with dawn now, and he felt her trembling, the rigid shaking that he did after long sobbing. He heard the ragged tear of guns, the airplanes far away, and then a steady sound like a zipper being torn across the morning.

It was the sound he and the other boys made with their tongues thumping their hard mouth roofs to make machine guns in the war. "Mama," he said, to her shuddering back.

"What did you see?" She didn't turn around. She whispered it to the room.

"I seen a man try and take Daddy's gun. And then people start shootin." Hosea smelled the doorway, dank and close. "And Maceo don't know neither."

"I heard Maceo on the porch," she whispered. "You daddy must be hidin somewhere 'til they stop." She was silent, and Hosea heard the airplanes droning through the sky like great, furious wasps. France. They were in the war.

He stood up, pulled at her shoulders, but she lay on her side still, her eyes closed again. He ran to the front window, and Maceo was outside on the tiny porch, his France gun loose in his hands, his knees bent and crouching. Hosea opened the door, crouching, too, and Maceo saw him.

"Get back inside," Maceo said, looking across the field, and Hosea saw white men surrounding the choc house, saw the flames glowing bright squares in the windows. He heard trucks rumbling down the street toward them, and over the flat sky, pillows of smoke climbed and joined in billowing drifts.

"Go," Maceo said. "Stay down on the floor. I'm comin now."

He pushed Hosea back to the front room, and he told Hosea's mother, "You and the boy go in the back, to the kitchen. They lookin for men. Stay down."

Hosea heard the men shouting when they came to the houses. "Home Guard," they yelled. "Send the men out first, then everyone else. Now, dammit. All the men."

Hosea felt his chest would burst into flame. He heard the bullets strike the glass in the front, and then wood splintered at the door. "Send the men out, goddamnit, or we'll level this damn shack."

Hosea heard Maceo's feet slide across the floor, and he said, "I'm comin out. No gun."

When the door opened, the shots were like pepper raining across the walls. Hosea's mother gasped and pulled Hosea toward her. She backed toward the tiny cupboard in the corner where she kept brooms and mops, and they pressed themselves as boots scraped the porch steps.

"Ain't a damn thing worth it in here," a man said. "Check the bedroom for a trunk or something."

More feet came heavily into the bedroom. Hosea's breath rang in his ears. He felt his mother's belly against his face, and then a tremble began in her thin skin, through her dress. Hosea shivered, and the baby's elbow or foot thumped against his temple, drew a dull line down his jaw.

"Niggers on Detroit Avenue got something worth carrying," the first man said. "Come on. Get the stink out of here with that."

Their shoes sounded near the front door, and Hosea heard a soft kick. Then he smelled sharp liquid, and the smoke.

"They burnin, Mama. They burnin." She was still, frozen, and he could hear the glisten of flame gathering in the wood. Then he smelled scorching hair, and his throat closed with risen spit. Maceo. "Mama," he shouted, pulling her out the back door.

The flames were already rising in Miss Letitia's house, and one of the white men dangled her money box from three fingers, turning when he saw Hosea and his mother in the back, among the swaying shirts.

A man with a gun sat in the truck, staring at the women and children, his green eyes pale as marbles. Hosea saw white men hanging in the windows of the buildings downtown when the truck rolled slowly through the streets. He saw white women pointing and laughing from sidewalk corners, and he was afraid to look at his mother beside him. Then, on one street, he saw the charred coats and upturned faces of three men. He pressed his face to the wood slats. The hands were curled under like rabbits, held stiff to the sky. The feet were gone. The flames had burned away the flesh, leaving only stick-bones that ended in a straight nub like a hoof. His saliva rose again, flooding his molars with acid, but he swallowed again and again, his face turned to the others in the truckbed, and he felt the sting drop slowly through his chest to his breastbone, where it fanned heat under his ribs.

.   .   .

They slept under the grandstands at the fairgrounds, the dirt prickling under their sides, and when the shadows blended through the slats of wood and the whole park was full of faces, his mother began to hiss breath through her teeth. She called for Letitia, for Retha, but only strange women were there in the dank cave. Hosea saw two older women bend to hear her whispers, and one came to pull him away by the elbow. "Come over here, little man," the woman said. Her eyes were milky with film. "Come help me get your mama some water."

He sat with her against a fence, watching all the women and kids, and a few bent old men. He knew his mother was having the baby; he felt the tracing of foot nub against his jaw, the insistent movement against his side in the truck. He closed his eyes, listening for her, but in the babble and crying of lips all around him, he could hear only the hollow popping sound the old woman's lips made when she adjusted her mouth like she was used to smoking a pipe. He dug his hand deep into his pocket and pressed one of the copper balls hard into the whorls of his fingers.

All night he lay near his mother, in the smell of blood and salt and blue milk. She lay on coats, the baby hidden in the dress someone had brought her from the Red Cross; Hosea saw splinters of wood embedded in her loose roll of hair.

When daylight filtered gray through the roil of smoke and the loose breaths of all the people in the grandstand, Hosea saw white people at the edge of the fences. They would gesture to a face inside the fairground, and a guard would take the figure outside to the white person, who took sometimes three or four. Hosea was chilled with fear racing along his shoulderblades. Did the white people choose who they wanted to shoot now?

He stared at the bobbing pale faces gathering outside the fence. And he saw Retha's brown face in among them, her eyes meeting his, her finger showing him to the white woman.

When Retha bent down to his mother, she said, "Come on with me, Sophia. Only way to get out of here is have somebody vouchin for you. I been done talked to Mrs. Hefferon all mornin. She talkin bout you only done a few jobs for her, and I told her you ain't got nobody else. Come on. Let me help you up."

Hosea held his mother's dusty dress when she walked silently toward the gate. He felt the long badge pinned to his shirt. Police Protection, the man said. You can only go with an employer. Is this your employer?

His mother nodded, and Retha said, "She do the laundry for Mrs. Hefferon. We goin home now."

His mother winced at the words, and when the white woman stared at them from beside the car, he felt the acid rising again. Clenching his throat, he stopped. She stepped forward. "The French lace," she said, her voice flat. "It's probably burned."

Hosea's mother nodded, her mouth still sealed by a rim of shine between her lips, a sliver of damp Hosea could see when she tightened and then unrolled her mouth.

"I don't know what's wrong with everyone," the woman said. "People shouldn't be agitating niggers to think . . ." She stopped and put her fingers under her earlobes, pressing hard. "Now Retha says you want to come stay with us."

Hosea held his air inside. His mother was silent. The baby was only a slight lump in his mother's dress, under the coat Retha had put around her shoulders.

"Don't you know any other white people?" the woman said, moving her fingers to her temples, and Hosea saw red dents left there when she dropped her hands to her sides. "You have to crowd in with Retha."

"I don't mind, Mrs. Hefferon," Retha said. "We should get the baby out the air."

"He wouldn't open the door for me," the woman said, fixing her eyes on Hosea's face, and a lacing of heat crawled through his scalp at her chin twisting when she held her head sideways, staring at him. People passed all around them raising dust. "I hope he won't cause trouble. He can pick up the yard for today."

Hosea saw his mother's lips work, the shine spreading. "That lace," the woman whispered. "You have no idea. Mr. Hefferon's mother is . . ." Retha put her hand on his mother's back and propelled her toward the black car door, and the woman spoke louder. "Don't you want to say thank you, boy? You'll have a place and a job, a little man's job."

Hosea's mother turned and she met his eyes. Her skin was smudged with light dust like gold powder, and she wet her lips again. "He don't need to talk just yet," she whispered. "He just a baby."

"He's a little man. He's already looking for trouble," the woman said, holding her chin higher, waiting, and Hosea brought the copper balls out of his pocket in his clenched fingers, holding them fisted against his leg, imagining them sunk deep into a necklace in the folds of her throat. He blurred his eyes, so that she was only a shape, and passed her to stand by his mother.

A Worn Path

Eudora Welty

It was December—a bright frozen day in the early morning. Far out in the country there was an old Negro woman with her head tied in a red rag, coming along a path through the pinewoods. Her name was Phoenix Jackson. She was very old and small and she walked slowly in the dark pine shadows, moving a little from side to side in her steps, with the balanced heaviness and lightness of a pendulum in a grandfather clock. She carried a thin, small cane made from an umbrella, and with this she kept tapping the frozen earth in front of her. This made a grave and persistent noise in the still air, that seemed meditative like the chirping of a solitary little bird.

She wore a dark striped dress reaching down to her shoe tops, and an equally long apron of bleached sugar sacks, with a full pocket: all neat and tidy, but every time she took a step she might have fallen over her shoelaces, which dragged from her unlaced shoes. She looked straight ahead. Her eyes were blue with age. Her skin had a pattern all its own of numberless branching wrinkles and as though a whole little tree stood in the middle of her forehead, but a golden color ran underneath, and the two knobs of her cheeks were illumined by a yellow burning under the dark. Under the red rag her hair came down on her neck in the frailest of ringlets, still black, and with an odor like copper.

Now and then there was a quivering in the thicket. Old Phoenix said, "Out of my way, all you foxes, owls, beetles, jack rabbits, coons and wild animals! . . . Keep out from under these feet, little bob-whites . . . Keep the big wild hogs out of my path. Don't let none of those come running my direction. I got a long way." Under her small black-freckled hand her cane, limber as a buggy whip, would switch at the brush as if to rouse up any hiding things.

On she went. The woods were deep and still. The sun made the pine needles almost too bright to look at, up where the wind rocked. The cones dropped as light as feathers. Down in the hollow was the mourning dove—it was not too late for him.

The path ran up a hill. "Seem like there is chains about my feet, time I get this far," she said, in the voice of argument old people keep to use with themselves. "Something always take a hold of me on this hill—pleads I should stay."

After she got to the top she turned and gave a full, severe look behind her where she had come. "Up through pines," she said at length. "Now down through oaks."

Her eyes opened their widest, and she started down gently.

But before she got to the bottom of the hill a bush caught her dress.

Her fingers were busy and intent, but her skirts were full and long, so that before she could pull them free in one place they were caught in another. It was not possible to allow the dress to tear. "I in the thorny bush," she said. "Thorns, you doing your appointed work. Never want to let folks pass, no sir. Old eyes thought you was a pretty little *green* bush."

Finally, trembling all over, she stood free, and after a moment dared to stoop for her cane.

"Sun so high!" she cried, leaning back and looking, while the thick tears went over her eyes. "The time getting all gone here."

At the foot of this hill was a place where a log was laid across the creek.

"Now comes the trial," said Phoenix.

Putting her right foot out, she mounted the log and shut her eyes. Lifting her skirt, leveling her cane fiercely before her, like a festival figure in some parade, she began to march across. Then she opened her eyes and she was safe on the other side.

"I wasn't as old as I thought," she said.

But she sat down to rest. She spread her skirts on the bank around her and folded her hands over her knees. Up above her was a tree in a pearly cloud of mistletoe. She did not dare to close her eyes, and when a little boy brought her a plate with a slice of marble-cake on it she spoke to him. "That would be acceptable," she said. But when she went to take it there was just her own hand in the air.

So she left that tree, and had to go through a barbed-wire fence. There she had to creep and crawl, spreading her knees and stretching her fingers like a baby trying to climb the steps. But she talked loudly to herself: she could not let her dress be torn now, so late in the day, and she could not pay for having

her arm or her leg sawed off if she got caught fast where she
was.

At last she was safe through the fence and risen up out in
the clearing. Big dead trees, like black men with one arm, were
standing in the purple stalks of the withered cotton field. There
sat a buzzard.

"Who you watching?"

In the furrow she made her way along.

"Glad this not the season for bulls," she said, looking
sideways, "and the good Lord made his snakes to curl up and
sleep in the winter. A pleasure I don't see no two-headed snake
coming around that tree, where it come once. It took a while to
get by him, back in the summer."

She passed through the old cotton and went into a field of
dead corn. It whispered and shook and was taller than her
head. "Through the maze now," she said, for there was no
path.

Then there was something tall, black, and skinny there,
moving before her.

At first she took it for a man. It could have been a man
dancing in the field. But she stood still and listened, and it did
not make a sound. It was as silent as a ghost.

"Ghost," she said sharply, "who be you the ghost of? For I
have heard of nary death close by."

But there was no answer—only the ragged dancing in the
wind.

She shut her eyes, reached out her hand, and touched a
sleeve. She found a coat and inside that an emptiness, cold as
ice.

"You scarecrow," she said. Her face lighted. "I ought to be
shut up for good," she said with laughter. "My senses is gone. I
too old. I the oldest people I ever know. Dance, old scarecrow," she said, "while I dancing with you."

She kicked her foot over the furrow, and with mouth drawn

down, shook her head once or twice in a little strutting way. Some husks blew down and whirled in streamers about her skirts.

Then she went on, parting her way from side to side with the cane, through the whispering field. At last she came to the end, to a wagon track where the silver grass blew between the red ruts. The quail were walking around like pullets, seeming all dainty and unseen.

"Walk pretty," she said. "This the easy place. This the easy going."

She followed the track, swaying through the quiet bare fields, through the little strings of trees silver in their dead leaves, past cabins silver from weather, with the doors and windows boarded shut, all like old women under a spell sitting there. "I walking in their sleep," she said, nodding her head vigorously.

In a ravine she went where a spring was silently flowing through a hollow log. Old Phoenix bent and drank. "Sweetgum makes the water sweet," she said, and drank more. "Nobody know who made this well, for it was here when I was born."

The track crossed a swampy part where the moss hung as white as lace from every limb. "Sleep on, alligators, and blow your bubbles." Then the track went into the road.

Deep, deep the road went down between the high green-colored banks. Overhead the live-oaks met, and it was as dark as a cave.

A black dog with a lolling tongue came up out of the weeds by the ditch. She was meditating, and not ready, and when he came at her she only hit him a little with her cane. Over she went in the ditch, like a little puff of milkweed.

Down there, her senses drifted away. A dream visited her, and she reached her hand up, but nothing reached down and gave her a pull. So she lay there and presently went to talking.

"Old woman," she said to herself, "that black dog come up out of the weeds to stall your off, and now there he sitting on his fine tail, smiling at you."

A white man finally came along and found her—a hunter, a young man, with his dog on a chain.

"Well, Granny!" he laughed. "What are you doing there?"

"Lying on my back like a June-bug waiting to be turned over, mister," she said, reaching up her hand.

He lifted her up, gave her a swing in the air, and set her down. "Anything broken, Granny?"

"No sir, them old dead weeds is springy enough," said Phoenix, when she had got her breath. "I thank you for your trouble."

"Where do you live, Granny?" he asked, while the two dogs were growling at each other.

"Away back yonder, sir, behind the ridge. You can't even see it from here."

"On your way home?"

"No sir, I going to town."

"Why, that's too far! That's as far as I walk when I come out myself, and I get something for my trouble." He patted the stuffed bag he carried, and there hung down a little closed claw. It was one of the bob-whites, with its beak hooked bitterly to show it was dead. "Now you go on home, Granny!"

"I bound to go to town, mister," said Phoenix. "The time come around."

He gave another laugh, filling the whole landscape. "I know you old colored people! Wouldn't miss going to town to see Santa Claus!"

But something held old Phoenix very still. The deep lines in her face went into a fierce and different radiation. Without warning, she had seen with her own eyes a flashing nickel fall out of the man's pocket onto the ground.

"How old are you, Granny?" he was saying.

"There is no telling, mister," she said, "no telling."

Then she gave a little cry and clapped her hands and said, "Git on away from here, dog! Look! Look at that dog!" She laughed as if in admiration. "He ain't scared of nobody. He a big black dog." She whispered, "Sic him!"

"Watch me get rid of that cur," said the man. "Sic him, Pete! Sic him!"

Phoenix heard the dogs fighting, and heard the man running and throwing sticks. She even heard a gunshot. But she was slowly bending forward by that time, further and further forward, the lids stretched down over her eyes, as if she were doing this in her sleep. Her chin was lowered almost to her knees. The yellow palm of her hand came out from the fold of her apron. Her fingers slid down and along the ground under the piece of money with the grace and care they would have in lifting an egg from under a setting hen. Then she slowly straightened up, she stood erect, and the nickel was in her apron pocket. A bird flew by. Her lips moved. "God watching me the whole time. I come to stealing."

The man came back, and his own dog panted about them. "Well, I scared him off that time," he said, and then he laughed and lifted his gun and pointed it at Phoenix.

She stood straight and faced him.

"Doesn't the gun scare you?" he said, still pointing it.

"No, sir, I seen plenty go off closer by, in my day, and for less than what I done," she said, holding utterly still.

He smiled, and shouldered the gun. "Well, Granny," he said, "you must be a hundred years old, and scared of nothing. I'd give you a dime if I had any money with me. But you take my advice and stay home, and nothing will happen to you."

"I bound to go on my way, mister," said Phoenix. She

inclined her head in the red rag. Then they went in different directions, but she could hear the gun shooting again and again over the hill.

She walked on. The shadows hung from the oak trees to the road like curtains. Then she smelled wood-smoke, and smelled the river, and she saw a steeple and the cabins on their steep steps. Dozens of little black children whirled around her. There ahead was Natchez shining. Bells were ringing. She walked on.

In the paved city it was Christmas time. There were red and green electric lights strung and criss-crossed everywhere, and all turned on in the daytime. Old Phoenix would have been lost if she had not distrusted her eyesight and depended on her feet to know where to take her.

She paused quietly on the sidewalk where people were passing by. A lady came along in the crowd, carrying an armful of red-, green-, and silver-wrapped presents; she gave off perfume like the red roses in hot summer, and Phoenix stopped her.

"Please, missy, will you lace up my shoe?" She held up her foot.

"What do you want, Grandma?"

"See my shoe," said Phoenix. "Do all right for out in the country, but wouldn't look right to go in a big building."

"Stand still then, Grandma," said the lady. She put her packages down on the sidewalk beside her and laced and tied both shoes tightly.

"Can't lace 'em with a cane," said Phoenix. "Thank you, missy. I doesn't mind asking a nice lady to tie up my shoe, when I gets out on the street."

Moving slowly and from side to side, she went into the big building, and into a tower of steps, where she walked up and around and around until her feet knew to stop.

She entered a door, and there she saw nailed up on the wall

the document that had been stamped with the gold seal and framed in the gold frame, which matched the dream that was hung up in her head.

"Here I be," she said. There was a fixed and ceremonial stiffness over her body.

"A charity case, I suppose," said an attendant who sat at the desk before her.

But Phoenix only looked above her head. There was sweat on her face, the wrinkles in her skin shone like a bright net.

"Speak up, Grandma," the woman said. "What's your name? We must have your history, you know. Have you been here before? What seems to be the trouble with you?"

Old Phoenix only gave a twitch to her face as if a fly were bothering her.

"Are you deaf?" cried the attendant.

But then the nurse came in.

"Oh, that's just old Aunt Phoenix," she said. "She doesn't come for herself—she has a little grandson. She makes these trips just as regular as clockwork. She lives away back off the Old Natchez Trace." She bent down. "Well, Aunt Phoenix, why don't you just take a seat? We won't keep you standing after your long trip." She pointed.

The old woman sat down, bolt upright in the chair.

"Now, how is the boy?" asked the nurse.

Old Phoenix did not speak.

"I said, how is the boy?"

But Phoenix only waited and stared straight ahead, her face very solemn and withdrawn into rigidity.

"Is his throat any better?" asked the nurse. "Aunt Phoenix, don't you hear me? Is your grandson's throat any better since the last time you came for the medicine?"

With her hands on her knees, the old woman waited, silent, erect and motionless, just as if she were in armor.

"You mustn't take up our time this way, Aunt Phoenix,"

the nurse said. "Tell us quickly about your grandson, and get it over. He isn't dead, is he?"

At last there came a flicker and then a flame of comprehension across her face, and she spoke.

"My grandson. It was my memory had left me. There I sat and forgot why I made my long trip."

"Forgot?" The nurse frowned. "After you came so far?"

Then Phoenix was like an old woman begging a dignified forgiveness for waking up frightened in the night. "I never did go to school, I was too old at the Surrender," she said in a soft voice. "I'm an old woman without an education. It was my memory fail me. My little grandson, he is just the same, and I forgot it in the coming."

"Throat never heals, does it?" said the nurse, speaking in a loud, sure voice to old Phoenix. By now she had a card with something written on it, a little list. "Yes. Swallowed lye. When was it?—January—two-three years ago—"

Phoenix spoke unasked now. "No, missy, he not dead, he just the same. Every little while his throat begin to close up again, and he not able to swallow. He not get his breath. He not able to help himself. So the time come around, and I go on another trip for the soothing medicine."

"All right. The doctor said as long as you came to get it, you could have it," said the nurse. "But it's an obstinate case."

"My little grandson, he sit up there in the house all wrapped, waiting by himself," Phoenix went on. "We is the only two left in the world. He suffer and it don't seem to put him back at all. He got a sweet look. He going to last. He wear a little patch quilt and peep out holding his mouth open like a little bird. I remembers so plain now. I not going to forget him again, no, the whole enduring time. I could tell him from all the others in creation."

"All right." The nurse was trying to hush her now. She

brought her a bottle of medicine. "Charity," she said, making a check mark in a book.

Old Phoenix held the bottle close to her eyes, and then carefully put it into her pocket.

"I thank you," she said.

"It's Christmas time, Grandma," said the attendant. "Could I give you a few pennies out of my purse?"

"Five pennies is a nickel," said Phoenix stiffly.

"Here's a nickel," said the attendant.

Phoenix rose carefully and held out her hand. She received the nickel and then fished the other nickel out of her pocket and laid it beside the new one. She stared at her palm closely, with her head on one side.

Then she gave a tap with her cane on the floor.

"This is what come to me to do," she said. "I going to the store and buy my child a little windmill they sells, made out of paper. He going to find it hard to believe there such a thing in the world. I'll march myself back where he waiting, holding it straight up in this hand."

She lifted her free hand, gave a little nod, turned around, and walked out of the doctor's office. Then her slow step began on the stairs, going down.

Contents Under Pressure: White Woman/Black History

Catherine Clinton

A s a white woman in black history, I am frequently required to dispel myths—about myself as much as my chosen field of intellectual inquiry. When people I don't know call me at Harvard (where I taught for many years and now have a research association) to invite me to speak, I'll ask the program organizer if this panel, series, whatever, will reflect "diversity." Always protestations of political correctness follow and when I reveal to the caller that I'm not African-American, I am almost always dis-invited. I usually give them the name and phone numbers of colleagues who would fit the bill. I learned the hard way to raise my color over the phone rather than having it discovered in person. I have been up-braided—I taught black studies courses, I wrote books dealing with slavery and other African-American issues, I have a "black name." My résumé gave the impression that I was a black woman. Who do I think I am?

I am my own person and always have been. I do not like collard greens, I do not appreciate jazz, I am not a fan of rap music and I especially hate slapping hands as a form of greeting. I do like gospel music, having been raised Southern Baptist, but I keep it in the closet. Because, like a black man trying to hail a cab in Manhattan, it's everyday stereotyping that tatters the soul. I am constantly aware that no matter what the degree of nuisance I suffer—from ridicule to rancor from black or white colleagues—all of my slights and discomforts rolled up together can't compare to the level of discrimination endured by the average black American in a single day. Although it's not the reality I encounter, it's what I study, what I know, making me who I am.

Although I started out in African-American studies, my involvement has been periodic rather than persistent, woven into wider patterns—blending with Southern studies, women's studies, the history of sexuality, etc. Unlike most African-American colleagues, I was not born thinking about race. Race remained a relative abstraction for me during most of my sleepy Midwestern, suburban childhood. But even my hometown of Kansas City, Missouri, was rocked by the murder of Martin Luther King in 1968 when I was fifteen years old. I remember wondering why race unleashed so much fury and hatred within our society. The grown-ups I knew had few answers. Questions of "why" stay with me. Unfortunately, my own children have been subjected to repeated viewings of Rodney King being beaten. And we grown-ups still don't have many answers. As a parent sending her children to public elementary schools in the 1990s, I fear the debates from my childhood, when Linda Brown's parents sued on her behalf in nearby Kansas schools, ring depressingly similar.

When I was a teenager, my parents sent me to an exclusive girls' preparatory school because they felt a superior education was important. At the same time they warned me not to be drawn into the prejudices and pretenses which accompanied such a school. I was taught that country clubs, anti-Semitism and racism were unacceptable. When King's assassination sparked race riots, my parents discovered we were the only ones on the block without guns, and perhaps the only ones in the neighborhood unwilling to use them. Bomb threats interrupted my school day and when schoolmates laid blame for these events on African-Americans themselves, my dissent conferred upon me the status of outsider—something for which I have been grateful ever since.

As I marched off to college in 1969, my freshman year was considerably enhanced by the learning experience outside the classroom as campuses across the country exploded with protests. I well remember my first course in black history, which I enrolled in because I wanted all my courses on Tuesdays and Thursdays so I wouldn't have to be diverted by the classroom more than two days a week. (I frequently warn students who enroll in my own courses that they may have frivolous reasons for taking a class in black history—but be warned, exposure can lead to a lifelong involvement. Several, I am pleased to report, have proved me right.)

I ended up majoring in black studies in college for a variety of reasons. I had started out in English, with very decided opinions about literature and how to express myself. My enthusiasm waned as the department overflowed with dewy-eyed women swooning over arrogant male faculty. I was uncomfortable "giving good daughter," seemingly a prerequisite for success as a female lit major. I switched into political science and was extremely fired up by a charismatic professor whose interest in me, unfortunately, proved more than intellectual. His sexual harassment was a hideous episode of my undergraduate career and drove me right out of American political history and into black studies—a daunting field, but my introductory courses were eye-opening and electrifying.

Choosing to concentrate in Afro-American studies, a controversial department at Harvard University, during my junior year, I can now see how fundamentally foolish it was to think I could escape sexual politics (or sexual harassment) by becoming a white woman in black studies. I look back on episodes and am thankful for my oblivion, yet in several cases deeply regret my youthful ignorance.

During one of my first courses in the field I wrote a severe and lengthy attack of Eldridge Cleaver's *Soul on Ice,* taking the author to task for sensationalizing "rape as a political act." I never shaped my interests to suit the macho style of black studies in vogue. No one, especially the grader, appreciated my critique. When I was taking a course on law and race, I chose the Scottsboro case for my final paper. I did an incredible amount of work—reading local Alabama papers ordered on inter-library loan, scouring trial testimony and pouring over secondary and periodical literature. I completed what I thought was stellar work, but was surprised when I received only a "B." It took me several years before it finally dawned on me that *maybe* the Scottsboro case, replete with issues with which my black male professor had struggled all too painfully during his lifetime, was not the most appropriate topic for me. I certainly had the right to pursue these topics as my own interests, but I should have been prepared for the poor reception they received, especially when I refused to take a party line.

Sitting in classrooms which were almost always exclusively black except for me, I could not conform or hide, so I simply did the most work I could to demonstrate my seriousness of purpose, my total embrace of the field. My presence made me suspect to my fellow students, until I put in the time and energy—not to win anyone over, which was not my goal, but to show I was there to stay.

It was a lengthy hazing. I was not admitted to elective seminars in several cases. Once a professor grilled me on my credentials: had I been a freedom rider? was I a member of the Panther Party? I was often judged and found wanting. I decided against a course in black autobiography because the final paper required seminar members to write their own autobiographies and no whites needed apply. I was turned away from a lecture by Shirley Du Bois, W.E.B. Du Bois's widow, cosponsored by the department. The constant and persistent reverse discrimination was a powerful lesson for me.

I was a freak, a curiosity—an extremely pale, redheaded woman surrounded by various shades of black. The two other whites in the department were the invisible men of Afro-American Studies—never showing up and silent when they did. My department chair baited me in private and tried to humiliate me at our departmental meetings by holding discussions on whether whites should be allowed to participate in shaping Afro-American Studies. I never really understood the complex depths of his hostilities until undergraduates held a discussion about hiring a black professor who had a white wife—as did our department chair. This was an issue on which I kept absolute silence, while the black students conducted a vicious, verbal lynching of this distinguished African-American scholar. I think both the chairman and I were equally shaken by witnessing this bloodletting, but the experience polarized us even more.

At one point during my college career, another white woman joined the department. She was a member of Students for a Democratic Society and a melodramatic advocate of black rights. She always made theatrical references to "brothers and sisters," embarrassing all within earshot by failing to realize that "sisterhood" was earned rather than proclaimed. Even more distressing, she sought to expiate white guilt by working her way through the willing black male student body. As one of the black women in the department complained, "Why doesn't she just come to class with a mattress on her back?" I breathed a big sigh of relief when she left both the department and Harvard after a few short weeks. However, her "beat me, rape me, make me write bad checks" school of race relations gave me an unanticipated boost. She had made me look good to my peers.

I was mortified that this woman's style and lack of substance was the image of white women in black studies. My own long-term monogamous relationship with a white man during my junior and senior years at Harvard allowed me to dodge the subject entirely. I assiduously avoided even the appearance of impropriety in a manner that I now look back upon as ridiculous in the extreme. I did not want my intellectual commitment to African-American Studies dismissed as some kind of sexual proclivity. I allowed racism to affect personal relationships. I should have taken the opportunity to educate, to take a stand against slander—but I was more concerned with my relations with black women at this time, not black men.

Holding my ground in arguments with black women in the department, dozens of lively, enlightening and occasionally acrimonious exchanges ensued. We could and did tackle issues of feminism, class conflict and racial dynamics, in and outside the classroom. The subtext could and occasionally did turn unpleasant: "You're a honky bitch and I'm not." I remember a particularly savage exchange when one young black woman told me that Carole King had no business singing "Natural Woman" which was "owned" by Aretha Franklin. Even when I pointed out that King had composed the song and could record her own music, my classmate claimed King's rendition was an act of cultural imperialism. Our prolonged skirmish on this point reflected a larger battle.

I now appreciate that this particular young woman spoke to me through the subterfuge of academic debate. In the moment, I could not recognize her pain. I was all too preoccupied with my inflated sense of myself. I never reached out to her. Maybe there could have been no common ground, but I wish one of us, preferably me, had torn away the veil, moved beyond the wrangling and into communication. But I still learned from her and so many others.

Raucous debates over Imamu Baraka's *Dutchman*, feuds over strategies for Harvard's divestment, countless hours of discussion in and out of class provided me with important insight beyond the books I was reading, the papers I was writing. I got more than the education for which I had bargained. Many of these women taught me that my color could and did render me insensitive, maternalistic, and upon occasion just plain wrong. I could wear all the intellectual shoe polish I wanted, it was still a "white chick" saying it. People would see and not hear, and that was my failing as well, all too often.

I remained passionately committed to the intellectual integrity of the field, an articulate and dedicated champion of Afro-American history. (I never took a course in Harvard's department of history, recognizing its patent indifference to questions of both race and gender. Too little had changed when I returned to campus to teach in this department in 1983: I likened my experience to that of a fetus returning to an abortion clinic.) When Afro-American Studies came under academic review and the committee of student representatives needed to look diverse, I was drafted. When outsiders argued that black studies was nothing more than consciousness-raising for black students only—who you gonna call? So "mythbusting" became my specialty. I struggled with my token status, my absence of color highlighted in the campus's most colorful domain.

Once I had to speak not just for myself but all whites in black studies, I felt constrained, muzzled, forcibly removed from the free-for-all of open debate. Simultaneously, I was forced to abandon my initial, "color-blind" approach to black studies, especially with the exploding campus politics of the early seventies turning me into an outdated Pollyanna, in an era of deconstructing Huck Finn.

Undergraduate classes provided indelible memories, fostering the kind of riveting intellectual exchange to which I now aspire. My first course in African-American literature was a revelation. I was spellbound, transported by lectures and discussions in sections. To this day I can't reread Jean Toomer's *Cane* without hearing the melodious voice of my section leader reciting a passage. (He did much more than read aloud, as I was lucky to have Arnold Rampersad, now a leading authority in the field, as my first section man.) I was completely thrilled to take a class with an idol, C.L.R. James, who brought panache and passion to the podium. This razor-sharp septuagenarian enjoyed Socratic exchanges and made every class count. If I would raise my hand, hoping to be called on in a crowded field of frantic, waving arms, James might point over toward me, the only white in a sea of black faces, and gesture, "you, there, the one in paisley overalls," or "you, the one with the pen in her hand," or some other identifying trait—anything *but* race, a lesson I value down to this day.

At the same time, over the years I have often conducted an exercise where I ask two students (different colors, different sexes) each to read aloud to the class a brief statement: "Blacks/women are different. They have special needs which are not being met by this university. Blacks/women are better served by having separate educational experiences, which I advocate." Afterward we hotly debate what was said, what was heard—difference and meaning, sex and race, discourse in my course, and ploy to "let the thinking begin!"

I have a powerful weakness for words. They are my comfort and joy. They refresh and renew and revitalize, and each day I realize how lucky I am to be able to make my living in the world of words. The millions of words to which I have listened and the thousands of volumes I have read and the hundreds of pages I have written offer me a depth, a breadth, a range of appreciation of the black experience which I cherish. I have no peace but greater understanding.

After I graduated from college, I went to England on fellowship and earned an M.A. in American studies. By then I was drifting out of black studies and into women's studies, bruised by the Mau-Mau games necessary to get ahead. I went on to Princeton University for my Ph.D. in history, consumed with questions of race and region, sex and gender, a warrior on the frontier of the new Southern studies. At the time, Princeton was called "the last plantation." But as I conducted my research for my dissertation on the role of the slaveowner's wife and racial and sexual dynamics in the Old South, I could testify, after frequent forays on the Southern research trail, that Princeton was far from the last bastion of plantation values.

My first teaching post as a historian was at Union College, a liberal arts college in upstate New York, where my course in African-American history had no white men enrolled—at a college with over sixty percent males and ninety-five percent whites. I decided that no matter where I taught, I would be a magnet for those students who felt themselves disfranchised. I would attract those whose interests were not in the "mainstream," and it was my job to make them feel welcome to the table rather than having to wait upon it.

I have always tried to engage and even enrage my students —to trigger within them the unstoppable urge to learn, preferably about something that might change their lives. My methods vary, depending upon the class, the students, the taste and feel of the semester. When a campus cheerleader for a conservative magazine at Harvard unfurls a Confederate flag from her dorm room and tries to provoke a brawl, begging for a lawsuit, these issues invade the classroom. Not just campus politics but equally often the national spotlight focuses on racially charged incidents—Bernard Goetz, Tawana Brawley, Howard Beach, the Central Park jogger case, Anita Hill and Clarence Thomas, Mike Thomas (need I add, Rodney King) and the list goes on. Life must be a learning experience when we're studying the past, struggling in the present and trying to chart the future of race relations in America.

At the same time, I believe that the power of knowledge and a love of learning demand high standards, that rigor and discipline must prevail in my classroom. I resist the free-for-all where students remain untutored on the topic of the course for which they have enrolled. Brilliant, gifted and silver-tongued students may try to charm their way to a degree without doing the hard work of producing quality research and polished papers, without being pushed to their potential. Why should they, when a white professor can be guilt-tripped into giving him or her an "A" by pushing a few buttons? I let them know by the end of our first meeting that they are barking up the wrong "Little Tree" if they try to pull any scam on me.

At the same time that I advocate strict academic criteria, I do not remain unaffected by the kinds of personal and political problems minority undergraduates have to continue to face. One of my students was harassed in the local student bookstore, accused of suspicious behavior because she was looking at tapes and C.D.s for too long while wearing dreadlocks. Her case was splashed all over the campus paper and disrupted her term completely. Another was picked up by the campus police while trying to take the shuttle bus back to his dorm from the library. Another had his uncle shot by police over Thanksgiving break, and found it hard to concentrate on final exams. Another had to go home weekends because her father was getting out of jail and she feared for her mother and younger siblings. Many have come to me with the aftershocks of incest survival. Black men and women, just trying to do their best,

confronting extraordinary obstacles to having an ordinary semester.

And despite the very hard and at times tragic circumstances
surrounding these issues, a sense of humor seems my most
strategic asset, for teaching and learning. Blacks are more willing to listen if I am willing to laugh at myself ("melanin-
impaired"), and whites are better prepared to face their shortcomings if they are stung by wit rather than full frontal assault.
Teaching strategies have moved well beyond what I remember
being taught in seminars on methodology.

One of my friends has suggested that I work on a book
with a black co-author, satirizing the racial stereotypes and
prejudices we share about one another. "It's a White Thing,"
she has suggested we call it. ("Why is it you people put may-
onnaise on everything?") Because, of course, although both
blacks and whites may condemn racial stereotyping, it infects at
the core of so many interracial interactions. Our inability to
laugh, our inability to share, allow our problems to fester.

Even more imbedded in our conflicts is what the great
James Weldon Johnson once suggested: at the heart of the race
problem is the sex problem. A colleague in English confided
that he thought so much writing in African-American Studies
on "mulattoes" and "miscegenation" came out of literature
because scholars have an easier time with interracial sexuality if
it's fictional. Dealing with historians' reticence on this topic—
indeed the entire spectrum of issues dealing with sexuality—I
think he's more right than he knows. ("It's an uptight thing!")

I have been dealing with interracial sex in my research and
writing for about ten years now and I find no topic more
disconcerting, a subject which can provoke equally strong and
negative responses from both blacks and whites. At a conference where I was invited to offer a paper on Southern families
I was asked if I would talk about white families or black

families. I told them I would do both. When I did not speak sequentially, but instead about the sexual intersection of black and white in the Old South, many listeners were offended. I was pregnant at the time, and my Southern aunt, who accompanied me, had been taken into the fold by many of the blue-haired female set in attendance. She told me they clucked sympathetically after I concluded, wondering how a niece could shame her family so. It is my philosophy that someone who looks just like me, someone about whom there are such preconceived notions, can and should make it her life's work to demolish comfortable clichés about sexual and racial dynamics.

When I first began researching black women during Reconstruction, my data revealed the depths of devastation that post-Civil War poverty wreaked for African-American women, but it also revealed ways in which black women's actions in the past do not always conform to our politically correct expectations in the present. I penned a letter in 1986 warning a friend that I had found that "not all historical truths will emerge politically correct." I was unearthing post-bellum letters from freed women who saw their children as commodities, bartering them as they would livestock. Even if I could provide a full context for appreciating these cases, what would the response be to my discovery of a mother who was told if she had another child she would be thrown off the postwar plantation where her family lived. She secretly gave birth in the woods and killed her child. She was put on trial for infanticide, found guilty and sentenced to hang. When I delivered a paper in 1987 citing such cases, my presentation provoked sharp response, and anger from black women especially. It was ironic to me that the next year when Toni Morrison's *Beloved* was embraced, and won her the Pulitzer Prize she deserved, my findings were given a new lease on their historical life. Morrison's brilliant novel, which explored a black mother's murdering her child, ironically paved the way for some measure of acceptance of my historical evidence as emblematic.

In 1988, while teaching at Brandeis, I read an article about the low number of black Ph.D.s nationwide. I had been aware of the problem, particularly at Harvard, where the number of black faculty in the Faculty of Arts and Sciences was on the decline. The Harvard Afro-American Studies department was having a difficult time recruiting, and the department was dealt a near-fatal blow when its chairman and my good friend Nathan Huggins died suddenly in the fall of 1989. I remember feeling completely devastated by his memorial service; indeed, when my husband forced me to go to the doctor, despite my protestations that I was just feeling blue, it turned out that I had scarlet fever, which plagued me well into the new year.

The acting chair asked me to return to Harvard (from scarlet fever to scarlet woman, I imagined) to the department from which I had graduated nearly twenty years before. I accepted with great trepidation, but I knew the students needed attention, the department needed warm bodies, and I was willing to step into the breach to preserve morale. I was also eager to serve as a cheerleader for students seeking to go on to graduate school and become educators themselves. I sought Ford money for students to work on projects, I set up luncheons and meetings with visiting black faculty, I organized an ongoing workshop—I threw myself into the task at hand and found considerable reward.

I organized a seminar in black women's history, hoping to confront questions of gender and sexuality, color and race. Again, humor was a powerful resource. Turning people's assumptions inside out was the best way to peel away layers of resistance, to stimulate discussions. Trying to provoke open forums, I would warn students that everyone's ancestors came out of Africa—making us all, in some sense, African-Americans. Yet we must recognize that ethnicity and religion are dramatically different categories from race: the day a person talks about having a black grandmother the same way we regard having a Hispanic grandmother or a Jewish grandmother, then we have shifted gears.

Before the end of my semester teaching black women's history I would always ask, "What would you say if I told you I was a black woman?" This elicits a wide range of responses. (My all-time favorite being a spontaneous outburst from the front row: "I'd ask, who does your hair?"). By my breaking the ice, the floodgates could and almost always did open. Sometimes people would resent what seemed flippancy on my part, but I reckoned any figurative body blows I took to get people talking—even if only to discuss the professor's being a horse's ass—were well worth it.

Some graduate students worried about these charged exchanges and I warned them that the thickness of your skin and not its color was a useful measure for success in the field. Students feel freer to debate openly the meaning of color and definitions of race if the professor, black or white, takes the initiative. Shock tactics usually subside after the first few meetings. From then on, I usually spend a lot of my semester writing notes to students, perhaps making calls, holding conferences and passing out Kleenex. All of this proves worthwhile if I can create an atmosphere of open exchange, to make seminar participants willing to express diverse and even conflicting views.

Watching several of my students win fellowships and undergraduate prizes for their work in black women's history—indeed nearly a dozen are now in graduate programs scattered across the country—I feel a renewed sense of hope. Former students are writing on interracial sexuality, women in the Black Panther Party, black and white relations in Civil War

Tennessee, the influence of Caribbean writers on African-American literature, sex and race in nineteenth-century Mississippi, and I know significant books and more prizes are in the works. The fact that many of these students are black women again boosts my sense of wonderful possibilities. I have learned as much from my students as they have learned from me, if not more. My greatest gift to them was not imparting wisdom, but listening and encouraging them to listen as well.

As a white woman in black studies, my relationship with black women continues to be complex. I have had more problems with colleagues than students. Many black women academics who don't know me stereotype me and build up a wall between us as they lay eyes on me. At conferences there have been threatening questions from the audience, covering a range from "You're a honky bitch and I'm not" to "Who do you think you are?" I have learned, especially with people I don't know who enjoy lecturing me on the basis of my skin color rather than what I have to say, the value of letting other people have their say, just let it all spill out. If their ideas seem to me to be particularly racist or mean-spirited, I might attempt reasoned response. But too often it's not what I've said, it's what they haven't been allowed to say. Offering them the unimpeded opportunity to challenge my views can clear the air and perhaps lead to dialogue and future communication.

Many of my black women colleagues in African-American Studies have generously shared their ideas with me and have treated me with friendship and respect. Some show their goodwill in their writing or in public, and to them I am enormously grateful. Others are willing to offer me only covert support, unable to demonstrate openly any regard. This kind of behavior gets in the way of our academic progress, but it rarely wounds me the way it used to. A number of them have expressed strong disagreement with my interpretations or find my work unconvincing, weak, wrong-headed or bad, completely within their professional right. Some just plain don't like me and I applaud them—that's why I love America.

A few years ago a group of my students came to complain to me about a student who was non-African-American who was joining all the black campus groups and black cultural associations at Harvard that were open to any student. The student was writing a thesis on a black topic and the group who came to me feared that this student was acting like an anthropologist, doing fieldwork and exploiting them. They proposed that some kind of rule be invoked to prevent "students like these . . ." I interrupted to ask them what they thought of the student, and they all agreed the student was a jerk. They agreed their complaint revolved not so much around race as around the fact that the student got on everyone's nerves. So I told them I was sorry, but I couldn't help them legislate against jerks—who we know come in all colors.

We talked about alternatives to public diatribes, like trying to hold an intelligent conversation with the student. I explained that if they chose to become academics, like me they would be forced to spend a good deal of the work week dealing with jerks and they might as well recognize this as an opportunity for on-the-job training. One sensitive soul took a Gandhian approach, but the others really worked over this student. I'm afraid they all went on to become lawyers—but bloodshed was avoided and a valuable lesson learned.

I have proposed several panels at conferences where historians working on black women—blacks and whites, men and women—might have open dialogue on the topic of political correctness, racial dynamics and feminist interpretations. I think it would be productive to take on the questions of voice and authority, color and representation which have sometimes provoked violent and unplanned eruptions at conferences. The Women's Studies Association has been battered in recent years by charges involving racism. The Southern Association of

Women Historians suffered minor seismic disturbances at its first national conference in 1988. I saw these as opportunities to engage in meaningful exchange.

So far, my proposals have fallen on deaf ears. I have received carefully worded letters explaining what troubling times we are going through: Oh, really, and did I sleep through a golden age? How we wouldn't want to undermine the wonderful progress being made, and other lame excuses. We are always going to be engaged in struggle, and if we want to keep our fields productive we must expect disagreement and once in a while a little scorched earth. The passive forms of preservation—letting things lie fallow—haven't worked in the past. So why not let some fertilizer get flung around, in hopes of a new crop of ideas? Let a thousand arguments bloom.

Those heated exchanges echoing in lounges and corridors are long overdue as part of our public discussion. Leadership must encourage us to abandon forms of censorship which stifle the free exchange of ideas on race, which privilege one view over another, and essentially produce Kabuki theater rather than the fireworks our topic should salute, not douse. Blacks and whites convening in the fields of black studies and women's studies well know the power of dissent, which gave birth to their intellectual enterprises. We must embrace risks and get back to our unselfconscious, rowdier roots. Not all historical truths will emerge politically correct. Not all questions are asked to be answered. If I were to solve all the intellectual puzzles with which we struggle, what would there be left for you to do? I tell my students.

I want to promote a groundswell for political incorrectness, for making mistakes and learning from them, for showing your true colors, whatever your skin color. I want my students to feel the strengths African-American studies has brought to me —to be pushed along their own paths, by ambition, by example, free to soar by the time they graduate. I want them to be confident when our views diverge and prepared for challenge in any arena they choose. I want them to understand the irony and delight I experienced being declared an "Honorary Octoroon" at a departmental celebration. Contents under pressure has its glory days. And as long as those hundreds of students I've taught are still out there, persisting if not prevailing, I can count on more glory and those better days, yet to come.

Reaching Across
the Feminist Racial Divide

Dorothy Gilliam

The splendid, snow-capped Teton Mountains of Jackson Hole, Wyoming, framed the semi-rustic Sojourner Inn, site of the annual Journalism and Women Symposium known as JAWS. Inside, a room was crowded with white women and a sprinkling of black and other women of color.

The year was 1992, and we'd come to network and assess how women were faring in the media. We'd gathered at a panel discussion featuring Nan Robertson, a former *New York Times* reporter who had written that season's hot new media book, *The Girls in the Balcony*. It was about that newspaper's discrimination against its own newswomen, and how women at the *Times*—from female journalists to clerks and accountants—had, through a class action discrimination suit, pushed that newspaper, kicking and squirming, into a fairer treatment of women.

In her remarks, Robertson bemoaned the stereotypical male

talk show host she'd met on the book promo circuit who "only wanted to talk about bimbos like Jennifer Flowers" when she wanted to talk about women like Anita Hill. Then Robertson launched into effusive praise of Hill.

As she talked, I felt myself getting annoyed—a feeling rooted in historical and sociological rage. During the question-and-answer period, I rose and faced Robertson. "When will white women have a sense of quid pro quo with black women," I asked, "and return the debts they obviously owe women like Hill by joining with us in attacking some of the problems that afflict our communities?" In other words, I wanted to know why white women didn't feel a need to build coalitions with black women based on equality and power and shared agendas.

Roberts seemed taken aback, even deeply offended, by my words. Her hand flew up to her bosom as if I'd triggered a bullet her way. Her smooth articulateness melted into stammers and stutters, and her response was vague, something to the effect of, "Black and white women have to communicate more with each other."

After the session was over, several black and brown women came up to me. They shook their heads in dismay, complaining that my question had not been answered. But they brightened as they expressed how much they appreciated the dose of reality that it had injected into the discussion.

Unexpectedly, Robertson's presentation—and my reaction to it—gave me a way to think about a peculiar form of racism among white women of which they seem largely unaware.

Black women have often been forerunners on issues—abolition and civil rights, for example—that in turn lead to benefit to the white woman. The reverse is not often true. With the clear exception of the issue of abortion, there does not seem to be an equivalent way in which black women benefit as directly or as dramatically from white women's leadership or actions in the white women's movement.

This produces hurt, frustration and pain in women of color, particularly those who are in the work world with white women or in relationships that are professional, personal, and sometimes intimate. The result is often a deep, hidden anger and a sense of betrayal.

Black America was still reeling from the aftershock of the Hill-Thomas earthquake when I traveled to Wyoming. I was told I was in the largest group of women of color who'd ever attended the annual symposium—courtesy of a special grant that provided partial funding. When the Hill-Thomas story dominated America, I'd been on leave from the *Washington Post* on a residence fellowship in New York City. So instead of writing about the event, I'd had countless discussions, over cups of coffee and glasses of wine, with my black female friends. One point we made was how Hill was in the tradition of black women who galvanized an issue vital to the interests of white women, a phenomenon that was rarely acknowledged. We also took note that Hill had given white women an avenue to attack white men.

Looking around at the space we women shared that day, I thought, how near we are, yet how far apart in experience and understanding. How many of them, I wondered, realized how much the story of black women's beginning in America was a part of some of us still—as victims of colonization, slavery and segregation? How many would fathom how this trio of horrors was made worse by lies we were told about how our African past was inferior and best forgotten?

How could they ever understand how it had seeped into our bloodstreams, this shared slave and segregation history with black men?

The handful of women of color in that room who, like me, were over forty had all directly experienced segregation and racism in the 1950s and had come of age during the black consciousness era of the 1960s, when we began to reclaim the identity that the collective weight of church-stage and society had forced us to surrender. The quest black women dealt with in the sixties was to dissolve the myths and lies many of us had internalized that had produced a strain of self-hatred. My three daughters were born in the mid- and late sixties, so I saw my role as seeing to it that they never internalized the lies and that they developed a healthy sense of identity. But it was hard, given the pervasive white images that surrounded them.

Black women like me asked ourselves what was our role in the revolution, and how could positive relations with our men be built and used as a vehicle to move us toward liberation?

It was not until the 1970s that we faced such questions as what, if any, was our responsibility toward the women's liberation movement and whether we could successfully build bridges with white women. In answering this question, many of us took note of historical credits. We remembered the New England schoolmarms who went South during Reconstruction, and the women like Mary Chesnut, the Grimké sisters, Harriet Beecher Stowe, and suffrage movement leaders Elizabeth Cady Stanton and Susan B. Anthony. We remembered the 1960s white women's activism that eventually made abortion legal and helped halt the growing stream of black women entering hospital emergency rooms after faulty self-induced abortions.

But black women never forgot how the wondrous Sojourner Truth, abolitionist and suffragette, was ignored by Susan Anthony when she called for all women, black and white, to be enfranchised along with freed men. "In some respects," wrote Jeanne Noble astutely in *Beautiful Also Are the Souls of My Black Sisters*, "Miss Anthony can be likened to many white women's liberation leaders who worked so diligently in the student nonviolent movement but left in anger at the onset of the Black Power thrust."

Black and white women also worked together in the grad-
ual desegregation of some women's organizations such as the
YWCA, and the rights of women and blacks were fused. And
while we mutually faced job discrimination and false stereotypes, overall history didn't give us much reason to feel that
white female's causes were that much more humanistic than
white male's. Meanwhile, we were struggling to stabilize black
families and eliminate racial prejudice for all blacks, regardless
of sex.

Yet when Rosa Parks ignited the civil rights movement by
her refusal to move to the back of a Montgomery bus, she
simultaneously lit the fire of desire for freedom in white
women. Some lib leaders equated their powerlessness to a
"niggerization" and referred to themselves as "niggers"—
much to the chagrin and revulsion of black women, who didn't
see them as all that powerless and definitely resented the pejo-
rative racial comparison.

Despite our double jeopardy as blacks and females and our
shared need of such stated lib aims as equal pay, we could all
identify with the question Noble, the historian, asked in 1979:
"What assurance do we have that Miss Ann will want to share
whatever other advantage she gains with us? Does she really
want us to have the kind of power we want for ourselves?
Given, say, the anti-busing stance of white women, for example, those questions were largely rhetorical.

Despite many black women's view that continuing racism
prevented them from giving first priority to the elimination of
oppression because of sex, black women felt they "knew"
white women pretty thoroughly. As playwright Lorraine Hansberry put it, "Our lives have been intertwined with white
women—in the kitchen, in the schoolroom, in the marketplace,
and in the volunteer board room. We probably know Miss Ann
better than Mister Charlie does, and surely far better than our

black brothers do—because sex has little to do with knowledge of total life styles—positive or negative. The roles we have played in society give black women a special vantage point of observation."

During the conservative 1980s, when greed, me-ism, and self-interest became the country's watchwords, affirmative action laws benefited white women even more than blacks, yet blacks became the chief victims of the negativism the term evokes today.

So I was thinking of a lot of things that day in 1992 when I raised the question.

Ironically, there was another woman on the panel who was less taken aback, not because of the question, but because she knew me better than Robertson did. Betsy Wade was a *New York Times* journalist who had taught me when I was one of two blacks at the Columbia University Graduate School of Journalism in the sixties. When I saw her at Jackson Hole, she told me, "You were always pressing . . . pressing . . . you wanted it . . . you were the kind of person I wanted to give to because you wanted it so badly."

I didn't consider myself as having pressed particularly hard that day. But why did I feel the white women were looking at me as if I'd brought a skunk to a black-tie party? It was the same feeling I'd had during my 1991 fellowship when I would ask white media executives about their racial hiring policies or their coverage of communities of color. Neither white men nor white women seem to know how to talk about issues of race. But for black women, race is the omnipresent fact of our lives.

Because we're affected by what's going on in our lives when we deal with issues like this, let me say that personally I was not in the best space when I went to Jackson Hole. I was suspended between two deaths—one that had recently occurred and another, more symbolic one that lay ahead. Feeling vulnerable, I was not in the best of spaces to be rubbed raw. I never like to feel vulnerable when I'm interacting with large numbers of white women.

I'd recently returned to the States from Trinidad where I'd gone to say a final good-bye to my friend Wilfred "Freddie" Cartey, the late great poet. Freddie had died in March of that year and was buried in his native Port of Spain. Unable to attend his funeral at the time, I'd descended into the moist, salty air of that island in August as if entering a womb. I carried asterium to his grave, cried, and my soul felt peaceful. Cartey always reminded me to relate what was happening to the poorest of our people, and that trip reinforced the already existing tendency.

"You were brave," said a young Pakistani woman. "I'm glad you asked it," said another. "Good question," said still another black woman, lamenting that it was not answered. I felt that I'd touched the right nerve, but the coldness I sensed from the white women left me in need of hearing a friendly voice. When I went to my room later, I called the man with whom I was in final stages of ending a nearly two-year relationship. I needed some TLC. But he was cold and unresponsive. His reaction hurt. Two misconnections in one day!

Later, when I shared this and similar incidents with white feminists—how we as black women feel so excluded from the experiences they're sharing when we come together in settings like the one at Jackson Hole—they bemoaned the chasm that exists between us. "They were all good people in the room," said Harriet Woods, head of the Women's National Political Caucus, shaking her head sadly, "and this was not happening among ideological enemies or people who were ill-motivated."

Yet this was the backdrop against which the Anita Hill-

Clarence Thomas drama played out. Black America looked on in amazement as white feminists embraced her as their own—Hill became a symbol for every woman. One friend of mine who was working on a doctorate in Illinois said that when discussions arose in class, the white women dominated the conversation so much that she felt her comments were unwelcome.

Yet black women are still in double jeopardy—being black and female, still counted as two by the affirmative action folks and pitted against our own brothers by those who enjoy seeing the friction. Still not respected for our brilliance, beauty, intelligence, stamina and the harsh unrelenting fact that we have had to climb the rough side of the mountain . . . climbed a staircase that was bare with torn-up places . . . climbed a ladder that had rungs deliberately taken out so we could stumble and fall. We're still given European definitions of beauty, charm, fashion; still remain at the bottom of the economic totem pole; and our family problems are given a fancy label like the "feminization of poverty."

As a Chicago preacher put it, black women are "messed over, disrespected, abused, used for lust and then left in disgust. Some have accepted the enemy's definition and don't know what their potential strength and possibilities are."

So with the black family in a deadly battle for survival, with the life-threatening problems in the black community, we are in no mood to waste time on the niceties; we need help. White women who have themselves faced oppression should be our natural allies as we challenge the issues of poverty, injustice, media inequality and other challenges. But it sometimes seems as if white women are too busy buying guns to protect themselves from crime, and as the newest "feminist" statement, to recognize black women's pain at knowing the targets for those guns' bullets are our own sons and daughters.

I recognize the links between racism, sexism, classism and
homophobia and pray for healing between black and white
women that will finally allow us to work together on common
agendas from a position of shared power. White women have
long talked the talk. If there is to be progress in this country,
they now have to walk their talk.

Feminism
in Black and White
bell hooks

Even though I have taught Zora Neale Hurston's *Their Eyes Were Watching God* for twenty years, it is a book that continues to astonish, fascinate and delight me. I am awed by Hurston's prophetic vision. She used the writing of this novel to critically reflect on one of the most significant feminist issues: what conditions must exist for female creativity to nurture and sustain itself. In search of the "horizons" of that liberatory location where she can construct self and identity, find against that "jewel down inside," Janie leaves familiar places, communities, comfort and status in search of freedom. Her love relationship with another artist/adventurer serves as a catalyst for her self-actualization.

Ultimately, Janie finds that simply longing to be free is not enough. She finds that she must consciously choose to break the chains that bind her—that she must act. She finds that action requires courage, commitment, risk. Faced with the possibility that she might meet her death questing for self-realization, for freedom, Janie declares: "If you kin see de light at daybreak, you don't keer if you die at dusk. It's so many people never seen de light at all." To Janie the light is awareness, that quality of insight and vision which enables her to see clearly what she must do, how she must, what it means to live as a liberated black woman.

My twenty years of teaching *Their Eyes Were Watching God* overlap with twenty years of passionate commitment to feminist politics, to feminist thinking and practice. The joy that is present in Janie's life when the novel ends mirrors the joy that I feel in my life right now. I believe that this feeling of joy and fulfillment is a direct consequence of my sustained engagement with feminist politics and feminist practice.

Over the years I have been consistently called upon to justify remaining loyal to feminist politics, given the racism of white women active in the movement. Questions like, Are you black first or a woman? Don't you think you are weakening the black liberation struggle by supporting feminism, betraying the race? were where the discussions of feminism often began with black and white audiences twenty years ago. While the questions are the same today, it is most often assumed, especially by black audiences, even before I answer, that none of my explanations will be adequate, that I am a man-hating sell-out, a traitor to my race. Usually my interrogators speak with confidence, provide documentary evidence of white female racism within the feminist movement, sometimes drawing that evidence from my work or that of other black women engaged in feminist activism, sometimes referring to personal experiences in feminist settings or with feminist individuals.

Significantly, no one has ever insisted or assumed that black women should cease supporting the black liberation struggle because of black male sexism and misogyny. Indeed, it is always assumed that aware, politically progressive black women will be capable of separating the political shortcomings and failings of some black men from the more important political ideals and beliefs that are the ideological foundation of our collective continued participation in the black liberation struggle. Respect for black female political acumen is most often suspended when the issue is support for feminist politics. Suddenly we are seen as capable only of being dupes, puppets, slaves controlled by more powerful white women. During the Thomas hearings, it was common to hear black folks dismissively describe Anita Hill as only "a puppet of the white power structure." Why was it so difficult for folks to see Hill (whether we agreed with her or not) as a thinker, making choices rooted in her own strongly held political beliefs about the way government should work, about the ethical dimensions of political work, and most especially the extent to which leaders should be accountable to the public? Why was it so impossible for this public to accept that a black female of her own accord could believe with all her mind and heart that men, not just black men, who use sexual harassment as a strategy of patriarchal terrorism in the workplace should be unable to occupy powerful positions in a democratic government? And why was it difficult for everyone to understand that seeing sexual harassment as criminal not necessarily mean that one advocates feminist politics. Public response to the Thomas hearings exposed the extent to which our culture has difficulty respecting the political actions of black women.

The place where one might imagine that black women might be respected would be in the realm of feminist politics. Yet from the beginning of the contemporary feminist movement to the present day, black women have had to struggle to gain political recognition of both our commitment to feminist politics and our contribution to the feminist movement. Without the radical interventions of those black women who demanded that the feminist movement rethink its construction of female identity to take into account the complexity of female experience, feminist politics would not be inclusive or visionary. Most white women do not praise black women for renewing and revitalizing feminist politics. Even though black women/women of color have challenged the feminist movement to acknowledge the political significance of racial hierarchy, to this day most white women resolutely refuse to change their thinking about the direction and agendas for feminist politics. African-American refusal to see black females as capable of choosing engagement in nonexclusionary feminist politics, as well as recognizing our positioning as primary participants in the development of feminist theory and practice, mirrors assumptions many white women make, assumptions informed by both racist and sexist thinking. No matter the number of books I write on feminist thinking, the lectures I give, wherein I share the reality that feminist politics is not a country occupied and owned by white women, that it is not a door marked "whites only" that women of color are seeking permission to enter, many white women see it as just that. They continue to regard me and other women of color as meaningful presences within the feminist movement only to the extent that we are willing to serve agendas they set. Continuing to feel as though they "own" the feminist movement, they make feminist locations sites where they assert coercive control, where they strive to unilaterally determine the direction of feminist theory and practice. Not surprisingly, women of color enter these locations feeling as though they have three choices: to assimilate, to wrest control away from the existing hierarchy, or to refuse to participate and start separatist organizations.

Significantly, those white women who were and are willing to learn from and grow with black women/women of color, who called for a reconceptualization of feminist constructions of female identity so that race would be considered and concrete changes in feminist politics would take place, often do not occupy positions of power. All over the United States feminist organizations collapsed or were severely weakened in the wake of power struggles over agendas. In retrospect, it is evident that many women who joined the feminist movement did not think differently from the dominating males in our society about the nature of power, about how organizations should be run. Indeed, women often duplicated in feminist settings the same conduct that took place in white supremacist capitalist patriarchal settings, with one crucial difference: men were not present. White women from privileged class groups usually occupied positions of power. In such settings, black women/ women of color were always in the minority. For the most part they were not any more committed to exercising power differently than were their white counterparts. This was indicated again and again when they responded to white supremacist thinking and action within feminist circles by withdrawing, abandoning all concern with the feminist movement, or by trashing feminism. These responses meant that they were always acting from the position of powerlessness that white supremacy defines as our place. Rather than assuming that they could act subversively to redefine and transform feminist politics, they acted as though if white women would not give over power to them they had only one recourse, to refuse to participate. When black women/women of color respond to racist aggression in feminist settings by acting as though we are always and only victims, never able to intervene and change existing structures, we help to maintain them. When black women/women of color act as though we lack the political vision to create an inclusive feminist theory and participate as leaders in the revolutionary feminist movement, we reinscribe the notion that the movement "belongs" to white women. Individual black women, like myself, who have consistently refused to abdicate our power to influence and transform feminist politics are often seen as threats. It is our voices that folks try to silence, our presence that is deemed difficult and undesirable, our work that is often appropriated to enhance the feminist movement even as our beings continue to be devalued. So far, despite our continuing effort to transform feminist thinking, we reside on the margins of the feminist movement in loose coalitions with those radical and visionary white women who are our comrades in the struggle. Overall, within most feminist circles power continues to be distributed in ways that maintain and perpetuate existing racial hierarchies wherein white women always have greater status and power than black women.

Significantly, institutionalization of feminist concerns in the academy and in various spheres of public life has made it difficult, if not downright impossible, for feminist reconceptualizations of power to alter existing arrangements. Since white women had greater status in those spheres than the majority of black women anyway, prior to the feminist movement, existing racial hierarchies were not only reproduced in these settings, they remained intact. Feminist advocates seeking to "make it" in mainstream settings were and are often reluctant to try to do things differently, or structurally find it impossible. For example, most women's studies programs and departments are currently run in the same manner as traditional patriarchal departments and programs. While this is problematic for some feminists, reformist feminist activists who believe gender equality will become a reality only if women show ourselves capable of imitating successful men are eager to conduct feminist business in a manner that mirrors the status quo. This being the case, it should no longer be a shock to feminist sensibility that individual women often use feminist platforms to propel themselves forward into previously male-dominated positions of power only to abandon those platforms when the desired outcome is achieved.

Reformist feminist thinking and practice have had a greater impact on society than radical/revolutionary praxis because it was based on a willingness to compromise, to embrace existing structures. Its primary goal was to help women gain equality with men of their class. Hence, it was that strand of the feminist movement that was dominated by white women from privileged classes that was least willing to incorporate an analysis that included race. Advocates of feminist politics need to openly acknowledge this if we are ever to fully understand why the feminist movement did not overcome the alienation that black and white women feel from one another. The vast majority of people in our society, women and men, understand feminism to be only about women gaining equality with men. It is this understanding of feminism that is taught via mass media, reinforced by popular feminist literature; that literature rarely acknowledges race or racism as factors that also determine female status, and consequently does not highlight the voices and experiences of black women. From a revolutionary feminist standpoint, which I embrace, this literature potentially undermines the revolutionary feminist movement since it keeps us stuck in outmoded ways of understanding woman's reality. Susan Faludi's *Backlash: The Undeclared War Against American Women* is a prime example. No one reading this book comes away imagining that feminist advocates wish to transform society rather than simply to gain greater social mobility, power, and equality with privileged men. No one reading this book comes away with the awareness that there has been major feminist critique of universalizing the category "woman" or that there has been a theoretical revolution calling for a recognition of differences in female social status created by race, nationality, class, etc. These differences mean that anti-feminist backlash does not have the same implications for all groups of women. While this critique is not meant to invalidate the important thesis of Faludi's book, its failure to be inclusive legiti-

mizes biases. Mass media's exclusive focus on reformist feminist thinking and writing acts to obscure more complex radical
feminist politics.

Reform efforts are central to the feminist process, but feminism is essentially a revolutionary politic, one that demands
more than reform. Popular insistence that there be as many
"brands" of feminism as there are of any other "product"
undermines the feminist movement that seeks to end sexism
and sexist oppression. When feminism is represented as being
only about gender equality with privileged classes of men (i.e.,
white males) there can be no mass cultural recognition of the
need to eradicate patriarchy or to reconceptualize power. And,
most important, if this marks the limit of feminist vision there
need be no change in the ways white women relate to black
women/women of color, no interrogation of the status and
privileges given white women by white supremacy, a status
that enables the exploitation and/or oppression of nonwhite
women and men.

To build feminist solidarity, we must be willing to acknowledge the ways politics of difference have created exploitative and oppressive power relations between women that must
be contested and changed. Individual white women active in
the feminist movement who are not committed to altering these
hierarchies, who accept class hierarchy and desire to exercise
class power were and are threatened by those critical interventions within feminist politics that call for an interrogation of
the universal category "woman," a recognition of difference
that would include understanding how racism and white supremacy are primary determinants of female status, as well as a
revision of feminist scholarship so that it would be more inclusive and more accurately address female reality. White women
who think this way distort the importance of these interventions. They wrongly interpret them as a bid for power, an
attempt by "misguided" women of color to gain control over

and destroy the feminist movement by deflecting attention away from gender to race. Of course these misguided interpretations advance their own class interests. Unfortunately, they are often the white women who speak publicly for and about feminist issues.

Within more radical feminist circles, there has been a genuine concern on the part of many white women that we create a feminist movement that is more inclusive. That concern was not always linked to a willingness to make serious changes in thought, structure, and leadership. Many of these women felt threatened when confrontation happened around issues of difference, especially when the issues were race and racism. Some white women were overly proud of feminist generosity when they were willing to invite "others" into the sphere of feminist power. There was often an expectation that these "others" would be grateful, passive participants, not folks who can confront, challenge, and demand change.

It saddens me to reflect on the many moments in feminist settings where opportunities to grow and learn, to enhance our understanding of the politics of difference, were undermined by the fact that most of us had no understanding of how to manage conflict, reconceptualize power, while simultaneously creating a spirit of community that could serve as a basis for building solidarity. I am saddened because we did not all have the skills to remain rock-steady when the ground began to shift and shake. In large numbers many women have drifted away from the organized feminist movement. Some of that drifting was a direct response to struggles for power, attempts to confront issues of race and class. While most white women in the feminist movement had no difficulty acknowledging that racism and/or white supremacy were institutions of domination that needed to be changed, difficulties arose when they were asked to examine their own politics, their being. When individual white women were challenged to consider the ways their lives were informed and shaped by white supremacist power and privilege, breakdowns in communication happened. And, more important, when white women were challenged to divest themselves of those privileges, it was evident that many of them were more comfortable with a reformist politic that did not embrace issues of race and racism and therefore did not require them to change racist and/or white supremacist thinking and action. Those white women, many of whom were and are lesbians, who were and are committed to radical and revolutionary feminist politics, developed strong solidarity with black women/women of color who did not have access to the same spheres of media power to project this vision of the feminist movement. The work of white women like Barbara Deming, Zillan Eisenstien, Donna Haraway, Adrienne Rich, Elizabeth Spelman to name only a few, has not been given mainstream attention. Their collective work has not countered the prevailing assumptions about feminist politics projected in the mainstream. And even within feminist circles their commitment to anti-racist politics has not transformed structures or served to counter the negative experiences of either white women or women of color who feel that the feminist movement has yet to fully address these issues in a constructive way. Sadly, the feminist movement did little to really bridge the political gaps separating black women and white women from one another. And in its worst manifestations of the existing racist structure, it created new gaps.

Often we black women/women of color found ourselves expending energy working to intervene in feminist settings only to find that our interventions were either appropriated or not appreciated. Many of us were truly shocked by the will to power we confronted in individual white females. It was a stance completely antithetical to all the theory we had read in white feminist literature about feminist ethics and the feminist process. This will to power was in many cases separate and distinct from a lack of understanding about racism. Individual black women/women of color did not know how to strategically intervene within the feminist movement when we were not confronting white women who were ignorant about racism but instead were facing individuals who simply did not want to relinquish power, even if that meant their continuing support of existing racial hierarchies. For example: How do we respond to white women scholars who initially refused to take race seriously but who later found that they could actually strengthen their career status by focusing on race without in any way changing their racism? It was difficult for individual black women to know how to confront powerful white women who spoke in the name of feminism, who changed their work to include race while continuing to behave in an exploitative and/or oppressive way in their interactions with black women. This was especially the case among academic women. Since conventional academic structures of competition promote the kind of jockeying for power wherein one seeks to project the assumption that work is unique and not overly influenced by the ideas of peers, it meant that many white women found it useful to appropriate the work of women of color in such a way as to make it appear that their own work was really better, more academically substantive, etc. Not surprisingly, many black women felt that their only choice was either to divorce themselves from the feminist movement or to focus on separatist models. Of course many white women were very accepting of those black women scholars who were willing to institutionalize a separate but distinct "black feminist movement," for that meant that there was no demand that the mainstream (i.e., the white-dominated feminist movement) would need to undergo major changes in theory and practice.

Those black women, women of color, and white women

who remain committed to transforming feminist thinking and practice in ways that make it more inclusive still find ourselves engaged with a revolutionary feminist politics that deepens our bonds with one another. Confrontation and contestation have made us more powerful. Our solidarity has been strengthened by our passage through trials and tribulations. We found and find ourselves on the other side of troubled times—transformed, as excited by and as committed to feminist politics as we were when the contemporary movement began.

Our faith has been renewed because of the changes we witnessed. I witnessed white women who initially closed their minds and hearts to discussions of race and racism shift their thinking—change. Many of these women are now able to talk openly and honestly about the intensity of their previous denial, the violence of their resistance. They are proudly anti-racist. We are proud to be comrades in struggle. We continually regret not having access to mass media that would project our triumphs, our revisionings of feminist theory and the feminist movement rather than a reformist vision that undermines all that we work for. I witnessed myself and other black women/women of color sustaining our commitment to feminist politics despite white racism because of our political commitment to transforming sexism and sexist oppression. Black and white women who remain committed to revolutionary feminist politics hold on to feminism and each other because we know that feminist solidarity is life-affirming, necessary for the transforming of patriarchal society and the healing of our planet. Many of us have the good fortune to see a new generation of revolutionary young feminists coming to power who eagerly embrace standpoints that include recognition of race and class. Over the years, all of us in our diversity of location, standpoint, experience, etc., who remain passionately, fiercely committed to the feminist movement understand more fully (like Janie in *Their Eyes Were Watching God*) what is needed if we would be liberated women, if we would be liberators. It is the sweetness of that understanding, the power, that will be the heartbeat of the future feminist movement, affirming in unprecedented ways love and solidarity between black women, white women, and all women.

Hello, Stranger

Gayle Pemberton

One of my favorite stories is Flannery O'Connor's "Everything That Rises Must Converge." It is not the most deadly encounter between black and white strangers in American literature, but it is a most compelling and chilling one. The story is a tragicomedy about parents and children, race, self-delusion, class and the South. In it, Julian, a boring, patronizing young white man, reluctantly accompanies his mother on her trip to the Y for a weight-reducing class. She has refused to go alone, because the buses have become integrated. She decides to wear a new hat, which is a ridiculous-looking purple-and-green-velvet affair. On the bus, wearing a duplicate hat, is a large black woman accompanied by her very young son. Unable to contain what she sees as a grotesque mirror of herself, the white woman resorts to a sentimental "habit of being"—ogling, smiling and fawning over the young black child. As they all get off the bus together, she goes to give the child a coin, paying no heed to her son's warning not to do it. In righteous indignation and fury, the black woman— her fist and red purse joined into one weapon—hits the white one, knocking hat and woman to the ground. This act precipitates a stroke in the white woman, and the confrontation is symbolically the last one she will have in this world. The story ends with her face distorted and her mind lost in her distant past, as she calls for "Grandpa" and someone—I bet I know who—named Caroline, to come get her.

Julian's mother smiled at the black child—a nervous reaction in the face of what she feared was a changing social order. The stroke sent her back to a secure childhood, when servants and grandparents were, for her, at beck and call—when social relations in and out of family, in and out of race, were guided by custom and ritual. When the black woman hit her, she hit at that custom and ritual embodied in the white woman. And the punch didn't just knock the white woman to the ground, it knocked her out of time, place and history smack-dab into the middle of a sentimentalized past. All that started with a smile.

Smiles, like humor, are the most serious and complex forms of communication used by human beings. When we consider the range of the smile—from the ecstatic and joyful to the horrifically malignant—frowns and grimaces in their totality seem limited and quite incomplete. Supreme innocence resides in the smile of a baby, and yet how many millions have died with their last image a smiling murderer, either carrying out his own or the state's bloody desires? When I was a child, I was curious about the lines from bad western movies—the "Smile when you say that, pard'ner" moments—because I knew that a smile would not turn an insult into a benign comment. On the contrary, it would make the insult worse.

When I became an adult, I discovered that most of my

chance encounters with white women involved their smiling at
me. I may have a mordant sense of humor, but it is not discern-
ible just in passing. I see many things in my face, as do my
friends and family, but, in general—and unless I do something
to encourage it—my expressions are not causes for unbridled
laughter, or even grins. As a result, I have long since stopped
trying to discover what the stranger's smile means. Does it
camouflage a joke, an insult, guilt, friendliness—or fear?

Sometimes the smile ushers in some passing concern that is
domestic and ritualistic because I am shopping, and there is
something a little too familiar and informal in the exchange.
"How do you cook that?" from the white smiling woman at
either the fish, meat or fresh produce section of the supermar-
ket, is the equivalent of her giving me a penny or a nickel.
Without so much as a "Pardon me, but . . ."—and invariably
there are other white women, perhaps even physically closer,
that she might choose to ask. The intervention is based upon a
complex of assumptions and a series of reactions that constitute
our brand of American racism. As much as I would love to
hear her say, "Pardon me, but I'm an idiot," or, "I can't boil
water," or, "I hate this stuff, but they want it; how do I make it
edible?"—I never do. And my position as culinary authority is
meritless, like white-skinned privilege, and it stands for nothing
I have earned by my own labor or character. I am a black
woman, read *cook*. I am not a small black woman, read *really
good cook*. My responses in such encounters can never be truly
instructive; seminars require captive and willing audiences. It is
unlikely anyone but me would get the joke if I were to suggest
the use of a large pot, onions, a couple of ham hocks, and
cornbread on the side, regardless of whether the sought recipe
is for broccoli, red snapper, parsnips or Belgian endive. Instead, I furnish the simplest good recipe or technique I know,
and let it be done. Gourmeting-it-up does not resolve the issue
either: fancy and foreign foods in my basket precipitate smiles

and wonderment expressed at how one learns to cook such things.

Some would call these brief, coffeeless klatches benign, and certainly they are when compared to other standard, more pernicious assumptions made when black and white strangers meet. ("Is she going to buy that standing rib roast with food stamps?") But whether a black male is assumed to be criminal by a white female stranger, or I am perforce a good cook, both inferences spring from the same source, and the man and I are just as likely to receive a nervous smile as a hedge against her fear.

What is so dispiriting about all this is that culturally we have not progressed beyond sentimentality—the default societally-induced emotional response—between strangers of different races. That sentimentality expresses itself in a variety of ways: arrogance, fear, hatred, curiosity and pity. More frustrating, smiles are exactly what we would seek in a perfect world as strangers greet one another. But to be the recipient of a smile usually reserved for babies, at best, or for puppies and kittens at worst, challenges the potential for women to meet on grounds of equality and humanity.

The place where white and black women meet as strangers is a product and consequence of history. As a society, we delude ourselves about many things—we talk about teenage pregnancy, domestic and other kinds of violence without contesting the ways in which males are socialized to be aggressive. We contend that women are the bearers of civilization, and teach their children kindness or whatever empathy they can muster. In matters of race, we say it is the white men who stand out as lynchers, shooters, in white and blue collars, in racial melodramas of power and subordination. White women —who have been oppressed for being women, and powerless —we say have more natural understanding of the plight of oppressed others. But we make a grave mistake of history, if nothing else, when we make such generalizations and assumptions. Just as some white women have fought valiantly for their own, and others' rights, who have seen as sister a black stranger, a greater number have not, and most have been at the sides of men—in back or sometimes front, leading and following them—in literal and figurative assaults on black people, and in resisting changes to make society more equitable.

I am reminded of such an encounter in Chicago some years ago, when on seeing me, a white mother, smirking, arranged to have her teenaged daughter removed as the co-patient in my hospital room. My mother, sister and I were affronted, and then mused about what would have happened had we transposed the characters and situation by insisting that I not be in a room with a white person. We understood racial power dynamics and realized, as most blacks do and most whites do not, that reversing the circumstances cannot and does not produce the same effect. There is no mystery to what the hospital authorities would have said; we would have been encouraged to find another facility for my surgery. It would have been an exercise in, and a tribute to, democracy had we complained to the hospital about the complaint. Doubtless the results would have remained the same; I would have had my single room and perhaps some patter about how not all white people thought like the woman. But I did not challenge the woman's smirk, which was the emblem of her sense of racial superiority and privilege. Instead, factoring all the factors, I acquiesced to the rude reality and went about relishing my new single room bought by an insult. I fantasized that the daughter—who had shown no signs of discomfort in my presence—would instead find a chatty roommate, who loved to talk about her many and various, all dreadful, diseases.

This episode came from a northern, urban city. On many occasions I have heard black people say that they much prefer the tough, straightforward exercise of racial bias they find in the South, to the coded and layered Northern varieties. Conversely, more than one white woman has told me that she prefers the veneers of gentility and manners of the South to the direct, blunt style of Northern race relations. Needless to say, I have always mistrusted such categorization, unless of course it means that people find psychological comfort in having their defenses already in place, so that they will be ready to field the inevitable racially charged volley. Region, it would seem to me, is not the most significant aspect of this larger issue. Race is. What happened to me in Chicago was *Northern* perhaps only because the hospital officials acted as if the facility were actually integrated.

I witnessed another chance encounter between black and white women in the gift shop of a museum in Memphis. The clerk was a college-age white woman, who by all outward appearances was nauseated by either her job, the reading on her lap, some memory, or the large numbers of African-Americans visiting a special show that day. Suddenly a group of fifteen or more young black children walked into the gift shop. The clerk halted them verbally, and smirking, told them quite rudely that they could enter only three at a time. They stopped their chatter and hesitantly backed up. The black woman supervising the group rounded up her charges and, in loud tones, told them that they needn't go where they weren't wanted— that there would be nothing in the shop desirable for them anyway. That was the extent to which she was willing to encounter the white stranger.

The black woman erred on a count or two: first, the museum *did* want their business, having brought an exhibition of African-American photography to town, and the cultural mores of Memphis suggest that a successful run would be unlikely with only white patrons attending the show. Whether officials sought to make the black community feel that the museum was "theirs" all the time is an unknown. There was little evidence to support or to deny it. Second, inside the gift shop were a number of souvenirs of the exhibit, of good quality, too, that even children, poor or otherwise, might afford. The encounter with the white female stranger—someone low on the museum's chain of authority—was nevertheless both sentimental and resigned. The white woman won her battle without so much as having to produce evidence that the three-at-a-time policy was other than her own capricious want. The black woman diverted the children's curiosity about trinkets to the more familiar territory of racial code. Both women trusted their reflexes, born of a history of inequity and reaction, and a good day went sour. I thought it would have taken both very little, and perhaps everything, for either woman to have moved to mitigate the confusion. Of the fifteen or so children turned away at the door, I am sure some percentage will remember the day by the encounter with the white stranger, and not by the vigorous imagery of historic black struggle caught on celluloid. I wrote the head of the museum a letter relating what I had seen, and I asked about policies, but I never received an answer.

There is something heroic about the black woman's swing of fist and purse in the O'Connor story. It's an old-fashioned feminine gesture: flinging the purse—joined by a just bloomed sense of empowerment: throwing the fist. The act, too, is from a member of a class that has been routinely de-feminized and rendered powerless. The black woman, in resisting the sentimentality fused with measly charity, strikes a blow for her child's dignity and for her own. One would not want to have to do that every day, even though daily the dignity of countless black women is affronted by white strangers. And daily, white women are insulted by black female strangers who, sometimes righteously and rightfully, and sometimes not, insult and strike in anger from a pain born of and by many generations.

Smirks should be challenged or avoided. But what is to be done with the smile? Perhaps it is only to smile back, because whatever the smile means is something quite personal with the white woman who has given it. It may indeed be a reaction that carries no thought with it. Or it might be a way of deflecting fear. Quite possibly it may be the only way she can communicate some appreciation of a black woman's reality as she struggles with her own—an attempted solidarity of sorts that has no context for more engaged interaction. Smiling back means as much or as little as what has been sent.

I have to know that the woman who approached me in the aisle carrying a can of greens and asking me if I had tried them because a friend of hers said that they made them just like the black Southern people did, with fatback and seasonings—I have to know that she was trying to communicate, I have no idea what. She was quite crestfallen when I told her that I didn't eat canned greens. I noticed that she held her head down as we passed each other in paper products first, and then in frozen food. I wondered if she wanted me to tell her that the greens were great, authentic, delicious, and in doing so, she would be revealed as someone great, authentic, and perhaps delicious to me, too. But I left her, as the black woman in Flannery O'Connor's story left the older white woman, reckoning that her images and illusions probably had nothing to do with either the fictional or the real black woman, in this case me.

When black and white women meet as strangers we carry with us parcel and sum of all that our families and this society have made of us. Sometimes, at odd moments—like the Freedom Marches of the 1960s—the context is certain and it suffices: we know what the smile from the white stranger walking arm-in-arm with us means. But at more common moments our encounters may bring smiles, frowns, confessionals or rebukes.

As women, who are socialized to distrust each other—and who do so even as we witness the enormous power of male bonding —we may never reach that point in an ideal world when strangers greet each other with a smile that we know means simply, "Hello, stranger."

"Are We So Different?"

A Dialogue Between an African-American and a White Social Worker

Cathleen Gray, Ph.D.,
and Shirley Bryant, D.S.W.

As university professors and colleagues at a medium-sized private university, the authors have worked together on the same faculty for nearly ten years. One of the authors, Cathie, is white, a therapist, and a professor of clinical social work practice. The other, Shirley, is African-American, a specialist in organization development, a student of the African-American family, and a professor of "macro" social work practice (policy, administration, community organization). We are both involved in research on marriage and divorce among middle-class women, African-American and white. Although we have always been friendly we only recently became friends by the sharing of ourselves and our work. In working in research on marriage, we began the important dialogue about the similarities in African-American and white women, in our work and in ourselves.

We present the following as a dialogue between us on some

similarities and differences that we have found between white and African-American middle-class women in their marriages. Cathie recounts her observation from clinical work with an African-American professional woman who was experiencing problems in her marriage. Shirley reflects on Cathie's discoveries in light of her own and others' research findings regarding middle-class African-American and white women in their marital relationships.

CATHIE: Some years ago I received a call from Margaret, who was seeking psychotherapy. Over the phone she said that she was having marital problems and was questioning her commitment to her marriage. She also mentioned that she was an associate in a major law firm and was hoping to become a partner in the firm the next year. We scheduled a consultation to talk in person and decide what would be the best course of therapy for Margaret. When I hung up the phone I noted to myself that Margaret sounded as if she were under a lot of stress and, like many young female attorneys in Washington, was hard-driven and in conflict about her roles and relationships. When Margaret's appointment time arrived I opened the door to my waiting room and registered to myself a bit of surprise: Margaret was also African-American.

As the consultation progressed, Margaret spoke of the stress not only of working toward the partnership, but of being the first African-American woman who was near partnership level in her firm. She had sacrificed a great deal to pursue a law career, and now at thirty-six found she was conflicted about many things. She wanted a baby, but had questions about her marriage to James. They had married while both were undergraduates, and James was now a high school English teacher. Margaret knew that James loved her, but she felt that he wanted more from her than she could give, was too dependent on her, and really wanted to stay home and raise children.

Margaret was clearly under stress, having symptoms of anxiety and depression, and was also facing a major life transition.

As I listened to Margaret I was asking myself the questions I always do during a consultation: What seems to be the source of the problem? What can I offer her? Although I felt very clear on the first question, I struggled with the second. I kept asking myself, how can I possibly put myself in the shoes of an achieving and pressured African-American woman? How could I know what she is experiencing? Would she be able to trust me, a white, somewhat older, professional woman? Would she see me as biased? Would she see something in me that I might not yet even know about? I decided, or rather rationalized, that Margaret had enough to work on; she didn't need to also work out racial issues with her therapist.

After giving Margaret feedback on what I thought the source of the problems might be, I went on to say that, although I would like very much to work with her, I thought that she might want to work with a therapist who could also be a more appropriate role model and who could clearly understand the conflicts encountered in being the first African-American woman to achieve high status in a previously mostly white, male arena. I then suggested that Margaret might want to work with a colleague of mine who was very talented and also African-American. Margaret said that she would consult my colleague, but asked if she was also an academic, as she felt that someone who was both a practitioner and an academic, as I was, would better understand some of the pressures within a law firm. My colleague was not, but I suggested that Margaret see her once, and then she would more actively decide for herself what was in her best interest. We concluded the consultation, I wished Margaret well and we said good-bye.

I thought a lot about our consultation after Margaret left, and I reflected most on why I had referred her on. I thought there were many ways in which she and I might work very well together, but some words of Harry Stack Sullivan kept coming back to mind: "We regard the stranger as our enemy."[1] I also reflected on how I went about teaching my students about conducting therapy with people who are different from ourselves. I never was comfortable setting guidelines for how to "do therapy" with minorities, since every person is unique and we never know what is unique to a person until we work with him or her. I have always taught that bias is our projection onto another of what is unacceptable in ourselves, and that in working with anyone different from ourselves we must always look inside and examine our own projection process. The stranger is our enemy only so long as they are the stranger. Why was I reluctant to get to know Margaret? What did I not want to look at in myself? My conclusion was twofold. At that moment I was unwilling to look at my own projected bias, but I also saw a lot of myself in Margaret. This was a time when I was undergoing my own internal struggle related to my work at the university in that I was a regular faculty member but did not yet have my Ph.D. Internally, I often felt I was not qualified for my position, in spite of all external positive evidence. This was the struggle I found in Margaret that also belonged to me—am I really qualified or am I fooling a lot of the people a lot of the time?

After this time of introspection I concluded that I had learned something about myself, but that I would not see Margaret again, since I believed the African-American therapist I had referred her to would have more to offer her just in being African-American. To my great surprise Margaret called two weeks after our initial consultation. She reported that seeing the other therapist had been very informative, but that she still wanted to work with me because she felt intuitively I had more to offer her. She also said that she appreciated why I thought she might want to work with an African-American therapist, but she had learned from the consultation that she needed to work with a woman therapist who was not African-American, although she didn't know why. I was intrigued, not only with her statement of what she had learned in the other consultation, but with what I supposed we both had to gain from the experience. An important therapeutic relationship was about to begin.

As I worked with Margaret, I was able to see more of why she felt we should be working together. It was important for her to be able to put issues of race on the back burner for a while, though not permanently. I perceived two possibilities that might account for Margaret's reluctance to work with an African-American therapist. One was based on her fear (or projection) that she would have to prove to an African-American therapist that she was a strong African-American woman when internally she didn't feel strong at all. The other possibility was that she would have to protect the African-American therapist from her internal rage and also from her internal strength. I became curious about Margaret's relationship with her mother, as I perceived that Margaret felt she might be letting a lot of people down and maybe felt let down herself. She clearly had conflicts over wanting to be strong, yet also wanting permission not to be strong.

Margaret wanted and needed to work on several issues in her life, but the most pressing issue at this point was her relationship with James. When she fell in love with James, she had seen him as the handsome, athletic hero, while she had always seen herself as bright but not very attractive to men. She now was in great conflict about feeling that she had clearly surpassed James professionally. She mentioned almost in passing that she earned quite a bit more money than James did—an issue that they hardly ever discussed. She also felt conflicted about her role as wife. Margaret was uncomfortable and very angry. She was working very hard, yet she was doing most of the household chores as well. She was terrified of having a baby, and her fantasy was that she would break apart from the added pressure.

Earning more than James was perhaps the source of one of Margaret's greatest conflicts. The fact that this issue was virtually undiscussed led her to internalize her anger. Outwardly she was very attentive to James, while internally she saw him as dependent on her and having a "fragile male ego." By not talking or even fighting with James around these issues, Margaret held on to her projection and her pain.

I could also relate to Margaret's conflict over responsibility within her marriage. Recently I was talking with a friend about the stresses in our lives. Both of us are university professors, and she is African-American. We both see our husbands as being caring and very involved in child care, but when the discussion got to our everyday lives we realized that both of us had appointment books filled not only with professional business, but also with unending child-related tasks—"plan carpool"; "make dentist appointment"; "buy fabric for Halloween costume." The endless list was a metaphor of our lives. When we went home and looked at our husbands' appointment books, each of us found they were both also filled with appointments—business appointments.

Since Margaret's top priority was her relationship with James, that's where we began our therapeutic work. My thought was that if this marital stress could be relieved a bit, Margaret could feel freer to make the important decision about whether to have a baby. I also perceived that Margaret could build trust in our relationship by working first on her relationship with James.

Margaret seemed to be in conflict about nurturance—her need both to nurture and be nurtured—and also about her own anger. We started with nurturance, as this was less frightening for her. Underneath her wish for James to take more care of the house, she really wished for James to take more care of her. She felt, however, that she would have to be fragile and dependent to be given that care. This is where Margaret's mother's messages appeared. Margaret's mother and father were divorced, and in exchange for no child support payments, the mother had full custody of the children and the father had no visitation rights. Margaret was the youngest of three daughters, all of whom had graduated from college. Her mother was very strong-willed, self-contained and strict. Margaret admired these qualities, but they also conveyed to Margaret that life was hard and work and schooling were critical because a woman, especially an African-American woman, cannot count on any man. Margaret could not remember her mother ever laughing or being cuddly with the girls. Her mother's message helped Margaret to work hard and achieve, but it also helped Margaret to feel guilty about playing or being at all frivolous, and to feel uneasy about being dependent. Margaret had never seen her father and mother model a good relationship. She had heard from her mother only how irresponsible men were. The feelings she developed from this experience interfered greatly in her marriage.

If she were to change her relationship with James, she might have to give up some control of her life and trust that James could first negotiate with her, then be able to accept some of her dependence. Margaret harbored two contradictory fantasies—one of being the first African-American woman senior law partner in her firm, the other of being at home full-time caring for her children. What she couldn't fantasize was anything in between. She had also constructed an "all or nothing" concept of her relationship. Either she accepted the status quo or she would have to leave James.

These fears of Margaret's were very familiar to me. I had heard them repeatedly from women clients over my many years of practice. The basic conflict was experienced as one of either accepting the current pain in a relationship or leaving the relationship.

What Margaret and I worked on was dealing with the notion that any change involves loss. This meant that Margaret might have to change her perception of James's dependency and "fragile male ego" if she began to negotiate for change in the relationship. She said she couldn't stand the way things were and decided that she would risk facing the changes.

Margaret began to tell James of her sadness and anger, and she also began to act angry, yelling and demanding that he take some responsibility. James was shocked to hear of Margaret's rage, as he was quite satisfied in the marriage and thought she was too. By letting out her feelings with James, Margaret began to see that he was not the enemy she had perceived, but was rather confused himself and wanting to improve their relationship if Margaret was unhappy. They renegotiated all the household chores into areas of responsibility. James didn't always do his chores the way Margaret liked or considered "right," but he did them. After several months of upheaval and conflict, Margaret began to feel much more relaxed at home and more intimate with James. Then they began discussing money and its power. James revealed that he actually wanted to talk about money but was very uncomfortable about it. He felt his job was less adequate and that because of this, maybe he was less than adequate himself. Opening this discussion led to much more openness in general between Margaret and James.

As Margaret and I went through this early process of the therapy, I continued to see her as being in a familiar, "race-less" conflict—familiar to me, to my friends, and to the other women I saw in therapy. I wondered whether I was seeing beyond racial issues or was really denying their existence. My conclusion was that I was doing both.

Margaret needed to work on the marital issues as strictly issues of marriage and gender. And in this first phase, my projection was that Margaret was of no particular race, just a particular gender. I could easily identify with her gender issues, as I had been down many of these paths myself and with so many other women I had worked with. On reflection, I think that this early work enabled us to form the bond we needed. I had mastered the difficult task of gaining Margaret's trust. Now I also had to trust her to go on the journey we had to go on to help her resolve other levels of her conflicts and disappointments, including her anger at women. It was going to be important for me to be open to let Margaret lead into her anger and into the issue of race, knowing that she would see me both as who I am and as what she projected onto me. We were both going to have to deal further with our projections.

I found Margaret to be a very gratifying client to work with. She valued my thoughts, reported positive change, and credited our work with saving her marriage. What lay beneath this gratification was her belief that she had to "be nice and work hard" to be accepted. Her inner self believed that if she got angry with me, she could "wipe me out" and I would severely retaliate. She had been assimilating all her life, had always gone to predominantly white schools, had always had white friends and colleagues, and had also always harbored resentments and the belief that all of these people saw her as incompetent and surely unequal.

When Margaret began to get angry with me it was expressed in the form of, "How would you know . . . you're not black . . . you have never experienced discrimination . . . your life is easy." I couldn't escape a lot of self-reflection while working with this aspect of Margaret's anger. My first thoughts were reflections on my own childhood in a relatively poor family living in an affluent community, or not having the same clothes and toys my friends had, of feeling I had to assimilate all the time. As most therapists do, I wanted to be seen as thoughtful, calm, and caring. But Margaret was seeing

another part of me which was hidden—the part that was also
angry at having to assimilate and be "nice." In Margaret's own
anger she was tugging at mine, and I was internally angry at
her for forcing me to feel some of my unacceptable feelings.
Now I knew why I had initially referred Margaret to another
therapist. I had unconsciously and immediately intuited her
rage and wanted to avoid it. But here it was. She yelled and
screamed at me for weeks. Now I attempted not to hide behind
a screen of "this has nothing to do with you, this has only to do
with her mother" and not to take this as a battle just between
us, thus fully engaging in the fight. I remained calm, absorbing
her anger, and I neither refuted it nor agreed with it. Rather, I
attempted to be accepting of this part of her, a part which she
was not accepting of.

After several weeks of rage, Margaret entered a period of
sobbing throughout her entire treatment hour. She was con-
vinced that I would not continue to see her through the
rageful period, that if she was so "mean" I would abandon
her. Finding our own anger unacceptable, we had both unconsciously resorted to denying it, avoiding it, and projecting it
onto others. Now we had to allow the mutual caring to
come out, a caring for each other in spite of weaknesses
and biases.

Carl Jung talks of how therapists must constantly be willing
to regress with their clients—to enter their neurosis in order to
help offer a cure.[2] Margaret forced me to rework issues that I
thought I had long ago resolved—to see myself as biased and
as having projections. But, most important, I once again had to
accept the sense of being not perfect but "good enough." This
was also the real Margaret that emerged at the end of her
therapy—a real woman who has softness, anger, success, failure, and who in the end is good enough. We both emerged
having grown by the experience. Now there was mutual caring

and respect, as well as what I enjoyed most—Margaret's self-acceptance.

Margaret and James did decide to have a child, and Margaret was made a partner in her law firm. James took on much of the child care and the household tasks, and Margaret found a way to be both an attorney and a mother who was home (sometimes) with her daughter.

SHIRLEY: From my own research perspective, what I find most intriguing about Margaret's experience is that as an African-American middle-class wife, she handled her issues in a way that fits neither the stereotypical model of the black matriarchy, nor the empirical model of egalitarianism, which is said to more accurately approximate the power structure in African-American families. Margaret is neither the domineering matriarch nor the rational negotiator. Instead of either asserting her independence and making her decisions regardless of their impact on her husband, or arriving at a mutually satisfying decision with him, she initially internalizes her struggle and wrestles inwardly with her choices and her fears. In this moment, in this act, she is every woman—neither African-American nor white.

What I have learned from my study of women's roles is that there is much less difference between the roles African-American and white middle-class women play in their marital relationships than is popularly believed. Although African-American women, regardless of social class, have been portrayed as dominant and white women are portrayed as subordinate in their marriages, neither has been shown empirically to be accurate. Over the past three decades, a substantial body of research has emerged that challenges these long-held assumptions.

Research has demonstrated that even when middle- and upper-class women, either black or white, earn more than men in their marriages, these women experience anxiety about being perceived by others as unfeminine or domineering. They also feel guilty about not being a "good wife and mother." Robert Staples, an African-American sociologist and scholar of the African-American family, has also observed that although early in their own lives African-American women express expectations of gender role equalization, as African-American males reach middle-class status they prefer wives who are subordinate. In fact, many middle-class males avoid self-actualizing, assertive African-American women.[3] An African-American middle-class wife in such a relationship would experience pressure to defer to her husband's needs, to adjust herself to fit with her husband's priorities. Margaret's fears about exploring her own ambivalences with her husband may reflect her unconscious awareness and acceptance of the role prescriptions that Staples describes.

I also was struck by the dynamics of the relationship between Cathie and Margaret. I was greatly interested in her apparent discomfort with an African-American female therapist and her obvious comfort with a white one. The paradox of this is that she felt safer transcending the barriers of skin color (albeit artificial ones) than exposing her vulnerability to a member of her own race and gender.

I sensed that the "strong black female" mythology and expectation may have played a role in this. It made me wish that Margaret could find a comfortable resting place on either side of the artificial divide. But it also reminded me of the power of our habits of survival. For African-American women this has translated, all too often, into the need to hide our pain from each other. So, as I see it, a part of Margaret's struggle is to break through the wall of fear that African-American sisters don't contain the pain, and to overcome their fears of each other—that their strength does not permit them to share each other's tears.

The broader base of social research describes for us the social and cultural mythologies that drive the behavior of individuals. It is important for therapists to be familiar with these myths as they are played out in the lives of their clients. Especially for white therapists working with African-American women, the mythology of the "all-sufficiency" or superwoman qualities of the African-American woman can have serious implications for the client-therapist relationship and the healing that these women seek. Coupled with the awful burden of self-sufficiency that African-American women have been made to carry has been the equally burdensome responsibility to be the glue that keeps their marriages together. As Evelyn Lee observes, "The bottom line for black women has been to sympathize with their men for the devastating oppression the larger culture has caused them . . ."[4] When their marriages fail, African-American women have been made to feel doubly responsible for the failure.

The tendency of wives in general to deny their own needs for the sake of their husbands' needs derives in part from the reluctance of both wives and husbands to acknowledge that power relations and normative preferences play a central role in their relationship. Margaret's internal conflict over the organization of roles and responsibilities in her marriage reflects the normative ambivalence that confronts many American couples today. It results from what some call cultural lag—i.e., a situation in which the old cultural norms no longer fit new social realities. As more women enter the workforce and gain economic parity with or surpass their husbands, they expect more equality in their marriages. H. Rodman explains this dynamic from a normative resource perspective, which holds that a person should gain in power in direct proportion to the ability of his or her resources to satisfy the needs of the marriage partner. Resources are defined as economic, intellectual, physical, emotional, or status factors that hold the potential of con-

tributing to the fulfillment of the needs of the marriage partner
or the family in general.[5]

Margaret no doubt feels that her financial contributions
should be reciprocated by greater role flexibility on her husband's part. She should not have to bear the sole or even the
major responsibility for household chores in addition to working full-time at a job that brings home more money than her
husband does. When she thinks of adding the responsibilities of
a baby to her current responsibilities she experiences anger,
fear, abandonment, and a whole host of other emotions that
come from being unable to negotiate a more tolerable role
arrangement.

The fact that Margaret internalizes her feelings rather than
discusses them would seem to confirm Rodman's theory that
cultural norms related to marital power may account for more
of the variation in the family power structure than the relative
resources of the spouses. It certainly confirms research that has
found that both African-American and white women, regardless of income distribution, believe they are responsible for
more of the household tasks than their husbands are. Other
studies show that among women who earn most of the family
income, the division of labor is along quite traditional lines.
Wives are more likely to be responsible for shopping, cleaning,
cooking, and laundry, and husbands more likely to be responsible for car maintenance, household repair, and yard work.[6] As
recently as 1992, Colburn, Lin, and Moore found that 89.2
percent of women believed that they were primarily responsible for household tasks; only 9.8 percent believed the responsibility was joint, and only 0.7 percent believed their husband
was primarily responsible. In this study 78 percent of the
women were employed and 24 percent had most of the responsibility for earning the family's income.[7]

My own research on African-American middle-class couples shows similar patterns of women's allegiance to marital structures that are at variance with their normative beliefs. The wives in my study were highly educated (over 70 percent had finished college or had professional degrees) and were well compensated in their jobs (median income was $26,000). Education proved to be a significant factor in determining the wife's beliefs about power and normative arrangements. The higher their education, the less they believed that the wife should cook and clean and the husband should provide the family income or make final decisions about family money matters. Also, the higher their education, the more these women believed that if the wife works, the husband ought to share in household chores and child care. The level of the wife's income also influenced her views on marital roles and responsibilities. The higher her income, the less she believed that the wife should cook and clean and the husband should have the last word in family or money matters. Conversely, the higher their incomes, the more they believed that the husband should share in household chores.

It is noteworthy that although the women believed they should have more power in their marriages (the higher their income and/or education), they still neglected to negotiate for it. Roles were organized very traditionally, with wives seeing themselves as in charge of the expressive functions of the family—e.g., buying the clothes, making decisions about dinner, choosing a doctor, and decorating the house, whereas husbands saw themselves as making the decisions about instrumental functions—e.g., what car to buy, what life insurance to get, and other money matters.

The women in my study, Margaret, and many other women in our society silently suffer from the strain of playing too many roles and carrying too many responsibilities in their marriage, without adequate regard or reward from their spouses for any of them. Froma Walsh, a leading family therapist, cites Beaver's (1986) research finding that couples in successful marriages are able to work out complementary roles in task performance and a sense of equitability and shared leadership. They avoid skewing the balance of power so that either feels that he or she is carrying a disproportionate share of the responsibilities.[8]

Essentially, women as a group absorb the same messages regarding role competency as wives, and learn at an early age that men's wishes and needs supersede theirs. These are attenuated, of course, by specific cultural prescriptions. The fact that African-American women have been in the work force longer than white women and continue to contribute proportionately more financially to their marriages than their white counterparts merely serves to obscure the reality of the power relationships within their marriages. The inability to openly discuss the divergence between the desirable cultural norm of egalitarianism of roles and the real life preferences of marital partners may contribute to the high divorce rates among both African-American and white middle-class couples. It might also relate to the increasing numbers of unmarried adults over eighteen, especially among African-American women and men.

The mythologies about African-American and white women in relationships, coupled with issues of social class, have driven a wedge between us as women and distorted the sameness of our experiences. These forces have also shut and often sealed the door of communication between women and their husbands.

We possess the power to liberate ourselves from the bondage of misperception and fear and to proclaim our oneness with each other as we renegotiate the rules of all of our relationships.

Our working together on this chapter and on similar research has forced the question of similarities and differences between ourselves as well as others with whom we work. The two of us have had different as well as similar paths and experiences. Before we could see each other clearly, we needed to attain our own self-acceptance, just as Margaret did. This is our real struggle—and it is an ongoing one.

[1] *Chapman, A.* The Treatment Techniques of Harry Stack Sullivan. *New York: Brunner/Mazel, 1978.*

[2] *Jung, C. G.* The Practice of Psychotherapy (2nd Ed.). *Princeton, N.J.: Princeton University Press, 1985.*

[3] *Staples, R.* Black Masculinity. *San Francisco: The Black Scholar Press, 1982.*

[4] *McGoldrick, M. Garcia-Preto; N. Hines, P. M. & Lee, E. "Ethnicity and Women."* In McGoldrick, M., Anderson, C. M., and Walsh, F. (Eds.). Women in Families. *New York: W. W. Norton & Company, Inc., 1991.*

[5] *Rodman, H. "Marital Power and the Theory of Resources in Cultural Context."* Journal of Comparative Studies. *3:50–67, 1972.*

[6] *Atkinson, M., & Boles, J. "WASP (Wives and Senior Partners)."* Journal of Marriage and the Family. *November 1984, 861–70.*

[7] *Colburn, K. Lin, P., & Moore, M. "Gender and the Divorce Experience."* Journal of Divorce & Remarriage. *17(3/4):87–108, 1992.*

[8] *Walsh, F. "Reconsidering Gender in Marital Quid Pro Quo."* In McGoldrick, M., Anderson, C. M., and Walsh, F. (Eds.). Women in Families. *New York: W. W. Norton & Company, Inc., 1991.*

Contributors

Shirley A. Bryant, D.S.W., is a professor of social work at the Catholic University of America in Washington, D.C., where she has taught courses in social welfare policy and services, community organization and administration for the past ten years. Dr. Bryant has a special interest in issues of family empowerment and social justice and has made numerous professional presentations as well as published in this area. She holds a doctorate in social work from Howard University in Washington, D.C., with a concentration in the area of families and children.

Catherine Clinton is a historian, a professor of African-American Studies and the author of many articles and books.

Ann Filemyr is a journalist at Antioch College in Yellow Springs, Ohio. For many years, Ms. Filemyr has worked with Native American tribes on land and political rights issues.

Dorothy Gilliam is a columnist for the *Washington Post*.

Marita Golden is the author of the novels *A Woman's Place*, *Long Distance Life*, and *And Do Remember Me*, and the memoir *Migrations of the Heart*. She is the editor of *Wild Women Don't Wear No Blues: Black Women Writers on Love, Men and Sex*, and the author most recently of *Saving Our Sons: Raising Black Children in a Turbulent World*. Her journalism has been published in the *Washington Post*, *The New York Times*, *Essence* and *Washingtonian*. She is a member of the faculty of the graduate creative writing program at Virginia Commonwealth University in Richmond.

Jewelle Gomez lives in San Francisco where she teaches popular culture and creative writing. She is the author of two collections of poetry and a novel, *The Gilda Stories*.

Dr. Cathleen Gray has practiced psychotherapy for over twenty-five years. She has also been on the faculty of Catholic University since 1975, where she teaches psychotherapy courses. Dr. Gray lectures throughout the country to professionals on areas of women's issues, marriage and divorce. She lives in Chevy Chase, Maryland, with her husband and three children.

Patricia Browning Griffith is a novelist, short story writer, and playwright. Her last novel, *The World Around Midnight*, was named one of the outstanding books of 1992 by the American Library Association. It is now in paperback from Washington

Square Press. She lives in Washington, D.C., and teaches at George Washington University and at the Writers' Center.

bell hooks is a writer, feminist theorist and cultural critic. Her essays, articles and interviews have appeared in *Z, Essence* and *Vogue.* She is the author of the following books: *Ain't I a Woman, Black Women and Feminism, Black Looks: Race and Representation, Feminist Theory: From Margin to Center, Talking Back: Thinking Feminist Thinking Black, Yearning: Race, Gender and Cultural Politics, Breaking Bread: Insurgent Black Intellectual Life* (with Cornel West) and *Sisters of The Yam.*

Beverly Lowry is the author of six novels—*The Track of Real Desires, Breaking Gentle, The Perfect Sonya, Daddy's Girl, Emma Blue, Come Back, Lolly Ray,* many articles and short stories, and one book of nonfiction, *Crossed Over: A Murder, a Memoir.* Presently she is the Jenny McKean Moore lecturer in Creative Writing at George Washington University and she teaches in the Master of Fine Arts Program at the University of Montana.

Mary Morris is the author of three novels *(Crossroads, The Waiting Room,* and *A Mother's Love),* two collections of short stories *(Vanishing Animals and Other Stories* and *The Bus of Dreams),* and two memoirs of a woman traveling alone *(Nothing to Declare* and *Wall to Wall).*

Toni Morrison, winner of the 1993 Nobel Prize for Literature, is the author of several novels including most recently *Jazz, Beloved,* and *Song of Solomon.* She has also written two books of nonfiction, *Playing in the Dark* and *To Come.*

Joyce Carol Oates is the author of short stories, novels, poems, plays, essays and literary criticism, as well as the winner of many prizes for her work. Her most recent novels include *What I Lived For, Foxfire, I Lock My Door Upon Myself, Black Water, Because It Is Bitter and Because It Is My Heart.*

Lisa Page has worked as a speechwriter, editor and freelance journalist. She lives with her husband, journalist Clarence Page, and their son Grady in Washington, D.C.

Gayle Pemberton is a chronicler of twentieth-century life in black and white in the United States. She is the author of *The Hottest Water in Chicago: Notes of a Native Daughter,* the forthcoming *And the Colored Girls Go . . . Black Women and American Film,* many essays and the play, *And I Am Not Resigned.* Currently she is the Kenan Professor of the Humanities in the English Department, and Chair of the African-American Studies Program at Wesleyan University. Pemberton earned Ph.D. and M.A. degrees at Harvard University and a B.A. at the University of Michigan. She is a former John Simon Guggenheim Foundation and W.E.B. DuBois Institute Fellow.

Retha Powers is a writer and editor whose journalistic work and essays have appeared in *Ms., Essence* and *Glamour* as well as *Body & Soul: The Total Health and Wellness Book for African-American Women,* edited by Linda Villarosa. She lives in New York City.

Susan Richards Shreve is the author of ten novels, most recently *A Country of Strangers, Daughters of the New World,* and *The Train Home.* She has written seventeen books for children and appears occasionally as an essayist on the MacNeil/Lehrer News Hour. She is a professor of English and on the faculty of the Institute of the Arts at George Mason University.

Susan Straight is the author of *Aquaboogie, I Been in Sorrow's Kitchen and Licked Out All the Pots,* and *Blacker Than a Thousand Midnights.* She lives in Riverside, California.

Alice Walker won the Pulitzer Prize for the novel *The Color Purple.* Novelist, essayist, short story writer and activist for global women's and human rights, Walker is also the author of *Meridian in Love and Trouble, The Temple of My Familiar, Possessing the Secret of Joy,* and *Warrior Marks,* an examination of genital mutilation.

Eudora Welty, one of the preeminent writers of the South, is the author of the novels *Delta Wedding, The Robber Bridegroom,* and *The Optimist's Daughter,* among others, and several collections of stories and other writings.

Naomi Wolf is the author of *Beauty Myth* and *Fire with Fire.*